GREAT
COLLEGE FOOTBALL
RIVALRIES

GREAT
COLLEGE FOOTBALL
RIVALRIES

by Ken Rappoport

tempo
books

GROSSET & DUNLAP
A FILMWAYS COMPANY
Publishers • New York

Once again,
for Bernice

Great College Football Rivalries
Copyright ©1978 by Ken Rappoport
All Rights Reserved
ISBN: 0-448-14624-X
A Tempo Books Original
Tempo Books is registered in the U.S. Patent Office
Published simultaneously in Canada
Printed in the United States of America

CONTENTS

A selection of photographs follows page 152.

1
OHIO STATE—MICHIGAN
The 100-Yard War

Michigan is the state that Woody Hayes loves to hate, and Ed Ferkany can sign an affadavit to that effect. The one-time Ohio State line coach drove the Buckeye head coach through Michigan on a recruiting mission one year, and on the way back through the southern part of the state, Ferkany noticed that the gas gauge was running low.

"Woody," he said, "I think we'd better stop for gas at the next station."

"Naw," said Hayes, in a hurry to get home. "Keep going. We can make it."

So Ferkany passed the next station, if a little apprehensive.

About a half-hour later, Hayes' assistant glanced nervously again at the gas gauge, and now the needle was almost on empty. Up ahead loomed the lights of another service station.

"Uh, Woody," Ferkany said, a little more edgy now, "there's another gas station up ahead. I really think we'd better stop this time and fill up!"

"No, dammit!" Hayes screamed. "We do not pull in and fill up."

"But, why? The tank's empty!"

"I'll tell you exactly why," Hayes growled. "I don't buy one damn drop of gas in the state of Michigan! We'll coast and push this damn car to the Ohio line before I give this state a penny of my money!"

Perhaps that famous Hayes story has been enhanced a bit as the years go by, but it still has a ring of truth to it and for good reason. The Michigan football team has often stood in the way of some of Hayes' grandest schemes, including Big Ten titles, Rose Bowl berths and national championships. The Michigan–Ohio State game has decided no less than seventeen league championships with the Rose Bowl and national title often hanging on the outcome, and since coming to Ohio State as coach in 1951, Wayne Woodrow Hayes has been involved in the majority of those. Some of these 100-yard wars between two of college football's superpowers have transcended the field and become significantly bitter issues between the schools.

Thus Hayes is noticeably involved in a year-round cold war with Michigan, actually refusing to utter the name of his fiercest rival, as if it would leave even more of a bad taste in his mouth. Hayes simply refers to the University of Michigan as "that school up north." And Michigan football coach Bo Schembechler, a one-time athlete and assistant under Hayes, continues to be, in public, anyway, a no-name to his former boss, just "the coach from the school up north."

Schembechler doesn't mind being anonymous as far as Hayes is concerned, so long as he can beat him. And he has done that often enough.

At Ohio State, Schembechler apparently learned his lessons well, for his image mirrors that of the hard-driving Hayes, and his success has been equally astonishing, although in a much shorter time span. Their histories are remarkably similar. Both are small-town Ohio boys who were football and baseball players at small-time Ohio colleges, who entered military service after graduation, earned master's degrees in education at Ohio State and have become successful coaches. They have explosive tempers, hearty appetites and a manic devotion to work. Each has been national Coach of the Year, each has suffered a heart attack and each is a militant leader. Hayes has been known to beat his players with his fists, while Schembechler favors a rubber bat. They are no doubt two of the most combative coaches in the business, to which a scene in their early, explosive relationship attests. Once, during an Ohio State staff meeting, Hayes threw a chair at Schembechler and the young assistant coach threw it back.

Hostility apparently still lingers between the two, adding spice to an already flavorful rivalry. To his undying chagrin, Schembechler is yet called "a chip off the old Woody" and "Little Woody." His public remarks about their relationship are often sharp, even if spoken in a humorous vein. At the 1975 Heisman Trophy dinner in New York, Schembechler sat next to two-time winner Archie Griffin of Ohio State and cracked: "Archie and I have a lot in common. We both played for Woody Hayes. He brags about it and I can't live it down." Schembechler concedes that the influences stemming from his close association with Hayes were not always positive. Hayes puts in his two cents in this regard: "I know Bo drives his players. I think maybe he has learned some of my bad habits."

Schembechler is open-faced in his criticism of Hayes, although his most persistently made point might be turned against himself. "I don't think anyone is as completely engulfed in football as Woody," Schembechler says. "I've tried to keep my sense of humor and have some other interests." The fact is, though, Hayes can be extremely charming when he wants, and at times as funny as a stand-up comic, while maintaining passionate interests in reading, writing and history. Schembechler's concerns do not extend much beyond athletics and his own family.

Since Schembechler was an offensive tackle under Hayes at Miami of Ohio in 1949-50, Woody's graduate assistant at Ohio State the following season and the Buckeye line coach in the years 1958-62, it is no surprise that his football style closely resembles the old master's. Both Ohio State and Michigan play prudent, conservative football and this has resulted in a series of low-scoring, high-tension games between the Hayes- and Schembechler-coached teams. Also, with the opinionated Bo and Woody involved, the series has become a bit more controversial than the school administrations would prefer. Unfortunately, the Ohio State–Michigan games have often brought out the worst in both men.

The impulsive, quick-tempered Hayes was never one to hide his frustrations and the 1971 meeting, won 10-7 by Michigan, triggered a childish display by the Ohio State coach that ended with him attacking the sideline markers. Schembechler had his naked moment in 1973 when, after the teams tied 10-10, the Big Ten Conference voted to send Ohio State to the Rose Bowl for the second straight year. Bo's verbal tirade against the Conference officials caused him to be put on probation for excessive behavior.

While such bizarre adult behavior is usually frowned upon, it is sometimes understandable in the case of these two coaches because of the high pressures and stakes present most every year in an Ohio State–Michigan game. Since Schembechler has taken over at Michigan, there has been only one season that his Wolverines and Hayes' Buckeyes have not fought it out directly for a Big Ten championship—in 1971. Their combined winning streak of Conference titles has been unmatched in the eight-decade history of the Big Ten.

Hayes was just as cantankerous—and just as successful—before Schembechler came on the scene. Prior to Bo's coaching career, Hayes matched guile and brawn with Michigan's Chalmers "Bump" Elliott for many years, and before him, Bennie Oosterbaan. Their extraordinary games provided some brilliant highlights during the fifties and sixties in the Big Ten, adding to the growing legend of one of America's greatest football rivalries. Oosterbaan, in fact, brought a sense of history to these contests since he had played in the first Ohio State–Michigan game back in 1926. Even then, the Buckeyes and Wolverines were settling championships in a compelling manner.

Ohio State was not one of the original members of the Big Ten when the league was formed in 1896, and by the time the Buckeyes were included in the standings in 1912, Michigan had temporarily withdrawn. When they finally met in 1926, however, the game was worth waiting for. Both teams were undefeated in the league standings when they met in Columbus on the next-to-last game of the season. A record crowd of 90,411 watched Ohio State shock Michigan with ten points in the first twelve minutes and all signs pointed toward a Buckeye rout. When Michigan took a timeout, Wally Weber said to Oosterbaan, "At this rate they're going to drub us by forty points." The highly competitive Oosterbaan was flabbergasted. "Dammit, Wally, we haven't even had the ball yet!"

When Michigan did get the ball, Bennie Friedman threw it for a touchdown pass to Oosterbaan, his favorite receiver. And when the Wolverines got the ball again, they kicked a field goal with thirty seconds left in the half to tie the score 10-10 at intermission. Attached to the kick is an often-told Oosterbaan anecdote.

As the Wolverines took their positions in placekick formation, Oosterbaan paused a moment, then hurried over and whispered something to Friedman. "Fake, fake, watch Oosterbaan!" cried the once-stung Buckeyes, thinking that the Wolverines were cooking up a running play for their famous back. The ball rested on the Ohio State forty-three-yard line as Oosterbaan returned to his position on the flank. Holder Lou Gilbert took the snap from center and placed the ball down as Friedman, without the normal pressure of a blitzing Ohio State line, sailed the ball through the uprights for the tie. When asked later what he said to Friedman, Oosterbaan confessed, "I merely asked him if he didn't think that was an awfully long way to kick a football."

In the fourth quarter Michigan got its break when Sid Dewey recovered an Ohio State fumble on the Buckeye six-yard line. Four plays later, Friedman lobbed a pass over the middle to Leo Hoffman for a touchdown, converted the extra point, and now the Wolverines led 17-10. That extra point was just enough to withstand an Ohio State comeback. The Buckeyes moved from deep in their own territory on a brilliant, sustained drive late in the game and hammered their way to the Michigan six, from where fullback Marty Karow blasted over the goal to cut the Wolverine lead to 17-16 in the last minute. But the game ended on that note when Ohio State placekicker Myers Clark missed the extra-point try, precipitating an audible groan of despair from the partisan Buckeye crowd. Michigan historians still place that game high among the school's most dramatic victories.

Michigan won Big Ten titles and national championships in 1932 and 1933, but not without some hardfought victories over Ohio State. Among some of the superb players who engineered respective 14-0 and 13-0 triumphs over the Buckeyes were Harry Newman, John Regeczi, Chuck Bernard, Willis Ward, Ted Petoskey and Francis "Whitey" Wistert. Those two straight shutout defeats, and Michigan's early domination of the series, provided Ohio State with some incentive for revenge later in the thirties, when Francis A. Schmidt changed the direction of Buckeye football into an upward flow. Nicknamed "Close-the-Gates-of-Mercy" Schmidt for the way his Buckeyes scored touchdowns in bunches, the Ohio State coach elevated football to a new stature at Columbus. In the seven years that Schmidt was at Ohio State, from 1934 to 1940, his teams had a 39-16-1 record, won or shared the Big Ten championship three times, and was runnerup three times. His impressive record included four straight, heady, lopsided victories over Michigan, from 1934 through 1937.

It was Schmidt who launched Ohio State's modern era of football eminence. A World War I bayonet instructor with a loud, raucous and colorful approach to the English language, Schmidt was one of the most talked-about coaches in the nation during his time. One historian described him as "the zaniest, maddest, most imaginative football coach ever to hit the Big Ten." Schmidt's genius was in offense, as displayed by his production of points in those four games while dominating Michigan by a combined score of 114-0. In his first season at Ohio State, Schmidt startled the opposition by wheeling out—in the same game—the single wing, the double wing, short punt and, for the first time, the I-formation.

His teams played the most wide-open football ever witnessed in the Big Ten, and rarely seen anywhere else. Spinners, reverses and double reverses were the order of every game. Schmidt's Buckeyes, it seemed, were the most lateral-pass conscious team in history. "His backs threw laterals, and then laterals off of laterals downfield," said one historian. "It was not uncommon for three men to handle the ball in the backfield."

Just as Schmidt was the dominent figure at Ohio State in the thirties, so was Fritz Crisler at Michigan in the period thereafter. Crisler arrived at Ann Arbor in 1938, concurrent with Tom Harmon's sophomore year, and for the next ten years helped field some of the strongest teams in Michigan's history. During this decade Ohio State was able to master Michigan only twice and the Crisler years triggered an era of Wolverine domination over the Buckeyes through the forties and into the fifties. After Crisler's teams defeated Ohio State for the third straight time in 1947 en route to a brilliant 10-0 season, Oosterbaan took over and prolonged Michigan's mastery into 1951. During that seven-year period, Ohio State was able to manage only one tie with the powerful Wolverines.

Crisler's appearance at Michigan in the late thirties represented a new cycle in Wolverine football. A successful coach at Princeton, Crisler was recruited to replace Harry Kipke, whose Michigan teams had gone through a protracted slump in the thirties. In a sense, Crisler was also replacing Fielding Yost, whose dominating influence had been felt at Michigan for almost forty years as coach and athletic director. A commanding personality, Yost was the power behind the three football coaches who succeeded him after 1926 and he made certain that they followed his policies and played his brand of football.

The vision of Yost's iron hand on his shoulder was actually a deterrent that made Crisler hesitant to take the coaching job. But Crisler finally accepted, after assurances that he would have complete control of the football program.

The suave, urbane Crisler brought his spinner-cycle offense to Ann Arbor. One of the most eye-catching in football, it required meticulous execution, flawless faking and perfect timing. Such a complicated attack could not have been used with ordinary players, but then, Crisler did not have ordinary players on his team. Among them was Harmon, a fusion of exceptional speed, power and deception. Before he retired his famous No. 98, Harmon scored three touchdowns against Ohio State in 1940 to lead Michigan's 40-0 romp and bring his three-year TD total to thirty-three, three more than the immortal Red Grange.

It was quite natural that Harmon would be compared to the Illinois great, since they were both from the same conference and more significantly, because their styles were so similar. Like Grange, Harmon's favorite running maneuver was the cutback over tackle, going to either side. And like Grange, he had similar power, elusiveness and a variety of football talents. Harmon had a theatrical personality as well and was aware of his own importance to Michigan. However, his roommate, Bob Ingalls, worked hard to keep Harmon's head in the right place. Once when Harmon was late for practice, Ingalls called out: "Everybody make a low bow, please. Here comes the Michigan football team."

That 1940 game was particularly irritating to Schmidt as that rout resulted in Ohio State's worst defeat since it entered the big time. While scoring three times to break Grange's career touchdown record in that game, Harmon also passed for two more scores. That defeat, some say, cost Schmidt his job at Ohio State. The proud Schmidt knew that the Ohio State athletic board was debating his future, and resigned before they could fire him. When news photographers came around for farewell pictures, his good-byes were filled with bitter sarcasm. "You guys have dozens of my pictures in your files," he said. "Just dig out one of them and use it. And while you're at it, just caption it, 'Rest In Peace.' " Three years later, at Idaho, Schmidt died of a heart attack.

When Schmidt packed his bags, Ohio State signed youthful Paul Brown, a giant in Ohio prep-school circles. Brown, whose Massillon Tigers had won six straight championships, continued his success at Columbus with a national championship in 1942, including one of the Buckeyes' few victories over Michigan in that period. Ohio State's 21-7 victory over the Wolverines in 1942 was another of those games that had a bearing on the title, even if Michigan wasn't involved in the race this time. The Buckeyes nosed out Wisconsin for the Big Ten championship by virtue of that decision.

The Wolverines and Buckeyes continued their hot rivalry through the forties and it seemed as if every game during that decade meant something. In fact, most every one of them did. In 1943, Michigan defeated Ohio State 45-7 to tie Purdue for the Conference title. In 1944, Les Horvath and Ollie Cline keyed an 18-14 victory as Ohio State scored in the last three minutes to win the title over Michigan. In 1945, Michigan defeated Ohio State 7-3 to give Indiana the clear championship. More heat was added to the rivalry in 1946 when Michigan walloped Ohio State 58-6, rubbing it in with Jim Brieske's twelve-yard field goal with ninety-six seconds left. "That field goal would fester in the football blood of Columbus," said one writer, and "On, Ohio, Fifty-Eight to Six" became a rallying cry of the Buckeyes. The 1949 game resulted in a 7-7 tie and a shared title for Michigan and Ohio State. However, the Wolverines would have won the title outright had it not been for a penalty in the fading minutes of that game. The Buckeyes marched eighty yards midway through the fourth period to score. When Jim Hague missed the extra point, it looked as if Michigan had a 7-6 victory. But the Michigan penalty gave Hague a second chance and he made that one count.

The title was also at stake in 1950 when Ohio State met Michigan in the famed "Snow Bowl" game in Columbus.

The season in the Big Ten, then called the Western Conference, had followed the national trend of shocks and surprises and by the last day of the year, three teams were still in contention for the championship. However, Ohio State could decide everything with just a victory over Michigan, a team with few redeeming features that had been beaten three times and tied once in eight previous games. The only gems that might be found in the Wolverine lineup were the two exceptionally fine backs the team had in Chuck Ortmann and Don Dufek, a superb tackle in Allen Wahl, an excellent end in Lowell Perry and a very good center named Tony Momsen, whose brother, incidentally, was a starting guard in the Ohio State line. Meanwhile, the Buckeyes were one of the Conference's strongest teams, led by their "Mr. Everything," fullback Vic Janowicz. In a savage mood over a defeat by title contender Illinois the previous week, the Buckeyes couldn't wait to get their hands on their underprivileged Michigan rivals.

The day before the game, snow began falling over Ohio and nobody paid much attention to it until gale-force winds made their appearance and lifted snow drifts to unbelievable heights. The day of the game, snow was hip-high.

More than nine inches of snow had fallen by Saturday morning, and the situation was further complicated by a stiff wind and a midmorning temperature of seven degrees.

Suddenly, tickets, which had been impossible to procure for months before the game, were readily available. In restaurants they were offered at list price to customers waiting for their tables and one scalper, afraid he would be burned, tried to sell a pair for less than the box-office price, but had no luck. Meanwhile, those fans willing to brave the elements started to file into the stadium, sweeping snow off their seats in order to find their seat numbers.

The Michigan team, making the trip aboard a special train from Ann Arbor, had spent the night in Toledo. By Saturday noon, railroad travel was coming to a halt all over Ohio, but the football special miraculously got through somehow, and together with two or three trains loaded with fans from Detroit, pulled up on a spur a quarter of a mile from the stadium. The Michigan players climbed out and fought their way to the football field, and it was the toughest touchdown drive they had to make all year.

For a while there was doubt that the game would, or could, be played. Ohio State coach Wes Fesler did not want to go on, but he was overruled by the athletic directors of both schools. After all, they pointed out, no Western Conference game had ever been postponed. It took until two o'clock to bare the field and when the tarpaulins were finally hauled away, the Ohio State band bravely marched out and, putting frozen lips to mouthpieces, sent the "Buckeye Battle Cry" riding on the wind. Members of the band said later that their lips peeled when they began to play their instruments. Yet the bandsmen went on, and so did the football game.

The game itself was no doubt as grotesque as any on record. According to an account in *The New Yorker,* "The players all wore gloves, including the ball-handlers. Every few minutes, the ball became covered with a thin coat of ice, like frigid cellophane. A kerosene heater was set up on the sidelines, and after every two or three plays a warm ball was put into the game and the old one thawed out and heated."

Operating at a minimum of offensive efficiency, the game developed into a kicking duel. Ortmann punted the ball twenty-four times, the most ever in a conference game. Janowicz kicked twenty-one times for Ohio State. However, one of the kicks was blocked, and therein lies the real story of the 1950 "Snow Bowl" game.

The Buckeyes were ahead, first 3-0 with a twenty-seven-yard field goal by Janowicz, then 3-2 after the Wolverines scored a safety. The game was decided when the Wolverines blocked a third-down kick by Janowicz and Momsen fell on the ball behind the Ohio State goal line. The play occurred with just forty-seven seconds left in the first half. Michigan claimed the 9-3 win and Fesler no longer had a job at Ohio State. The Buckeye coach later resigned for "personal reasons," but the general opinion was that he couldn't live with the memory of that blocked punt against Michigan.

Uniquely, Michigan won the game without making a first down and had a mere total of twenty-seven yards in the grim, surrealistic battle. Ohio State got all of three first downs, but Janowicz, the Buckeyes' brilliant backfield star, wound up with a minus total in rushing yardage that day— losing nine yards in nineteen carries. Eighteen passes were thrown by both teams that day. Michigan didn't complete one and Ohio State, only three.

The official attendance was announced as 50,503, meaning that almost 32,000 persons had not shown up. But thousands more, unable to sit in the bitter cold, left by halftime. And a few left before that, but not under their own power—two women, with frostbitten feet, were carried out of the stadium by policemen.

Big Ten watchers would perhaps attach some symbolism to that 1950 game, for it was the very next season that Woody Hayes came to Ohio State and started causing a blizzard of his own. Two years after the "Snow Bowl" game, Hayes' Buckeyes kept the title from Michigan with a 27-7 victory on Fred Burney's brilliant interceptions and John Burton's sensational passing. Burney picked off three passes in the end zone while Burton, only a sophomore, fired three scoring strikes and scored once himself.

Hayes' teams got steadily better and by 1954, he had a national champion. The Buckeyes capped the perfect regular season with a classic 21-7 victory over Michigan, with the help of a controversial goal-line stand and the running of Howard "Hopalong" Cassady, a former local high-school star who was nicknamed after the cowboy movie idol. After Ohio State's gallant line turned back Michigan fullback Dave Hill inches from the goal line, Cassady helped turn the game around with a sixty-yard dash that set up the tie-breaking touchdown late in the game.

Ohio State's goal-line stand became a *cause célébre* between the schools, since many Michigan men to this day still believe that Hill had made it into the end zone, despite what the officials ruled that day. Among those believers is Lou Baldacci, the Michigan quarterback from that game. The Wolverines had driven ninety-nine yards and eleven inches and stood on the threshold of a tie-breaking touchdown, and Baldacci recalls:

"Dave tried to dive over the goal line. He got to the top of the pile and I thought he scored. I know one of the officials did also. But the head linesman said he was short of the goal. So we gave up the ball and even though we still had time left we lost the momentum—that intangible factor in every football game."

By 1955, the Buckeyes were Big Ten champions again and once again beat Michigan to do it, this time by a 17-0 score. But Hayes started to hear the now-familiar criticism of his plodding offensive style, scornfully dubbed "three-yards-and-a-cloud-of-dust" by outsiders. Hayes liked to batter opponents with his fullbacks running behind devastating blocking. There was little need to pass, Hayes reasoned, if one could move the ball safely and sanely on the ground. The philosophy behind his winning teams bored the fans, but bullied opponents.

Win or lose in subsequent years, Hayes' burly figure was a menacing shadow in Big Ten football. Michigan, meanwhile, went through a mild slump in the late fifties and early sixties, succumbing to many teams, including Ohio State. From 1957 through 1963, Michigan was able to manage only one victory over the Buckeyes and during that period lost several lopsided games, including a 50-20 decision in 1961.

Finally, Coach Bump Elliott put some bounce back into Michigan's deflated football with his "five-year plan," even if it was running a little late. Elliott had replaced Oosterbaan in 1959 and promised dramatic results in five years. By 1963 nothing positive had happened on the field for the Wolverines but Elliott stated that, "The parts are beginning to fit into championship design. The talent, the drive, the desire are all there."

Most importantly, the players were there, and the following year Michigan had a championship team. Criticized by some for playing "dull football" in his early years at Michigan, Elliott displayed more flamboyance than ever before with his 1964 team. "My philosophy did not change, my people did," said Elliott, in explaining his dramatic change of pace. Among his people was quarterback Bob Timberlake, who, according to one writer, "ran like a fullback and scared the pelts off his own kind with reeling option-pitchouts and off-balance flip-laterals." The six-foot-four, 215-pounder also led the team in rushing and passing and kicked extra points and field goals.

With Timberlake keynoting the finest offense in the league, Michigan had won seven of eight games coming up to the Ohio State confrontation. The Wolverines' only loss had been a 21-20 squeaker to Purdue, when they flipped the ball around too carelessly and too often for killing interceptions. Ohio State, meanwhile, was undefeated in league play and stood as the last hurdle in the way of Michigan's road to the Rose Bowl. This meeting on the last day of the regular Big Ten season marked the tenth time that Ohio State and Michigan had played against each other with the Big Ten title on the line. The game, fast becoming a Big Ten classic, had loomed even larger with the arrival of Hayes in 1951. Impressionable Michigan fans tended to think of Hayes as indestructible and cold-blooded and many would never forgive him for that 50-20 pasting in 1961 when the Ohio State coach put his first team back in for a last-minute touchdown and two-point conversion.

Hayes would have no such luxury this day, however. Not only was he unable to run up the score on Michigan, he was not able to score at all. Michigan, it turned out, scored the only touchdown of the day on a pass from Timberlake to Jim Detwiler. The Wolverines also had the only field goal, on a Timberlake kick, and emerged with a 10-0 victory and the Big Ten championship. Everything broke right for Michigan that afternoon, including the movement of the wind, which helped set up the winning touchdown.

The victory gave the Wolverines one of their few moments of glory against Hayes in the pre-Bo Schembechler era. Under Hayes, the Buckeyes had defeated the Wolverines eleven out of fifteen times, from 1954 to 1968, including Elliott's humiliating title-costing 50-14 defeat the last year. That streak had reversed a long period of Michigan supremacy and it took a man like Schembechler to start tipping the balance of power back to a more equal basis. Schembechler promptly won two of the first three games from his old teacher, including Michigan's dramatic victory in 1969 that cost the Buckeyes the national championship.

Schembechler's game plan had gone into effect the week before, right after Michigan had walloped Iowa 51-6. "We knew right then that we were going to beat Ohio State," said Schembechler, who personally kept the fires burning by making his players wear a tiny No. 50 on their jerseys during practice, a gentle reminder of Ohio State's rout the year before. Schembechler had it all figured out how he would beat his former boss—concede Ohio State fullback Jim Otis his usual high-yardage figure and concentrate on stopping Buckeye quarterback Rex Kern.

"We didn't want Kern running the football," Schembechler pointed out, "so we set our defenses to stop him. We felt that our secondary could stop his passing, and we felt that we could score against their defense by running at 'em, which is something nobody had done."

That game plan was right out of the Woody Hayes textbook on winning: attack an opponent at its strongest point. Of course Schembechler was right that no one had been able to run through Ohio State in twenty-two previous games, including eight that season. The all-conquering Buckeyes had marched into that big game with the number-one ranking in the nation and the fiercest of reputations—a "worthy opponent for the Los Angeles Rams," someone had suggested. But Schembechler had a unique team himself. There was the pass defense built around Tom Curtis and Barry Pierson and a slick passing attack with quarterback Don Moorhead and tight end Jim Mandich. In addition, tailback Billy Taylor had emerged in mid-season as an extraordinarily good runner, giving the Wolverine offense a new dimension.

When the teams came out for warmups at Michigan's cavernous old stadium, the Wolverine fans threw snow-balls at the Buckeyes. Later, the Wolverine players threw something far more powerful at Ohio State, their defense, and thus established the tempo of the game. When the Buckeyes moved to the Michigan ten early in the contest and were unable to score from there, that provided the Wolverine players with all the confidence they needed for the rest of the afternoon.

"We knew we had 'em right there, when we stopped their regular stuff," Pierson said.

Even after Ohio State's second series of downs, when Otis plunged in from the one for a 6-0 Buckeye lead, the Michigan team's confidence was not shaken. Moorhead directed the Wolverines on a fifty-five-yard drive, mostly with his passes, and sent fullback Garvie Craw over from the three for a 7-6 Michigan lead. It was the first time that Ohio State had trailed an opponent all season.

The Buckeyes didn't let that bother them, though, coming right back to take a 12-7 lead on the first play of the second quarter with a neat passing play from Kern to tight end Jan White. Their extra-point try was blocked, but Michigan was offside on the play. Taking the penalty, the Buckeyes went for two points on the second try, but Kern was smothered by Michigan's defensive end, Mike Keller. Symbolically, that play told the story for the rest of the game.

For the rest of the afternoon, Michigan pushed Ohio State around as no other team had done that season. The Wolverines moved to the Ohio State twenty-seven and Tay-lor, breaking three tackles, ran to the five to set up Craw's scoring smash two plays later. That gave Michigan the lead back at 14-12. And the Wolverines continued to pour it on. When Ohio State could not move and had to punt, Pierson ran the ball back to the Buckeye three on what was perhaps one of the most important plays of the game, for it established Michigan's supremacy once and for all. Two plays later, Moorhead went over for a 21-12 Michigan victory.

While Woody Hayes was in seclusion behind closed locker-room doors, trying to figure out what had gone wrong, Michigan's players were laughing it up, singing "Hail To The Victor," and waving a bunch of plastic red roses, a reference to their forthcoming trip to the Rose Bowl. Schembechler took the traditional euphoric victory ride aboard his players' shoulders to the locker room, but was dropped along the way. It aggravated an old football knee injury, but hardly hurt his feelings. "He was the only thing his players had dropped all day," one whimsical writer observed.

Hayes' pain in defeat was not alleviated by an unsympathetic Columbus carpetmaker who later shipped him a rug with the score on it. The rug served as a perfect motivational prop for Hayes, who laid it at the door leading to the practice field so that his players had to stomp on it on the way to practice every day the following year.

Hayes' motives were apparent in 1970, when his goal for a revenge victory over Michigan sometimes bordered on the psychotic. Everyone knew that the Ohio State coach had suffered through a torturous year to get back at the Wolverines for that costly 1969 defeat, but some thought that during the rather insane week leading up to the game Hayes might have been guilty of overkill in his preparations and inspirations. The coaching staff was still working until midnight every day, still looking at films and diagnosing game plans right up to the last minute. There was no end to the gimmickery Hayes used to inspire his players. Along with the aforementioned rug, Wolverine jerseys were scattered on the floor and a Michigan recording blared endlessly through the dressing room. Then, too, there was a sentimental quiz. The Buckeyes were handed pencils and paper and asked to write an answer to the question, "What are you personally going to do to help win this game?" The Ohio State coaches knew they had their players motivated completely when one sub replied, "I know I won't play, but I'll yell 200 percent."

The crowd of 87,331 in Ohio State's throbbing stadium was thunderously wild and got even wilder when Michigan fumbled the opening kickoff. Ohio State jumped on the chance and kicked a field goal for a quick 3-0 lead. The tenor of the contest had been established. "Breaks will decide the game," Schembechler had said beforehand, and prophetically it came true for the Buckeyes. Michigan tied the score with a field goal of its own, but later ran into a series of bad breaks, including the biggest one when Paul Staroba's seventy-three-yard punt from the Wolverine goal line was called back because of a penalty. Staroba's second kick only traveled forty-two yards, and the opportunistic Buckeyes, led by Kern, scored a touchdown minutes later and continued on their way to a 20-9 victory that was one of the sweetest in Hayes' Ohio State tenure.

Starting in 1972, Hayes then put together a four-game unbeaten string against Michigan with the help of Archie Griffin, one of the Big Ten's most decorated runners. Putting to rest inevitable comparisons with other Ohio State greats like Jim Otis and Hopalong Cassady, Hayes stated flatly, "Griffin is the best back we've ever had." He was certainly the most prolific, breaking several NCAA records with his startling speed and winning the coveted Heisman Trophy two times. Griffin gave Michigan a taste of things to come in his freshman year in 1972, when he scored the winning touchdown in a 14-11 Ohio State thriller that ended the Wolverines' undefeated season and sent the Buckeyes to the Rose Bowl. In 1973, Griffin collected 163 yards as Ohio State and Michigan battled to a monumental 10-10 tie. Of course the tie was much better for the Buckeyes because they were ultimately given the Rose Bowl berth by a Big Ten vote over the loud protests of Schembechler.

Griffin's pounding runs helped set up four field goals in 1974, leading the Buckeyes to a 12-10 victory over Michigan and another Rose Bowl berth. Even in a minor role, Griffin usually was a major factor in the heated Michigan –Ohio State games of the seventies. So concerned were the Wolverines with Griffin's intimidating presence in the 1975 game that they overdid their defensive preparations for him, but forgot just about everyone else and as a result lost a 21-14 decision. Once more, the roses went to Ohio State.

Battles for the Rose Bowl in 1976 and 1977 between Michigan and Ohio State continued to fuel an already white-hot rivalry. It also led to joking comments that perhaps the Big Ten should be split into two leagues, the Big Two and the Little Eight.

These modern gladiatorial epics have inspired a genuine, mutual respect between Hayes and Schembechler, even if they still fail to recognize each other formally. Old ties and feelings are sometimes stirred and sympathy occasionally arises, as they did when each man suffered a heart attack. Schembechler sent Hayes virtually the same get-well note in 1973 that Woody had written him four and a half years earlier. Otherwise, they have little contact with each other —except, of course, one brutal Saturday every year in the fall.

2
TEXAS —TEXAS A & M
Deep in the Heart

The home of the Texas A&M football team, College Station, is roughly 100 miles east of Austin, out in the flatlands of the colossal state of Texas, on the other side of a colorful little town called Dime Box. Austin, University of Texas territory, is where the Texas hill country starts. A river runs through the football-feverish town, a cross between big city and small-college living. "The north side looks like Dallas, the south side like Houston and the middle like the University of Texas," someone once noted.

When the Aggies look at Austin, however, they only see red and the feeling is mutual from the Longhorn side. "The Aggies have always regarded Austin as sort of a bordello in which perverts violate every Spartan notion," an observer once wrote. "UT students view Aggies as simple-minded farmboys [A&M's first female student was admitted in 1963] who are thrilled to wear soldier suits."

The observation may be overstated and not entirely true, but the familiarity of the football teams has indeed bred contempt—and violence—through the years. The long football series was once canceled decades ago, because of warlike conditions. There have been many notable fights among students and it has not been uncommon for a Longhorn rowdie to beat up an Aggie senior and snatch his military boots as a souvenir. The Aggies once branded the Texas mascot, a longhorn steer, with the score of their 13-0 victory in 1915. Some UT intellectuals reportedly used a running iron to turn the numbers into the word "Bevo," which has since been the name of the Texas mascot.

Of course, coaching reputations have hinged more than one time on the outcome of the Texas–Texas A&M game. Time was when the coach staked his job on it and on one

20

occasion both coaches got fired because the teams played to a tie.

Clearly, the bitter Aggie–Longhorn battle has been the Southwest's counterpart to Harvard—Yale and Army—Navy, "an institution in the lives of many Texans," according to columnist Clark Nealon of the *Houston Post*. "This is a traditional event by which so many measure births, marriages, wars and other events to call to mind."

Season records have been trampled in the Texas dust and the best team has often lost in this traditional Thanksgiving Day series that has been largely dominated by the Longhorns. One of the several cherished traditions that have sprung up from the eight decades of this venerable rivalry was a mammoth Longhorn victory string on its home field, Memorial Stadium. The Longhorns won 7-0 to begin a stadium jinx over the Aggies that lasted until 1956, when the Aggies finally won on Texas's home grounds, 34-21. Until then, the closest that Texas A&M could come to beating Texas at Memorial Stadium was a 14-14 tie in 1948.

The Aggies would have to rate that 1956 victory right up there with the sweetest of their triumphs in this series, although the 20-0 decision in 1939, when they won the national championship under Homer Norton, was undoubtedly a euphoric moment. Most of the golden memories, however, have belonged to the Longhorns, who traditionally could beat the Aggies through good times and bad. One of the Longhorns' most significant victories in the series came in 1940 when they knocked the heavily favored Aggies out of the Rose Bowl with a 7-0 decision, the only loss that season for Texas A&M. In 1963, the downtrodden Aggies had an upset equal to 1940 in their hands, but Tommy Wade came off the bench in the last, frantic minutes to pull out a 15-13 victory for Texas that was a steppingstone to the national title.

No national title was involved in 1894 but the eyes of Texas football fans were still focused on the Texas–Texas A&M game if for no other reason than it was the first intercollegiate contest in the Southwest. In fact, not many of today's Southwest Conference teams had been born when the Longhorns and Aggies launched their series at Austin. The Texas team had been organized a year before Texas A&M took up the game of football in 1894, and although the Longhorns had played a weak noncollegiate schedule against such teams as Dallas and San Antonio, they showed the result of their experience with a 38-0 rout of the Aggies on October 9, 1894. It was quite a victory for the "Varsity Boys," as they were then known, considering that touchdowns only counted four points.

T. B. Ketterson (then A&M publicity director) wrote, "A crowd estimated at 500 piled into its buggies and drove back to town" after the game. Texas fielded a team of fifteen and, according to one partisan UT writer, the stars of the game were all from his side of the field: "[J. T.] Michelson, [John Frost] Maverick, [J. A.] O'Keefe, [Davil S.] Furman, [Wallace W.] Ralston, [Ray] McLane and [James S.] Jones." He did give Texas A&M credit for one thing, though—its "gentlemanly" behavior. "One thing that certainly can be said in their favor," he said of the Aggies, "and that is . . . their deportment during their stay in the city has been of the best, and we trust to have the team with us again."

The Texas A&M players were no less gentlemenly on the field of play, it seemed, suffering shutout defeats in the first seven meetings with their more unruly Texas neighbors. Not until 1902 could Texas A&M gain its first victory in the series, a 12-0 decision in the first of two games that year. Texas initiated another winning streak the following year, and the fourth straight Longhorn victory in 1906 marked the introduction of the forward pass in the rivalry, when UT's Winston McMahon threw to Bowie Duncan for a touchdown.

It wasn't until 1909 that Texas A&M could win another game, but by then the rivalry had gained an uncommon ferocity, owing to student unrest in 1908. One of two games between Texas and Texas A&M was played that year in Houston as part of the No-Tsu-Oh (Houston spelled backward) Carnival in the city's West End Park. Texas had taken a 14-0 lead by halftime when some of its 1,200 students who had made the trip paraded on the field with brooms fixed to their shoulders like rifles, in mockery of the Aggies' military-styled school. A group of Aggie Cadets, incensed at this display, jumped the fence surrounding the playing field and a battle that was to become typical of this Carnival was underway. Sparks and fists continued to fly in later years.

By 1911, emotions between the schools had reached a highly combustible state after another outbreak between the students at the game in the Houston carnival. The Aggies were heavy favorites then, but the Longhorns scored a 6-0 upset when a Texas great, Arnold Kirkpatrick, recovered a loose ball and raced across the goal line for the only score of the game. Three Texas players left the contest with broken bones, and the Aggie backers, tasting the bitter fruit of defeat for the first time in four games with Texas, tossed an enormous quantity of lemons at the Longhorn players. Texas students later added fuel to the fire of discontent by disrupting Texas A&M's military parade. Again, they followed the rifle-bearing Aggies with broom sticks on their shoulders and drove a hearse bearing the A&M "corpse" to climax the parade. Fighting later broke out between the rival students as they headed home from the game from the West End ballpark.

The following day, athletic relations were broken off between the inhospitable neighbors. "I beg to inform you that the Athletic Council of the University of Texas has decided not to enter in athletic relations with the Agricultural and Mechanical College of Texas for the year 1912," read the succinct official notice to Texas A&M from Dr. W. T. Mather, chairman of the Athletic Council. No reason for the break was cited in Mather's original letter to Texas A&M but after speculation appeared in print, Dr. Mather issued this statement: "The Athletic Council of the University of Texas greatly deplores the statement of charges in the press purporting to come from semiofficial sources. The action taken was based on the belief that in view of the heated state of opinion among students and alumni of both institutions, it was the wisest course to pursue."

As if Texas students did not harbor enough dislike for their Texas A&M counterparts, Charley Moran gave them more reason to feed their hate. Moran, one of the most successful coaches at Texas A&M, produced strong, swaggering teams during this period and helped the Aggies forge a three-game winning streak against Texas, including two victories within the span of a month in 1909. Actually, Moran's only loss to Texas came in the controversial game of 1911, and Moran's success over Texas was one of the sparks that lit the fight between the two campuses. While the A&M students expressed highly vocal delight over Moran's domination of the series, UT resentment of the turning tide was expressed in the following bit of poisonous verse:

"To hell, to hell with Charley Moran
And all his dirty crew,
If you don't like the words of this song,
To hell, to hell with you."

Relations were not restored between the schools until 1915, when a conciliation was effected through the efforts of Dr. Mather and L. Theo Bellmont of Texas and Joe Utay and Hal Moselye of A&M. Texas was a heavy favorite to win the game in 1915, first year of the Southwest Conference, but the Aggies scored a 13-0 upset in the first game played at College Station between the two teams.

That 1915 series renewal game was the setting for what is generally considered the greatest punting performance in Southwest Conference history. Harry Warren "Rip" Collins kicked the ball twenty-three times and most reports list the average for the Texas A&M kicker at fifty-five yards for the game. That generally accepted herculean figure is suspect, since there was no general rule for statistics in those days, but there was no question of Collins's ability to kick the ball as well as anyone. "The goal posts were on the goal line then but he could stand at midfield and punt the ball over either goal post and then he'd turn around and drop kick the ball over either one," said Rickey Key, a classmate of Collins.

The November 21, 1915, edition of the *Austin American* listed Collins, in his twenty-three punts, as carrying 1,026 yards, which would be nearly an average of forty-five yards per punt. Perhaps that tremendous average has been enhanced by time and legend, but Key insisted that Collins's performance that day was as good as generally accepted. "It was better than they say," said Key. "A&M didn't have much of a team and Texas had an awfully good one, but A&M won it largely because the Texas safety man couldn't handle his punts."

Clyde Littlefield, who played for the Longhorns that day, agreed: "It was a great job by Collins. Our safety man wouldn't leave the ball alone and he couldn't handle it."

Exactly how many muffs the Texas safety made isn't clear, but the supposedly sure-handed Longhorns fumbled the ball away twelve times in the game. The Aggies managed to hold onto the ball better and got two field goals in the first half and finally, a touchdown, which Collins scored.

The commonly accepted story for Collins's choice of Texas A&M over Texas is that Longhorn coach Dave Allerdice once cast slurs on Collins's competitive nature and the great kicker lived for the day he could gain revenge. He didn't have to wait any longer than his freshman year at Texas A&M.

Along with Collins's motives in the 1915 game, the A&M team had added incentive to beat the Longhorns because Aggie backers held Texas people responsible to some degree for having Charley Moran released as A&M coach after the 1914 season. Moran was charged with using illegal players or "ringers" (most people did in those days), and he was accused of coaching dirty football. Before the 1915 game with Texas, the Aggie players got a telegram, supposedly from Moran, asking the team to play the game for him, and Littlefield remembers them as being extremely emotional and ferocious.

"They were really in on us" said Littlefield. "I remember having to throw the ball earlier than usual and several times I hit the receiver in the back with the ball before he turned around."

The tradition of playing the game on Thanksgiving Day was born in 1916, when Texas administered a 21-7 beating to Texas A&M. Three years later, something even more significant happened at an Aggie–Longhorn game: the first sports event ever sent over the wireless (according to the Radio Electronics–Television Manufacturers Association in Washington). The play-by-play of the 1919 game was not a vocal broadcast from College Station to Austin, but was sounded on a telegraph key in Continental code of dots and dashes, using a long list of initials for each movement of the football. This was almost two years before the first prize fight and baseball game were heard over station KDKA in Pittsburgh, and it was three years later when WEAF in New York initiated voice broadcasts from football games.

William A. "Doc" Tolson was only a sophomore in electrical engineering at Texas A&M when he miraculously rigged up a crude but workable telegraph machine with the help of two assistants, Harry M. Saunders and B. Lewis Wilson. Tolson, later an eminent research engineer with the Radio Corporation of America, recalled that the original sportscast took a bit of doing. Most of the material for the telegraph machine was appropriated literally in bits and pieces, sometimes at night and occasionally when his professors looked the other way. "One vital part," he related, "came from an old electric fan which just accidentally fell off the windowsill of an instructor's office. When retrieved on the sidewalk two floors below, the fan's blades were irreparably damaged. But the motor worked fine!"

As an obviously biased observer of the game, Tolson had the opportunity to call the plays as he saw them—which, in this case, sent bad vibrations back to Austin. "Texas had a star quarterback named, I believe, Elam [Kyle C.]," remembered Tolson. "He was an excellent long forward passer and a fast man on his feet, carrying the ball for long gains around the ends. In reporting some of his plays, I would send, 'Elam passes fifty yards.' Then after half a minute just add, 'Incomplete.' Or, 'Elam long end run' and several seconds later report, 'No gain.' I knew these reports were giving Texas supporters at the old play-o-graph board in Austin a bad afternoon. At one point in the game, the University operator wired us and asked if we couldn't be a little less biased." The Aggies, by the way, won that game, 7-0, and really didn't need Tolson's help to do it. They were another of Dana X. Bible's stunning Texas A&M teams of that era, winning the Southwest Conference with an undefeated record (10-0 overall).

Bible's conference title in 1919 was one of five he collected in an illustrious, eleven-year career at College Station, where he won nearly seventy-seven percent of his games (72-19-9). Led by such players as Jack Mahan, Roswell "Little Hig" Higginbotham, Tom Griesenbeck, Scotty Alexander and Kyle Elam (a turncoat who later starred for Texas), the Aggies not only beat just about everybody but refused to let them score. In 1917, the Aggies swept through games with eight opponents, shutting them all out, and did the same with an enlarged ten-game schedule in 1919, when Bible returned from military service. The collective point differential in these remarkable seasons were, respectively, 270-0 and 275-0. By 1920, the Aggies amazingly were still not scored on under Bible, having run their brilliant streak under the defensive master to twenty-five shutouts, when they met unbeaten Texas in the final game of the season for the SWC championship.

Bible counted on a strong defense and the punting of Higginbotham to beat Texas, and it looked as if the game plan would work when the Aggies had a 3-0 lead at the half. The score for A&M was made on an early twenty-two-yard field goal by Bugs Morris.

But although the Aggies remained ahead through the

third quarter, it was obvious that the momentum had shifted in favor of Texas. The Longhorns drove to the shadow of the Aggie goal posts, only to be turned away inches from a touchdown as the third period ended. Then on their next possession, the Longhorns marched to the A&M eleven-yard line, Facing a fourth-and-seven situation, Texas made a first down by inches with a tackle-eligible play on the Aggie four. On the next play, Texas scored, kicked the extra point to make it 7-3 and collect its first SWC football championship.

"You can understand why it was such a bitter defeat," Bible recalled in later years, "and it was compounded by the loss coming late in the game." Added Bible, "That loss was the hardest to take of my coaching career."

Neither team was able to win on the rival's home field in SWC play until A&M came to Austin in 1922 and scored a 14-7 victory. The importance of the rivalry was underscored when Texas coach Berry Whitaker was fired shortly thereafter, despite posting a 7-2 record that season and an impressive three-year mark of 22-3-1, the best winning percentage of any Longhorn coach who served more than two seasons.

Texas scored its first victory at A&M's Kyle Field with a 6-0 triumph in 1923 on Lane Tyne's touchdown. After that, the superstition that neither team could win on the other's field remained intact until 1941. That year, to break the Kyle Field jinx, Texas students resorted to an old Chinese custom, many burning candles in their house for ten days prior to the Aggie game. Bible, then coaching the Longhorns, led them to a 23-0 triumph that day.

Although Kyle Field at College Station was the scene for many Texas frustrations, this was nothing compared to the psychic terror the Longhorns' Memorial Stadium held for Texas A&M. For four decades the Aggies could not win there, even with some of their grandest teams in history.

The Longhorns' best stands at Memorial Stadium in the jinx period from 1924 until 1956 were in 1936, 1938 and 1940. In 1936, the Longhorns went into the Aggie game credited with only one victory and a tie in seven games, but Red Sheridan, Judson Atchison and Hugh Wolfe collaborated in the first period for a touchdown, which Texas made good by repelling numerous A&M thrusts. The Aggies were again heavily favored in 1938 when they invaded Memorial Stadium, but the Longhorns beat their bitter rivals 7-6 with the help of Wally Lawson, Nelson Puett and Roy Baines. Bains was perhaps the most prominent member of that trio, climbing on a fellow guard's back to block Dick Todd's try for an extra point that would have tied the score for A&M. That victory, incidentally, was the only one of a dismal season for the Longhorns.

Two years later, the Longhorns and Aggies played one of the most exciting, and one of the most meaningful, games in their series. The Aggies were on the threshold of a second straight national championship when they came to Austin for their traditional Thanksgiving Day game with Texas. Unbeaten and barely scored upon in their first eight games of 1940 and boasting a nineteen-game winning streak as well, the Aggies had a Rose Bowl bid within their grasp and were overwhelming favorites to beat the Longhorns. Reflecting on the situation, end Dog Dawson says, "I don't think there was any doubt in anybody's mind that we would win." However, John Kimbrough, the superb A&M back who carried the appellation of "Jarring John" for obvious reasons, did not necessarily share the popular opinion. "We were far from overconfident," he says, "because Marion Pugh [the A&M quarterback] was injured and a very doubtful player."

Kimbrough's concern was well founded, it turned out. Texas started fast and ended with a big finishing kick, and the result was a 7-0 victory over the stunned Aggies. "They scored almost before the alma mater was finished," said Dawson about the Longhorns' touchdown strike in the first fifty-seven seconds. The Longhorns then dug in and held back repeated A&M threats spearheaded by a savage Kimbrough. Jack Crain, Malcolm Kutner, Noble Doss, Pete Layden and Buddy Jungmichel played leading roles for Texas in that stunning achievement. Soon after the game, the significance of the victory for Texas was emphasized when Dr. Homer P. Rainey, president of the university, and J. Howard Fouts, president of the Students' Association, declared the next day an official campus holiday.

Texas would continue to celebrate such occasions for many subsequent years, holding an unbeaten streak over the Aggies that extended until 1951. Texas A&M finally broke the eleven-game drought with a tension-filled 22-21 victory on a field goal by Olympic performer Darrow Hooper. Fighting broke out throughout the game and as the contest ended with Texas missing a desperation field-goal attempt, both teams charged onto the field in a wild free-for-all. The spirit of the day even caught Russell Hudeck, a big, jovial reserve tackle for A&M, who had played very little during his career, essentially because, some say, he was "easy going and not mean enough." He substituted in this game, however, and when a Texas player took a swing at him, Hudeck retaliated and decked his opponent. "Since we had seen Russell on so many occasions when the coaches tried vainly to get him fired up, it was surprising to see him take such an aggressive stand," says Glenn Lippman, the A&M fullback from that game.

After the war, pregame bonfires lent new spark to the rivalry, with each school trying to protect its wood supply from "enemy" sabotage. In 1949 an effort by four Aggies to sabotage a Texas woodpile literally backfired on the Cadets. The daring saboteurs drove by the mountainous stack of wood in broad daylight and threw gasoline onto it, but the flames leaped to the car, burning the back seat and two Aggies. Thwarted once, this did not stop the Aggies from trying again. The next day, they came in disguised as wood-gatherers and infiltrated the watchful defense at the Longhorns' Freshman Field. With the aplomb of cat burglars, they dropped two boxes of excelsior into the wood pile and ignited it.

Two students from Texas pulled off probably the most

daring prank in this regard. With one acting as a bombardier and the other as pilot, the two students flew in a two-seater private plane from about thirty-five feet over the A&M campus and dropped homemade incendiary bombs into the Aggie woodpile. The enraged Aggies jerked the flaming wood from their prematurely lighted bonfire and futilely returned the attack with sticks and stones.

In the ensuing years, the Aggies would be burned more than once by Texas on the football field, with Longhorn coach Darrell Royal boasting an overwhelming edge (17-3) in his twenty-year reign from 1957 through 1976. But if Texas A&M has had few satisfying moments against Texas in modern times, they have at least made them timely. The Aggies' 10-7 victory in 1967, fashioned on an eighty-yard touchdown pass from Edd Hargett to Bob Long, not only snapped a ten-game losing streak against Texas but gave A&M its first Southwest Conference championship in a decade. Then, of course, there was the Aggies' first victory in the Longhorns' intimidating Memorial Stadium. The Aggies, featuring future Heisman Trophy winner John David Crow, won the SWC title that year with the help of that exceptionally gratifying triumph over their arch rivals.

Bear Bryant, the renowned Alabama coach who was in charge of Texas A&M that season, remembers, "We were about five touchdowns better than Texas, yet I recall we were leading by only one touchdown as late as the fourth quarter. Texas was driving, but Lloyd Hale intercepted for us, and we added an insurance touchdown real late with Texas making a stubborn goal-line stand."

The Longhorns had one of their worst teams in history that year, winning but one game in ten, but as always the Aggie game brought out the best in them.

"I was impressed with how much the Longhorns played over their heads," says Jones Ramsey, the Texas sports information director. "A&M was really never in danger of losing, but Aggies who respected the Memorial Stadium tradition lived in fear until the end."

3
NOTRE DAME—ARMY
A National Issue

One evening at a New York bar, a burly longshoreman, his blood well above the boiling point, tackled the house on the subject of the Notre Dame football team.

"The Fighting Irish, they call 'em. Is that so, now?" roared the impassioned heckler. "Look at the names: Wisecowski, Filipowicz, Tamorczik, Holovak—where is there a bloody Irishman in the lot of them?"

Before his antagonized audience could reply, he continued in buglelike tones.

"Who have been the heroes of the Notre Dame team in the past twenty years? Eyetalians, Swedes—the likes of Carideo and Schwartz and Savoldi, Boledancewicz—a fine lot of Irishmen is all I can say."

At this point, the others in the bar challenged this giant intruder full-force, casting aspersions on his education, his ancestry and the like.

But the crusty longshoreman persisted in his unholy attack on Notre Dame and soon revealed his true colors as Army black, emphasizing that he was a lover of West Point football. To admit this in a bar that happened to be ninety-nine percent Irish took an enormous amount of courage and a great lack of tact. He topped off his vitriolic attack on the Fighting Irish with these fighting words:

"The Army will run them right out of the stadium tomorrow. It will be a 'massacray'—a 'massacray.' Fifty to nothing and more will be the score, and don't say I didn't tell you!"

It was not long afterward that the leather-lunged longshoreman found himself out on the street, much the worse for wear and tear. He had been given a version of the "flying wedge" by a half-dozen or so of the disgusted Hibernians at the bar, and sent babbling on his way into the night.

Such strong passion in the face of certain reprisal was indicative of the feelings long involved in the Army–Notre Dame series. The characters in the aforementioned scenario were representative of the fans involved, as well. Notre Dame's famed "Subway Alumni," never closer to South Bend, Indiana, than the sidewalks of New York, were loyalists purely by national identification, and this included just about every Irishman in the city. Army had its unofficial "alumni," too, and claimed a persistent national following, for the most part on the basis of its American military designation. One need not have attended West Point to be an "Army man."

Both schools, in fact, have been adopted nationally by many fans who never saw the inside of a college except in the movies. From 1913 through 1947, when the series was at its storied height, they flocked from all parts of the country to the game, which for the most part was played in New York's Yankee Stadium, and witnessed among other things the evolution of the forward pass, the birth of the Four Horsemen and the setting for some of Knute Rockne's most dramatic and eloquent moments.

For varied reasons, a temporary break in relations took place in 1947. The most common explanation, at the time, was that the series had become too one-sided in Notre Dame's favor. But there was a deeper, more complex answer. Actually, the series had gotten too big and too fierce for its own good and encouraged an uncommon hatred, not to mention a tawdry professional element. In a manner of speaking, they had taken the kids' game away from the kids.

The Subway Alumni, of course, have had their own individual heroes—from both schools.

For Army, the names of "Lighthorse" Harry Wilson, Chris Cagle, "Monk" Meyer, Hank Mazur, Doc

Blanchard and Glenn Davis are among the most prominent. Notre Dame would not be Notre Dame without mention of Knute Rockne, the famed Four Horsemen, Jim Crowley, Don Miller, Harry Stuhldreher, and Elmer Layden, and others of equal import that include George Gipp, Frank Carideo, "Moon" Mullins, Marchy Schwartz, Marty Brill, Joe Savoldi, Jack Elder and Bucky O'Connor.

Perhaps the most important name in the Army–Notre Dame rivalry, however, would be a non-player, Jesse Harper, the Irish coach who was the gadfly for the series. Back in 1912, Notre Dame had a far better football team than had been generally known, being rated even with Wisconsin, the Big Ten champions, by the *Spalding Register*, an official guide of the era. But the Irish had no national prestige and were several yards behind Army in this important public relations category. Army's reputation had been built on the wings of Eastern football, at that time the acknowledged geographical king of the sport.

Notre Dame got on the Army schedule by an accident of fate. Yale, an old West Point rival, had severed football relations with Army after their 1912 meeting and opened a date for another team. The powerful Cadets had some problems finding an opponent willing to play them, until they discovered Notre Dame. Harper, hoping to expand the football horizons of his relatively unknown school, had put out feelers for games to several colleges across the nation, including West Point.

"It was very simple," Harper recalled. "I wrote to Army to see if they had an opening on their schedule, and if so would they give us a game. No outside person knew anything about it until the game was arranged and contracts signed."

Harper was hardly shy about his dealings with the more significant football team. Obviously not dealing from a position of power, the plucky Harper nevertheless insisted on a fat guarantee for the game. He was offered $600 expenses for his squad, but he wanted $1,000. The fact that

Notre Dame expected to be paid at all for coming East was a distinct shock to the well-bred men of Yale, Harvard and Princeton, who always paid their way to West Point purely for the prestige of playing Army. Army at first balked at Harper's demand, but after a long and heated debate among members of West Point's athletic council, finally authorized the extraordinary expenses.

When Cadet Harold Loomis, the Army football manager, announced his 1913 football schedule, his satisfaction with having filled the open date with Notre Dame was soured by criticism from fellow corpsmen, who felt that West Point was stooping to "second-raters" to conquer. This thought was given further credance after an Army scout returned from South Bend in the fall of 1913 with an unimpressive report on the Fighting Irish.

"Eichenlaub, a big fellow, is a fine fullback," said Lieutenant Tom Hammond. "And the quarterback, Dorais, threw a number of smooth passes. He likes to throw to a fast, aggressive little end named Rockne. I don't believe they can beat us."

Certainly, the general appearance of the Notre Dame players did nothing to inspire awe when they stepped off the train from South Bend for their game on November 1 at Cullum Hall Field. They came in like beggars at the back door, some of them without a pair of football cleats to their name.

"We were permitted few luxuries on this trip from Indiana," Harper said. "The boys carried their uniforms in satchels—some wearing their jerseys under their coats to conserve space. Our only extra equipment was a roll of tape, a jug of liniment and a bottle of iodine. To cut expenses, we traveled by coach as far as Buffalo before changing sleepers."

Willet J. Baird, the wide-eyed Army mascot, who was on the train platform with other curiosity-seekers when the Fighting Irish arrived, recalled that Notre Dame "presented the usual appearance of a small college team which considered itself lucky to have so many players [18]. They came without the usual large trunks of baggage which were carried in those days by many leading Eastern teams. They were more impressed at having arrived at West Point and more concerned with the appearance of the academy than they were with the game that would take place."

Loomis, the only official Army greeter at the station, escorted the team up a steep hill, settled them in Cullum Hall and told them, "You'll spend the night here, and if you want a practice workout this afternoon, the field will be yours at four o'clock."

Apathy prevailed while the Fighting Irish went about their pregame business. Only a handful of Cadets and officers showed up to watch the Irish work out. Aside from Ray Eichenlaub, the burly Notre Dame fullback, the visitors from the unheralded Midwestern school appeared much smaller than the Army players.

After the Irish had eaten supper with the Cadets in Grant Hall the night before the game, Charles "Gus" Dorais, Knute Rockne and several other players looked in the New York newspapers for stories about their impending duel with Army. Dorais finally found a two-paragraph item hidden in the back of the sports section that gave the Irish ego a jolt. Their anonymity was underscored by a newspaper's mistaken reference to Illinois as the Irish's home state. "The fatheads!" mumbled Dorais. "Why, they don't even know where Notre Dame is located."

South Bend, Indiana, would be put on the map soon enough, however. Some 3,000 complacent fans, sitting calmly in the stands the next day looking for an easy Army victory, instead saw something that shocked them out of their seats. The fourth time the Fighting Irish got the ball, they drove eighty yards for a touchdown, mostly on the wings of the revolutionary forward pass. The Cadets were stunned by this explosion of air power as Dorais fired passes from any point on the field, many of them to Rockne.

"It was amusing to see the Army boys huddle after a first, snappy eleven-yard pass had been completed for a first down," Rockne later recalled. "Their guards and tackles went tumbling into us to stop line bucks and plunges. Instead, Dorais stepped neatly back and flicked the ball to an uncovered end or halfback."

When Army recovered from the shock and attempted to adjust to Notre Dame's spectacular passing game, Dorais cleverly took care of this West Point maneuver by shooting Eichenlaub through big, gaping holes up the middle for touchdowns. When Army closed in to stop Notre Dame's running game in the final quarter, Dorais again filled the air with footballs. The Cadets were completely baffled by this extraordinary air show, the likes of which had never before been seen in the East. And the Fighting Irish overcame Army's bulk and reputation and handed the Cadets a 35-13 beating, probably the most significant victory in Notre Dame history.

"The feature of the game that most amazed the sports fans in the East was the length of Dorais's passes," pointed out an observer. "Some of the spiral throws traveled thirty-five to forty yards to the receiver, an unheard-of distance in those days."

Dorais also threw an unheard-of volume of passes for those days. He completed fourteen of seventeen and compiled 243 yards through the air in the process. Bill Roper, the former coach of Princeton who was one of the officials at the game, said that he knew such play was possible under the new existing rules (the forward pass had been legalized in 1906) but that he had never seen the pass developed to such a state of perfection. Football men and the Eastern press marveled at such a concept. "The Westerners flashed the most sensational football seen in the East," the *New York Times* reported the next day.

What the story neglected to mention was the torturous, tedious work that had gone into the perfection of Notre Dame's passing game. For long hours daily in a gymnasium, Dorais worked with his two ends, Rockne and Fred "Gus" Gushurst, and halfback Tony Pliska. Outlines were drawn in chalk on the gym floor and the passes practiced to split-second count-offs. Dorais threw medium and long-range passes to his ends and hit Pliska with short lobs over the center of the line. Then, too, there was the Rockne –Dorais daring duo on the beaches of summer.

"That summer of 1913 at Cedar Point [Ohio], Rock and I practiced more than we ever had practiced before," Dorais pointed out. "Rock perfected his method of catching passes without tenseness in fingers, wrists or arms, and with the hands giving with the ball, just as a baseball should be caught. He also continued to develop his deceptive, stop-and-go style of going down the field for a pass, a style used by nearly all good pass receivers. I worked hard to increase both the accuracy and the length of my passes. A rule change that would become effective that fall had removed all restrictions on the length of a legal forward pass."

Such big Army stars as Lou Merillat, Vern Pritchard and Benny Hoge were dwarfed by the Irish élan. With Dorais passing to Rockne, Pliska, Gushurst and Charles Finegan, and Eichenlaub taking care of Notre Dame's ferocious ground game, Harper needed to use only one substitute that day, when Finegan broke a shoelace and sent an SOS to the bench for a new shoe or a new shoelace. Harper ordered Bunny Larkin to take off his shoes and send them into the game. But Larkin resisted.

"The hell I will," he said haughtily. "I didn't travel 1,000 miles to sit on the blankety-blank bench."

Harper looked at him and smiled. The scoreboard read: Notre Dame 35, Army 13, with less than a minute to go.

"Get in there at right half in place of Finegan, then, and be quick about it," Harper told Larkin.

On the Army bench sat a substitute who never did get into the game—none other than Dwight Eisenhower, who was to become the thirty-fourth president of the United States. While Eisenhower sat on the bench, Army coach Charles Daly "paraded up and down the sidelines nervously as he watched the depressing spectacle," said a newspaper. But Daly learned from it. Later in the year, Army used the forward pass almost exclusively while winning its big game against Navy, 22-9.

Notre Dame, which came into West Point like lambs, roared out like conquering champions, wasting little time getting back to a hero's welcome at South Bend.

"We were out of there the same night," said Rockne. "South Bend would have barred us for life if we hadn't hustled home right away. We were heroes—and they wanted us to know it!"

That particular welcome home remained one of Rockne's fondest memories, even if he was a bit nervous at the time. Remembered Dorais: "When we got out of our day coach at the South Bend railroad station, we found most of the town waiting for us. There was a parade with several bands and plenty of red fire, and of course, captain Knute Rockne was called on for a speech. He made one, but he was so nervous and embarrassed that he twisted most of the buttons off his coat while he was doing it; and no one in the audience could understand a word of what he said."

Because of this ringing success in Notre Dame's Eastern debut, Army immediately became the big game on the Fighting Irish schedule. And the Cadets, thirsting for revenge, eagerly awaited each succeeding game. The rivalry blossomed. In 1919, when Harper turned over the coaching reins to Rockne, he told him: "Rock, keep this Army game on your schedule. One day it might be big enough to play in New York City."

And so it was, promoted in part by the wildly exciting talents of George Gipp. His showmanship was so revered by football audiences that they sometimes sat in silent awe when he left a field. Remembers Buck Shaw, a teammate of the Gipper: "They felt that any demonstration would be a kind of sacrilege. It was eerie. I've never known another who got to people that way."

But despite his designation as an All-American, he was far from the general concept of the all-American boy. Too sophisticated for schoolboy pleasures and rarely a social mixer with teammates, Gipp searched for the conventional vices and found companionship among gamblers, pool sharks, and other unsavory, honky-tonk types. He readily admitted, "I'm the finest free-lance gambler ever to attend Notre Dame," and put his money where his mouth was time and again. Whether it was shooting pool, playing cards, or playing football, Gipp went for big stakes. It was not unusual for him to bet $100 on the flip of a coin or $500 on Notre Dame's ability to beat the point spread.

Gipp was at his classic best in the 1920 Army game, as Notre Dame trundled into the locker room at halftime losing 17-14. Rockne gave one of his most fiery speeches and when he was finished talking, looked around the room to note the effect of his words. He found every player fighting mad with the exception of Gipp who was lounging against a door with a look of boredom.

Rockne gave his star halfback a menacing look.

"I don't suppose you have the slightest interest in this game," the coach said.

"You're wrong there," said the swaggering Gipp. "I've got five hundred bet on this game, Rock, and I don't intend to blow it."

With that, Gipp returned to action and went to serious work. He ran a punt back thirty yards, threw a forty-yard touchdown pass, and kicked the extra point, then returned another punt fifty-five yards. He gained 236 yards on the ground and 96 in the air for a total of 332 for the day—more than the entire Army team. And Notre Dame won, 27-17.

It's probable that Gipp won a bundle on the Army game of 1919 as well. Inspired to greater heights by financial reward, Notre Dame's famous player used some quick footwork and fast thinking to help beat the Cadets 12-9. Remembered Rockne:

"The Cadets had us at a disadvantage of 9 to 0—and it looked at if they were going to hold it. Toward the end of the first half, the Notre Dame quarterback, Joe Brandy, opened up a passing attack—George Gipp throwing. This attack culminated with a cannon-ball pass from Gipp to [Pete] Bahan on Army's one-yard line. [Ojay] Larson, at center for us, awaited signals when Gipp called sharply, 'Pass the ball!' Gipp had had a flash of the head linesman lifting his horn to blow the end of the half. While both teams looked on in surprise, he grabbed the ball from Larson and dove over the goal line for a touchdown. The instant Gipp caught the ball, the linesman's horn sounded; but the half wasn't over until the ball was dead, and the ball wasn't dead until the touchdown was made. I've never seen a piece of quicker thinking on the part of a player."

The Army game seemed to be the stage for many of the stories surrounding Gipp's flamboyant career, and of course these colorful sidelights did nothing to harm the image of the rivalry. Once Gipp was playing safety against Army when he let a Cadet runner take the ball in for a touchdown without so much as making a move to get him. "The hell with him," Gipp said nonchalantly. "Let him go. We'll get it back and plenty more." Later in the same game, the Notre Dame star showed more of that unabashed ego that simply floored opponents. When Gipp's gorgeous forty-five-yard pass from his own end zone was dropped by Roger Kiley, he consoled his halfback with these words: "Don't worry about it, Rog. We'll call it again and stand them on their ear."

Gipp continued to play as hard off the field as he did on it through the season of 1920 and this extracurricular activity finally took its toll. A combination of high living and hard playing caught up with him after his extraordinary performance in the Army game and his health steadily moved downhill, until he developed pneumonia. Transfusions from his teammates prolonged his life as he lay stricken in a hospital, but Gipp continued to sink. He finally succumbed on December 14, 1920, at the age of twenty-five. His premature death came as South Bend, almost to a man, prayed for his recovery. As Gipp was on his deathbed, students were seen kneeling in the snow on campus, deep in prayer. Then the bells tolled, announcing the end for one of college football's most legendary players.

Attached to Gipp's death is the granddaddy of all sports stories, which perhaps more than any other had gained millions of uncommitted football fans for Notre Dame and focused special attention on the series with Army. While his mother, brother, sister and Rockne maintained a vigil at his bedside, Gipp supposedly made a memorable request in his last hour.

"I've got to go, Rock," he is quoted as saying. "It's all right. Sometime, Rock, when the team is up against it, when things are going wrong and the breaks are beating the boys—tell them to go in there with all they've got and win just one for the Gipper. I don't know where I'll be then, Rock, but I know I'll be happy."

Rockne of course made this famous by using Gipp's alleged request during a speech at the Army game of 1928. The "win one for the Gipper" appeal helped the Irish win a game against overwhelming odds and established an incomparable legend that was dramatized in movies and glorified in prose for years afterward. The "win one for the Gipper" request is almost too perfect to be true and almost too corny to be real; it would have been more in keeping with Gipp's flamboyant character to ask Rockne to put down a bet for him some day when the Irish were a sure thing. Likewise, it would have been more in Rockne's theatrical character to encourage his team to win one for the Gipper. For those who have had a hard time swallowing it, however, Rockne himself put the stamp of authenticity on Gipp's melodramatic statement. In his autobiography, Rockne insisted it really happened. A priest who was in the room said he heard Gipp say it. Rockne's assistant, Hunk Anderson, said that the head coach told him about it minutes after Gipp's death. And Notre Dame people, to a man, swear by it.

If there is some suspicion today about the request, there was certainly no question of its value as employed by Rockne in that 1928 game in Yankee Stadium. Coming in as the favorites, the all-powerful Cadets were led by Chris Cagle and a host of All-Americans. The Fighting Irish, in turn, were suffering through their worst season under Rockne. By early November, the injury-stricken Irish had already lost two games and a third loss seemed almost a certainty when they faced Army. Rockne knew that only a miracle could save Notre Dame that day, and he found one in his pregame speech. Ed Healey, the Notre Dame line coach that year, was an eyewitness to a magical piece of football history.

"Rock was terribly disturbed on the day of the game," Healey recalls. "About five minutes before game time, he spoke to the team. He prefaced his remarks on the terrific Army team. Finally, he recalled standing beside the death bed of George Gipp and told of reaching out his hand and listening to the dying athlete say, 'Coach, when the going gets rough, especially against Army, win one for me.' And of course, he repeated the word, 'Gipper.' And he went on to emphasize not only how important it was to them, the boys themselves, but likewise to answer the prayer of the Gipper, who was a convert to Catholicism on his deathbed. So you see there was a touch of the spiritual motivation about it all. And I'm telling you, there wasn't a dry eye in the house. We were all crying. I don't give a damn who it was. . . ."

Army could not have neutralized Notre Dame's emotion after that episode, even with tanks or guns. Sparked by Rockne's speech, the inspired Irish won the game 12-6 with two touchdowns in the second half. Jack Chevigny, who was just about Notre Dame's entire running attack that day, blasted over from the one-yard line in the third period to tie the score at 6-6. When the emotional halfback picked himself up in the end zone, he was supposed to have said, "That's one for the Gipper." Later, Chevigny helped set up Notre Dame's winning touchdown, although he was not there at its conclusion. Chevigny had to be removed from the game with an injury, leaving the hero's role to "One-Play" O'Brien.

Johnny O'Brien was sent into the game in the last quarter, when Notre Dame had the ball on the Army thirty-two. Too lean and willowy for steady football action, O'Brien was a track star with wonderful speed who could catch a football, and that was precisely what Rockne had in mind for him as precious time ticked away. On the first play, quarterback Pat Brady called O'Brien's play. Butch Niemec backpedaled and fired a long pass in O'Brien's direction. The ball arched over the head of Army's defensive back, stumpy Billy Nave, and hit O'Brien's hands on the ten-yard line. The receiver juggled the ball as he staggered toward the Army goal line. Finally, he clutched it firmly as he dived over the line, missing the straining grasps of two Army defenders.

Several years before the famous "Gipper" speech put the stamp of greatness on the Notre Dame–Army series, there were significant developments. Riding out of the Midwest on Grantland Rice's royal prose, the Four Horsemen had made Notre Dame most everybody's favorite and made the Notre Dame–Army rivalry a national institution. On October 19, 1924, sports fans picked up newspapers and read for the first time about the Four Horsemen outlined against Rice's "blue-gray October sky." That imaginative piece of writing was all that was needed to capture the public's fancy. Stuhldreher, Miller, Crowley and Layden did the rest, wearing their new title with style and elegance. After taking care of Army in New York by a 13-7 score, the "Horsemen" rode back to South Bend, where a smart publicity man put them on horses for a picture and a legend was made as quickly as you could snap a camera shutter.

While watching that historic 1924 clash from the press box, Rice began composing in his mind the most-remembered story in sports journalism history. And as the final gun went off, a telegrapher began punching out Rice's stirring report, which began: "Outlined against a blue-gray October sky, the Four Horsemen rode again. In dramatic lore they are known as Famine, Pestilence, Destruction and Death. These are only aliases. Their real names are

Stuhldreher, Miller, Crowley and Layden. . . ."

If ever a group of players belonged to an age, it was the
Four Horsemen. They were suited to the rhythm of the
golden twenties and danced to its rollicking tune in perfect
steps. Romance was in high gear and so was good, old-
fashioned corn. And sportswriters fed plenty of both to the
hungry masses.

Football fans eagerly swallowed the whole Notre Dame
image and built up a national following, orchestrated by
Knute Rockne, that was second to none in college football.
Followers of the South Bend institution were head-
quartered in New York under the impudent sobriquet of
the Subway Alumni but could be found in the four corners
of the land, whenever there was anyone named Ryan or
Rafferty, Clancy or O'Houlahan. Army's backers, if not
quite as large in number, were just as fierce. Yet there was
an element of warm affection whenever these teams played
in the twenties, a curious kind of sports love engendered by
Rockne's unique personality. The rivalry was more of a
happening than a game, engaging both the fan and the
non-fan, and became, according to one writer, an annual
sentimental jag that ". . . took on the quality of a pagan
autumnal rite and engaged the fervent observation of millions of people."

In the years that followed, Notre Dame's growth as an
outstanding educational institution was matched by its
ability to recruit the best football players in the country.
Army, for its part, went in exactly the opposite direction,
but somehow the Cadets managed to play excellent defensive football and kept the scores low and the drama
high. Despite the fact that Notre Dame won ten games and
tied two of the twelve meetings from 1932 through 1943, it
was undoubtedly the most bitterly fought series in the land.

The game was permanently moved to New York's gargantuan Yankee Stadium because of the unique demand
for tickets. But even this could not appease the voracious
public. "They could get 85,000 people into Yankee Stadium, and they wanted more people to see the game," said

one observer. "But that still left 120,000 prospective ticket-buyers who couldn't get any closer than Jerome Avenue." The annual game guaranteed a gate of at least a half-million dollars, but there was more being made on the outside by avaricious ticket scalpers, who pounced on the situation and shot seat prices sky-high. Fair distribution of tickets was impossible during the forties, at the euphoric height of the series.

Players were constantly hounded for tickets, and some moonlighted by selling theirs for $100 a seat. Notre Dame's Frank Tripucka recalls the pregame hysteria:

"The hotel lobby was so packed with well-wishers and people who wanted tickets that it was worth your life·to sneak out of your room for a drink of water. They even mobbed the practice field."

Ironically, though, the very fact that the series had gotten so large eventually led to its eventual curtailment. The game, it turned out, began slipping away from the schools because of its national importance. It drew a tawdry gambling element and, with these professionals on hand, it was estimated that something in the neighborhood of $5 million was wagered on the Army–Notre Dame contest each year.

The annual spectacle had become a blood war as well—and not only on the field. Zealots who attached themselves to Notre Dame became a constant source of embarrassment to the Fighting Irish and a continual pain to the Cadets. Their taunts from the stands were excessively spiced with sheer venom and born of uncommon hatred, it seemed to Army coach Earl Blaik.

"We never made a friend out of that game," Blaik would say later.

Notre Dame's Subway Alumni, who had virtually taken over Yankee Stadium, became a very real enemy for the West Pointers and their fans. During the years of the Second World War, the Subway Alumni hit at the national pride of the Army players, often chiding them as "draft-dodgers." From the moment the Cadets stepped on the field, the heated Notre Dame fanatics let loose with jeers. The cries became more intense as the game became more intense.

Blaik, an exceptional leader of men and like his Notre Dame counterpart, Frank Leahy, a brilliant football strategist, was sharply conscious of this strong anti-Army feeling. "The game has provided a form of psychological hatred detrimental to the best interests of the Army," he said, "and it could hardly tolerate a condition that bred such ill will for the service and the Military Academy." Blaik pointed to, among other things, piles of daily "hate mail" that Army players received.

Before these distractions drove a temporary wedge between the schools in 1948, the series itself had lost none of its supreme artistry. Such players as Johnny Lujack at Notre Dame and Glenn Davis and Doc Blanchard at Army would have their day, piling new legends on top of the ones etched by Rockne and Company.

The expression of Army football energy in the forties was channeled through Davis and Blanchard, two of the most exciting and proficient runners in Cadet history. Together they earned themselves the title of "Mr. Inside and Mr. Outside," the lithe Davis slicing around ends and the bullish Blanchard drilling through lines. Their talents were considerable. Blanchard was just as deadly off the ball as on, so powerful that a game film of him laying out two different opponents on a kickoff return is considered the classic demonstration of downfield blocking. Davis, a fleet halfback who went on to play pro football long after a torn knee and military service had made that kind of career seem impossible, was the highest scoring star to come out of the great rivalry with Notre Dame.

These were only two of many fine players who made the 1944 Army squad one of the most impressive college teams in history. Because of the Second World War, the service academies wound up with most of the country's football talent, and Army seemed to have prospered even more than Navy in this area. The list of talent under Blaik's command that fall was so staggering that the coach ran his rich team in interchangeable units. It was apparent that not even Navy would stem Army's march to the national championship that season and after the Cadets had humiliated Villanova 83-0 the week before the Notre Dame game, the deluge of vitriolic hate mail from segments of the Subway Alumni began to pour into West Point.

Notre Dame, with Ed McKeever serving as interim coach in the wartime absence of Leahy, had done deceptively well against other college squads equally decimated by the war effort. But the balance of power was painfully obvious when Navy's big gunners blasted the Irish 32-13. Sportswriters knew that Notre Dame would be overmatched against Army, and they weren't the only ones. A New York bookmaker, enraged over trying to balance the bets against a flood of Army money which continued to roll in, barked: "People who bet the Notre Dames are men. People who bet Army are mouses."

"He was wasting his breath," noted one sportswriter. "The Subway Alumni, which had thrived on a sure thing for so long, would not support its venom with its money."

When Army's superior forces led by captain Tom Lombardo came up the dugout steps and onto the field at Yankee Stadium, they bore little resemblance to the squads long-dominated by the Fighting Irish. Notre Dame had won ten and tied two of the twelve preceding games, and the Subway Alumni sensed that the string was about to be cut. The invective thundered out of the stands, directed at the Cadets.

The Cadets answered the best way they knew how, with an explosion of touchdowns. Army scored the first three times it had the ball. By halftime it was 33-0 in favor of the Cadets and during the second half it was just as bad. The West Pointers, as if purging the aftertaste of all those bitter prior defeats, added insult to injury by permitting a substitute tackle, Hal Tavzel, to catch a touchdown pass as the final touch in a 59-0 Army rout.

It was generally throught that Notre Dame had been deliberately humiliated and Blanchard conveyed this idea in the storm of indignation which followed. "If there was anyone to blame for the size of the margin, it was Notre Dame, which fired our desire to win with its long humiliation of Army teams," he said.

Following Blanchard's simple overstatement was Blaik's more pointed remark: "What Army did find sharply distasteful was that segment of the Subway Alumni, neither small nor quiet, which had, in the thirties and early forties, come to regard the Notre Dame–Army game in Yankee Stadium as a sporting event only so long as Notre Dame continued to win it."

The outrageous size of the 1944 score did nothing to deter the hard-core Subway Alumni of Notre Dame, who descended on Yankee Stadium the following year in hopes of a miracle. But the only stars shining on the field that day belonged to the Army and the Cadets administered another bad beating to the Fighting Irish, this time by a 48-0 score. The Irish were no more than another steppingstone to the national championship for Army's privileged team.

Those two rousing Army victories did as much to test the relationship of the schools as anything before or after. It was apparent after Army ran up 107 points on Notre Dame in the two seasons that nothing involving the united football fortunes of Notre Dame and Army would ever be the same again. It was a symbolic dark counterpoint to the mutual respect engendered during Rockne's fruitful days of the twenties. It was a rivalry born of love that had turned to hate, and Leahy and Blaik's relationship personified this fact. "There was no love lost between them," pointed out an observer.

In 1946, the two institutions would take part in one of the most emotional games ever played in college football.

"Before the 1946 season had begun," said a writer, "it had been accepted that Army–Notre Dame would be the game of the year, a vengeful vendetta in which Leahy and his legions, who had listened to these games overseas, would demand repayment in kind for the humiliation."

Among Notre Dame's Johnnies who had come marching home was Lujack, one of college football's most honored quarterbacks. Lujack was an inspirational play-caller who rarely did the obvious and his offensive genius sometimes overshadowed his brilliance as a defender. The 1946 Notre Dame team boasted certified All-Americans in Lujack, tackle George Connor, guard John Mastrangelo and center George Strohmeyer and a gaggle of other future prize-winners, including Bill Fischer, Leon Hart, Ziggy Czarobski, Emil Sitko, Jim Martin and Marty Wendell. The Army still had Blanchard and Davis, a talented quarterback named Arnold Tucker, and a skilled, deadly group of linemen judged among the best in the nation. New York bookmakers estimated that close to $25 million was bet on the outcome of that single football game in Yankee Stadium, and its buildup was incredible.

Preparations for the game bordered on the hysterical at Notre Dame. Running through formations, the Irish would stop every so often and bellow:

"Fifty-nine and forty-eight.
This is the year we retaliate."

Frank Tripucka, an understudy to the great Lujack, recalls: "The Sunday before we played Army, Jack Lavalle came in and gave us the scouting report and you could hear a pin drop. The next day we were on the practice field and Ziggy Czarobski was leading cheers in the huddle. Normally, Leahy never would have stood for that but he let us go and we got higher and higher. It was only Tuesday and we were acting like a pack of mad dogs."

Both teams were undefeated, but Notre Dame was made a slight favorite on the basis of having played a supposedly tougher schedule.

"I can remember the bus ride down to the ball park and I can remember the pregame locker room," Tripucka says. "I have never in my life seen a football team so emotionally high. Nobody had to tell us anything. I imagine it was the same way in that other locker room."

It was, but the game that was supposed to decide everything eventually decided nothing, except that here were two irresistible defensive giants. A crowd of more than 74,000 saw Army fail to cash in on six scoring opportunities, watched Notre Dame stopped on the Army three-yard line and witnessed Tucker of the Army and Lujack and Terry Brennan of Notre Dame dominate the defense with interceptions and key tackles. Perhaps the most remembered play was Lujack's one-on-one tackle of Blanchard in the open field that saved a scoreless tie for the Fighting Irish. Although Lujack tended to downplay his extraordinary effort as a "routine tackle," it was the most conspicuous thing that happened on the Stadium turf that day because of its effect on the game's outcome.

This is the way Bill Leiser described it in the *San Francisco Chronicle* on November 10, 1946:

"Felix (Doc) Blanchard, Mister Football of 1946, broke around right flank, sped fifteen yards down the sideline and headed for the touchdown that was to be the climax of all gridiron climaxes in this topsy-turvy football year. Johnny Lujack, the only man who could possibly have anything to say to the contrary, said no. The only man in position even to reach the flying six-foot, 205-pound one-half of the touchdown twins now on a rampage, Lujack didn't miss."

Lujack's heroic play was little consolation for him and the rest of the Fighting Irish, who straggled into their dressing room at the end, anguish and disappointment scrawled on their faces. They had stopped the nation's best running attack cold, but they had failed to win the game they wanted. Leahy closed the door to the dressing room and faced his tortured team resolutely.

"You played your hearts out, but you were not quite good enough today," he said softly. "Remember one thing now—the test of a champion is how he reacts to adversity on the days when it is bound to come."

It was the only tough game of the year for the Fighting Irish, who went on to edge Army for the national championship with an unwitting assist from Navy. The Midshipmen, who had been crushed earlier in the season by Notre Dame, fell only a few yards and a few seconds short of upsetting Army on the last day of the season. On the basis of comparative scores, the Irish were handed the national title.

Notre Dame's triumph over Army in the national polls only seemed to drive a wedge deeper between the schools. There were indications that Army wanted out of their renowned series because it was getting too lopsided in Notre Dame's favor, and this was perhaps one of many reasons for the intersectional powers to temporarily call off the passionate rivalry after the 1947 season. Actually, the more profound reason was that the series had gotten too big, too important, for its own good. In their joint statement to the public, Army and Notre Dame stressed this unwholesome conditions.

"Two reasons led to the decision," the statement said. "The first was the conviction of the authorities of both schools that the Army–Notre Dame game had grown to such proportions that it had come to be played under conditions escaping the control of the two colleges, some of which were not conducive to wholesome intercollegiate sport. The second reason was the desire of West Point as a national institution to achieve greater flexibility in the scheduling of intersectional opponents throughout the country."

Although announcement of the split was couched in friendly language, promising resumption of the series after a few years' cooling-off period, there were indications of great bitterness between the schools.

"There were signs that it wasn't all sweetness and light," wrote Lewis Burton in the *New York Journal-American*. "Harsh criticisms of Notre Dame's recruiting measures openly expressed by Earl Blaik, Army coach, could not be described as 'cordial' by any stretch of the imagination."

The divorce game of 1947 was taken out of the city and moved to the more prosaic surroundings of South Bend "out of consideration for the cordial relationships which have always existed between West Point and Notre Dame," the official announcement said. By this time, Army football had slipped a bit and to the disappointment of a superb Notre Dame team, Columbia had upset the Cadets two weeks earlier, thus denying the Fighting Irish the chance to personally end Army's defeatless string, which had reached thirty-three.

Notre Dame, however, did have the satisfaction of handing Army a shellacking. For all intents and purposes, the 1947 game ended almost before it had begun. Brennan, who in later years would rise to the position of Irish coach, ran back the opening kickoff ninety-seven yards for a touchdown while a record crowd of 59,191 went crazy. The play happened so quickly that Brennan's father, who had been delayed en route to the stadium, never saw it. Army never regained its equilibrium after that game-opening sock, although Leahy customarily fretted and fumed throughout. When the score was 14-0 in favor of Notre Dame shortly before the end of the first half, the Irish were in a fourth-and-one situation, which normally dictated a kick. Instead, Tripucka brought Notre Dame out in a straight T-formation and the B-unit quarterback could hear Leahy's trepidation all the way from the sideline. Tripucka probably will never forget it:

" 'Francis . . . Oh . . . no . . . Francis . . . don't. . . .'

"I popped our fullback, Floyd Simmons, off-tackle and he went for almost thirty yards. Then he fumbled. Army recovered. The noise was unbelievable, but I swear I could still hear Leahy. When I started to come off the field he ran out and grabbed me. He was saying things like, 'Oh, Francis, how could you, Francis? Francis, why do you hate me? You do, you know. You hate me. You hate your teammates. You hate Notre Dame. You even hate the Lady on the Golden Dome.

"Thank God Army didn't score but he followed me all the way into the locker room talking like that and all through halftime he told them, 'Look at this boy. This boy hates me. He hates you. He hates Notre Dame. He let us down. Why do you hate us, Francis?' "

Apparently Leahy didn't hate Tripucka, though, for he let him play the entire second half as the Irish won with consummate ease, 27-7.

Army and Notre Dame took a ten-year hiatus from each other, then resumed their series in 1957, when the Irish won a thrilling 23-21 decision in Philadelphia's Municipal Stadium. The break in athletic relations seemed to have had a wonderful therapeutic effect on the schools. The poison and bitterness were gone, and so was the wildly religious fanaticism engendered by the Subway Alumni. Somehow, it was just another passionate college football game played on a brilliant autumn afternoon. Knute Rockne would have liked that very much.

4
DUKE—NORTH CAROLINA
"Beat Dook"

The North Carolina–Duke series has been a rivalry made in heaven and appreciated by just about everyone but the management at the old Washington Duke Hotel. For years that venerable mansion in Durham, North Carolina, stood as the battleground for student celebration and sabotage. One year after a particularly exhilarating North Carolina victory, the Tar Heel celebrants in a fit of joy hurled all the loose furniture from the mezzanine down into the lobby, causing a good deal of commotion and consternation. This was an unusually lusty group. Usually, the most dangerous flying objects around the hotel were water-filled bags, toilet tissue and raw eggs.

Needless to say, the Washington Duke Hotel was forced to redecorate each year after the North Carolina–Duke game.

If the divine series has brought out the best in the players, it appears to have encouraged the worst in the camp followers. The aforementioned hotel pranks were tame compared to some of the action by wild-eyed partisans, particularly in the thirties—the Golden Age of this spirited, off-the-field feud.

The statue of Old Man Duke on the women's campus in Durham was a particularly enticing target for North Carolina raiding parties in the old days. An elaborate goal-line stand was usually set up at Duke to thwart the Tar Heel vandals. One year the Duke students surrounded the place with a board of nails to discourage automobile attacks and a firehose to discourage raiders on foot.

"If anyone got through the first two lines of defense,

there would always be a cordon of young toughs waiting with sand-filled socks," notes one North Carolina football historian.

A treasured statue, Silent Sam, and the Old Well at Chapel Hill were the main targets for Duke students directly before the game with North Carolina. But anyone attempting to deface North Carolina's prize landmarks faced the barbaric ordeal of kidnapping and a shaved and painted head.

Bonfire sites were also strategic points. A continual crossfire occurred, riots resulted and a lot more than feelings were hurt during these sorties. Rameses, North Carolina's mascot goat, was sometimes plucked off campus, no matter how well guarded, trundled off and released the day of the game, swathed in a painted coat of Duke Blue. The Victory Bell, the symbolic trophy passed to the victor each year, was never safe, no matter on whose campus it stood. Even those not directly involved in the emotional rivalry got a taste of its flavor. Movies in Durham were intermittently interrupted by demoniacal Duke students, who commandeered the projection booth, flicked on house lights, and chanted "Beat Carolina" from the stage.

In later years, the partisanship passions became more intellectual and less physical, but remained just as emotionally unstable. The Tar Heel mascot and Victory Bell continued to disappear mysteriously into the November night, the "Heel Howl" made thousands roar, the "Beat Dook Parade" lit up the town in Chapel Hill, and there were innumerable toasts of all varieties to both teams.

On the field, the rivalry has been equally as intense and unpredictable and immeasureably more vicious.

A classic rivalry because the schools are only eight miles apart, the Duke–Carolina series has been one of streaks. North Carolina won nine straight games between 1894 and 1929 and Duke won four straight beginning with two games in 1943. The Tar Heels won four in a row during the glamorous Charlie Justice years, 1946-49, and then Duke ripped off seven straight in the fifties. Bill Dooley's North

Carolina teams of the seventies took three in a row at one point over Duke and for the most part have dominated the Tar Heels' most traditional rival, a fact that has put him on solid footing with the powers at Chapel Hill.

Dooley's domination of Duke includes a 59-34 aberration in 1970, something that no doubt will be remembered as long as Don McCauley's records stand—which should be quite a while. That day, the magnificent McCauley hammered for 279 yards and five touchdowns in a glorious, record-breaking game. Called by Dooley "the greatest football player I've ever seen," McCauley finished his last game at Kenan Stadium owning twenty-three records, including the NCAA single-season mark of 1,720 yards.

McCauley, often mentioned in the same breath at Chapel Hill with Carolina's beloved Justice, the prototypical folk hero, remembers he was kept awake by a recurring nightmare on the eve of his biggest game in college.

"I had trouble sleeping," he recalls. "I was scared to death, thinking about this being my last game at home and everything. Going into the game, I wasn't even thinking about records. I remember there was a writeup the night before saying this one game I wasn't going to break any."

But it's possible that not even Justice in his finest hour ever received the thunderous ovation McCauley heard in the Duke game that day. For the last several minutes of the contest, the 48,000 fans chanted fanatically, "We want McCauley. We want McCauley."

One sportswriter remembers: "It sounded exactly like somebody trying to stampede a national political convention. If the voting age were lowered a trifle, and maybe even without the edge, Don McCauley could have been elected governor of North Carolina."

He certainly had the vote of just about everyone in Kenan Stadium that afternoon. The adoring fans couldn't wait to get their hands on North Carolina's All-American player, who had carried the ball forty-seven times—thirteen more than the entire Duke team. Three times the festive crowds flooded the field while the game was still going and had to be pushed back over the sidelines. At game's end, McCauley was swept up by his admirers and carried across the field on a wave of humanity. Even a Duke fan confessed that he had been caught up in the McCauley-mania. "I quit pulling for a Duke victory about midway through the third quarter," he said. "I just sat there and marveled at that guy running with the football."

Justice now sells insurance in Greensboro, North Carolina, but back in the forties, directly after the Second World War, he was selling football to the masses. And they were eating it up in big gulps.

"I never played before an empty seat in Kenan Stadium," he remembers with nostalgia. "We went to three Bowls when I was there. When our teams left Chapel Hill after 1949, they were $500,000 in the black."

Modesty prevents Justice from estimating his total impact on football in his time, but it is wholly insufficient to say that he was an All-American football player and that he ran and passed for 4,176 yards, averaged 42.5 yards on punts and 16.2 on kick returns, scored thirty-nine touchdowns, and threw for twenty-six more from 1946 through 1949. There were players who could pass better, others who could run faster and some who could kick farther, but there was no one who could do all these things as well in one man. Far from the classic runner, Justice nevertheless would leave infuriated tacklers in the dust with his gorgeous feints, a wiggle of the hip there, and a twist of the head there.

"He wasn't very fast," says North Carolina newspaperman Dick Herbert. "I mean, not real fast. And he ran a little spraddle-legged. But when he got hold of the ball, well, everybody got excited. In fact, his one run against Duke is regarded as one of the greatest of all time. I think it was for forty-three yards, and I think everybody on the Duke team had at least one shot at him. There was that old story about how one of the Duke players missed him at the line of scrimmage, and somebody said, 'Why don't you get up?' And he said, 'I'm staying here because he's going to come back this way again.' "

Justice, nicknamed "Choo Choo" because he ran like a train on a snaking, uneven track, was the ultraviolet ray at North Carolina during his time, a classic campus hero. Aside from his obvious talents as a football player, his enormous popularity was explainable. Justice thrived in a very romantic period of American life, points out Orville Campbell, a long-time friend: "He came along at a time when every little kid wanted to grow up to be somebody else, a football hero or even president. . . . Nobody captured the imagination of the American public the way he captured the imagination of the people in North Carolina."

For the first three years of his career, Carolina's most noble runner led the Tar Heels to rather handy victories over Duke. Then in the 1949 game, just when it appeared that the Blue Devils would turn the tables because Justice was lame, he dramatically led North Carolina to a fourth straight victory, 21-20, in one of the South's all-time classics.

The week before, Justice had been kept out of the Notre Dame game with an ankle injury, and it was not completely healed when it came time to play Duke. However, Justice was ready to play when he heard the thunderous ovation from the stands for his last game in Duke Stadium. Teammate Art Weiner recalls that the "Carolina fans got up and cheered solidly for fifteen minutes when we came on the field. They didn't sit down; it was a deafening kind of thing. It was unreal."

The way things started, however, it did not appear to be Justice's or Carolina's day. Duke's Billy Cox stunned the Tar Heels with a dazzling, seventy-five-yard touchdown run, although the shock was softened a bit when the Blue Devils missed the extra-point attempt. Another crippling blow then hit the Tar Heels when Justice aggravated his ankle injury and had to be carried off the field.

The game belonged to Duke until Justice got some Novocaine in his ankle and went back on the field. Then North Carolina's lame thoroughbred showed that he was as good on one leg as most players were on two—probably better. Justice passed to Weiner for a touchdown, and North Carolina had a 7-6 lead at the half. He later caught a touchdown pass from Billy Hayes, then threw another one to Weiner, expanding the Tar Heels' lead to 21-6 in the third quarter.

Duke was not finished, however, and just as the Carolina cheers were fading, they were drowned completely by roars from the Blue Devil supporters. It took their team just eighteen seconds to get back into the game, as Tom Powers returned the kickoff ninety-three yards for a touchdown and Mike Souchak kicked the extra point to narrow North Carolina's lead to 21-13 going into the fourth quarter.

From that point on, the game flourished at high-pitched insanity, and the crowd of 57,500 went berserk, as well.

The Blue Devils held the ball for most of the intense fourth period but were unable to score until North Carolina fumbled in the last few minutes. Four plays later, the omnipresent Cox went over right tackle for a touchdown, and Souchak kicked the extra point to bring Duke within one point with 2:55 remaining in the game.

Remarkably, Duke's inspired defense bottled up North Carolina's high-powered offense deep in its territory on two separate possessions in the final three minutes. After the second time, Justice tried to kick Carolina out of a hole, but it was a weak effort, and Powers returned the ball to the Tar Heel twenty.

Now there were only seconds left and Cox desperately threw an incomplete pass in an attempt to stop the clock. However, it appeared to be too late. The clock showed no time left and fans signaled the apparent end of the game by spilling on the field and embracing the North Carolina players. But they were told by Justice, "Please, please stand back!" Then they understood that victory was not theirs yet and melted back across the sidelines in shocked disbelief. Officials had ruled that time had stopped when

Cox's pass hit the ground, so actually the Blue Devils still had one play left in the game.

"It took police and groundkeepers and a frenzied appeal from the public address system about five minutes to clear the field," reported North Carolina's *Alumni Review*.

"I'll bet there was something like 15,000 people on the field," remembers Weiner. "They had to go back and round up some of the players, too."

All Duke had to do to win was get a modest field goal out of Souchak's toe from the twenty-yard line. The Blue Devils hurriedly lined up for what figured to be a cinch three points, but Weiner blasted through to block the kick and preserve Carolina's high-tension victory.

"Evidentally they had a mix-up in blocking assignments, because nobody even touched me," says Weiner, recalling one of the most famous blocked kicks in North Carolina history. "Paul Stephanz and one or two other Duke players have told me since that some of their players even left the field, as some of ours had, and when it came time to get the place-kicking team together, there was a lot of confusion, and I don't think they had their whole team lined up. Mike Souchak was to attempt a field goal from the twenty-yard line. But instead of lining up for a field goal, they lined up like they would for a punt, with both of their blockers on the right side and nobody on the left side where I was. I was very, very close to the ball, and I got there so fast that I almost ran on by the guy holding the ball. Had I done that, we probably would have lost the game, but I was lucky to stop and I sat on the ball, and Souchack kicked me in the rear end."

Such theatrical endings have not been uncommon in the Duke–Carolina series, played in a scenic splendor widely known as "the Southern part of heaven."

In 1957, the Blue Devils took a 13-0 lead and looked like they would chase the Tar Heels out of the stadium. But Jack Cummings later hurled North Carolina to a major upset, 21-13. North Carolina was fighting for a bid to the Gator Bowl in 1963, and appeared to be on its way with an

early 13-0 lead over Duke. But the Blue Devils rallied to
take a 14-13 lead in the last quarter. Then Junior Edge
passed Carolina into scoring range and Max Chapman
kicked a forty-two-yard field goal in the closing seconds for
a 16-14 Tar Heel victory. In 1969, Duke upset North Carolina 17-13 in the last period with the help of a trick play.
And in 1976, the teams played what some are beginning to
call the best game of this passionate, exquisitely competitive series. In that one, both teams repeatedly came
from behind and the game ended with controversy surrounding a pass-interference call that helped North Carolina to its final touchdown and a wild 39-38 victory.

If other Duke–Carolina games have not been as close,
they have usually been intriguing. Even the record books
have borne silent witness to a subtle Duke–Carolina controversy through the years. Until recently, each school had
claimed one more victory than the other in its football
guide books and the discrepancy was because of a game
that never came off in 1889. Each team insisted that the
game was supposed to be played on its home field. When
the other team didn't show up, each claimed a forfeit. But
the sports information directors finally got together and
decided to drop the "ghost" game from their books.

One year prior to the 1889 controversy, the teams had
started their series when Duke—then known as Trinity—
challenged North Carolina to a game which then re-
sembled rugby more than football. Steve Bragaw, newly
elected captain of the North Carolina team, pulled out his
rugby book and did some quick homework. Trinity,
though, had a big advantage because the game had been
practiced there for several weeks under the tutelage of a
Dr. Crowell, a Yale man, and North Carolina lost, 16-0.
The final score did not show it, but actually the boys from
Chapel Hill had put up stiff resistance. The university magazine was eloquent in its praise of the game:

"Well, we were beaten, and beaten fairly, and we say—
Hurray for Trinity! Sixteen points to nothing. It's funny,
but when we'd ask any one of the team about it, he'd say

—'we got beat, but boys—we had the best time!' And then would come into his eyes that mellow look which fellows have when they talk about a certain class of beings."

As far back as the 1890s, the Duke–Carolina games had as much significance regionally as they did locally. In 1893, "every noticeable play was wildly cheered," according to one newspaper, when Trinity's "navy blue . . . vied with the white and blue of the university . . . for the state championship." Typical of the series, Trinity won 6-4 with a second-half rally as, the paper's account said, "Daniels and Avery pushed Maytubby through to a touchdown, and Daniels kicked goal."

Even then, Duke–North Carolina battles were recognized for their aesthetic appeal. "The game is said to be the finest ever played in the state," the newspaper said.

Subsequent games between these two natural rivals would inspire similar reactions. Although the series was interrupted from 1895 through 1921 because Duke did not play football during this period, it did not lose any of its luster. By 1922, the Blue Devils and Tar Heels were back at each other's throats and watching them was the largest crowd thus far in the series, 4,000 fans. Each season thereafter saw a dramatic jump in attendance and as soon as 1928, 15,000 people were watching Chuck Erickson run thirty-five yards for a touchdown to help North Carolina subdue Duke 14-7.

The 1930 game enjoys enduring fame, if only for its weather conditions. Nothing was resolved in a scoreless tie, but the game won renown as the "Battle of Kenan Lake" as the teams played ineffectively through a sea of mud at Chapel Hill. The game seemed to symbolize the death of a football era at North Carolina, because the Tar Heels had unsteady footing the next few years and made perhaps their most significant coaching change in history. Replacing Chuck Collins in 1934 was Carl Snavely, a quiet Dutchman who had made a brilliant record for himself at Bucknell. Snavely's subsequent battles with Duke coach Wallace Wade would continually fuel the explosive series. However, when Snavely first came to Chapel Hill, he was more preoccupied with improving the quality of North Carolina football. This he did immediately with the help of George Barclay, an outstanding guard and linebacker who became the Tar Heels' first All-American player, and Crowell Little, a brilliant tailback.

By 1935, Snavely's Tar Heels had everything going for them, including an apparent trip to the Rose Bowl. All they had to do to finish unbeaten and untied was beat two underprivileged rivals, Duke and Virginia. After trouncing its first seven opponents by a combined score of 209-19, North Carolina came into the Duke game a heavy favorite with a Bowl invitation pending. A crowd of 46,880, largest ever to turn out for a football contest in the South, was on hand, along with a huge press contingent, including a national magazine crew sent to photograph the expected Rose Bowl entrant.

However, the only subjects worth photographing that day were the Duke backs, led by quarterback Ace Parker. They were the picture of perfection while helping the Blue Devils run away with a stunning 25-0 victory, one of the most humbling moments in Tar Heel history, and the *Durham Herald-Sun* issued the following subjective and colorful report:

"Although they tried hard, the Tar Heels were completely overshadowed as a hard playing Blue Devil machine, perfectly oiled, functioned beautifully. The Duke line, charging like a horde of maddened devils, cooperated beautifully with a half-dozen backs, who insisted on not being stopped. In the vanguard of those backs were Jack Alexander, Jule Ward and Ace Parker, who alternated at carrying the ball on reverses, spinners and end runs to keep the Tar Heels completely surprised."

The loss was considered a blow to the Tar Heels' Rose Bowl hopes at the time. But actually there would not have been a trip to California anyway, owing to the whims of North Carolina president Frank P. Graham. Outraged by high-powered recruiting methods and the increasing amount of money being spent in amateur sports, Graham was plainly against a Bowl trip for Carolina and would have insisted the Tar Heels stay home, even if tendered a Rose Bowl bid.

A rallying point for Duke Fans was the period from 1941 through 1945, when Eddie Cameron stepped in for Wade during the Second World War years and went undefeated against the Tar Heels, Snavely for the most part was gone, too, having left North Carolina to coach elsewhere, but his return in 1945 triggered a swing in the balance of power between the passionate rivals. During his time at North Carolina, Snavely earned several appropriate titles. The most obvious was "King Carl" for his haughty, royal demeanor, but others such as "The Gray Fox," "The Dutch Master" and "Mr. Single Wingback" clearly reflected the man's approach to football.

"He was a perfectionist," recalls one-time player Mike Rubish. "He was an excellent coach. He worked us hard in practice. We'd run wind sprints until we were blue in the face. At times we longed for a game. It was easier. He had only one vice. That was vanilla ice cream. He was crazy about it. I guess that was next to football."

Excellent as he was, however, Snavely was not a magician. And after the lush postwar period had provided him with an abundance of talent, he was caught in a football depression in the fifties. He left before Duke's domination had run its course, but the 1950 season signaled the start of a seven-game winning streak by the Blue Devils started by Wade and finished by his successor, Bill Murray.

Duke's 7-0 victory in 1950 was especially sweet for Wade, since it stopped Carolina's four-game winning streak in the series and was the first time the Blue Devil coach had beaten Snavely in their bitter rivalry at Chapel Hill. The score emphasizes that the defense played in that game in numbing cold, and Duke never played it better in this series. Two times the Blue Devils stopped the Tar Heels with magnificent goal-line stands inside their ten-yard line. And Duke also refused to budge when North

Carolina moved the ball on separate possessions to the seventeen, twenty and twenty-two-yard lines.

Duke's domination of the fifties ended with the appearance at North Carolina of Jim Tatum, fresh from building national powers at Oklahoma and Maryland. Tatum, soon to die from a mysterious ailment, abruptly ended Duke's seven-game winning streak with a 21-13 victory in 1957. Later, Tatum's successor, Jim Hickey, would really make up for past defeats with some of the most special North Carolina victories in the series.

The first one was called "Massacre In Methodist Flat," and the 50-0 decision in 1959 caused no end of consternation in the Duke camp. Not only was the score spectacular, it was controversial, because Hickey—already leading by fifty points—had inserted his first team back into the game at the end. Infuriated by this tactic, Duke coach Murray displayed a fit of anger at the game's end. As the two coaches walked to meet each other on the field, Murray snapped: "You sure wanted that last touchdown bad, didn't you!" In actuality, Hickey had no intention of getting another touchdown. As he explained to Murray afterward, he just wanted his seniors to finish the game and had in fact instructed them not to score.

If the two coaches appeared to kiss and make up, Murray had a hard time forgetting that fifty-point thrashing administered by Hickey's team, particularly since both squads came into the game rated dead-even with modest 4-5 records.

"Everything happened right for us that day," Hickey recalls. "They still talk about that game, and I can remember it vividly. We scored the first time we had the ball, and then Duke took the ball right down to our goal line, and we had a kid who made a good play on a pass in the end zone to keep them from scoring. Had they scored, well, you don't know what would have happened. But everything crazy happened in our favor after that."

After the game, Duke captain Mike McGee banged his helmet hard on a bench as he came into the Blue Devils' dressing room. Then the good-natured giant thought a while and grinned. "It was like being in a one-hour defensive scrimmage with the other team having the ball all the time."

The outrageous victory margin was clearly a freak of this fine series. Even when streaking, one team rarely destroys the other in these heavenly contests. From 1958 through 1964, for instance, no team won any game by more than six points, except for the 50-0 aberration. In this stretch, the Carolina–Duke series was not a place for weak hearts but strong stomachs—each team uniquely winning games by identical 7-6 and 16-14 scores.

Duke's narrow 7-6 escape in 1958 was mirrored by North Carolina's 7-6 thriller in 1960. In the 1960 game, incidentally, the Tar Heels pulled off an upset of great dimensions. They had a poor 1-7 record going into the game and Duke was a heavily favored bowl team, ranked sixth in the nation.

Duke won exciting 6-3 and 16-14 games in 1961 and 1962, using a total of merely fifty-one seconds to pull out both on the field-goal kicking of Billy Reynolds. The Blue Devil halfback kicked a field goal with only two seconds left to give Duke its three-point victory in 1961, then kicked one with forty-nine seconds left to erase a short-lived Carolina lead of 14-13 in 1962. One year later, Max Chapman kicked a forty-two-yard field goal with thirty-three seconds left for Carolina's 16-14 victory. That triumph, incidentally, earned the Tar Heels a bid to the Gator Bowl.

"We won it, we lost it, and then we won it again," Hickey remembers. "It took immense determination by the members of the squad to pull it out."

North Carolina had taken a 13-0 lead on touchdowns by Ken Willard and Eddie Kessler, but Duke came back on a seventy-yard scoring pass from Scotty Glacken and then went ahead 14-13 on a twenty-four-yard touchdown run by Jay Wilkinson. Then in the last two minutes, quarterback Junior Edge catalyzed the Tar Heels.

"I had confidence all along," he said later. "I told them in the huddle, 'Boys, we've got more than a minute and twenty seconds. We can do a lot of scoring in that time.' I just knew we could do it."

Edge then jauntily moved the Tar Heels into position for Chapman's kick, giving Hickey what he called "a more pleasing victory" then the spectacular 50-0 triumph in 1959. It must have been pleasing to Chapman, too, because he had kicked only one other field goal all season.

In keeping with the flamboyant character of this extraordinary rivalry, the 1969 game featured the now-famous "shoe-string play" that helped Duke upset North Carolina 17-13. The trick play occurred in the third quarter and provided Duke with its winning points. Recounting the bizarre moment Elton Casey reported in the *Durham Herald-Sun:*

"Duke was on its own forty-seven. With activity centered a few steps away from the end of the Duke bench, quarterback Leo Hart bent over to tie his shoe. As he did, Marcel Courtillet, playing the role of center, pitched the ball to Wes Chesson, the wide end, who in turn set out for touchdown territory. Chesson's run covered fifty-three yards.

"As Chesson circled left end, the Duke linemen peeled off and blocked off perfectly. Dave Pugh added the conversion for Duke and it was 14-7 in favor of the Blue Devils with but thirty seconds left in the third quarter."

That 1969 game, incidentally, was one of the few times that Duke has managed to beat Bill Dooley. Brought in to replace Jim Hickey in 1967, Dooley won but five games in his first two years at North Carolina, but two of them were over Duke and the pain of rebuilding was somewhat eased. On the anniversary of his first decade at Carolina, Dooley had won seven games and tied one with Duke in ten meetings. Easily the most memorable of those contests was the one in 1976, when the Tar Heels won 39-38 on a touchdown and dramatic two-point conversion in the last minute. The explosive offensive show was left undecided

until the last thirty-seven seconds when Mike Voight took
a last-second pitchout from Matt Kupec and crossed the
goal line to the cheers and joyful tears of North Carolina
fans at brimfull Kenan Stadium.

It was a highly emotional contest from the beginning,
with North Carolina virtually assured of a Peach Bowl bid
and Duke hoping to gain a measure of respectibility in a
modest season.

Each team had twelve offensive possessions in the game
and made the most of them, scoring five touchdowns and
one field goal each. The Blue Devils took advantage of
almost every scoring opportunity. They were in North Carolina territory seven times and failed to score only once,
when Vince Fusco missed a forty-eight-yard field-goal try.
Carolina was on Duke's side of the field eight times, but
fumbles by Voight stopped two first-quarter drives, one inside the Blue Devil ten. Voight would make up for those
fumbles later in the game—scoring four touchdowns, as
well as the winning points, and rushing for 261 yards.

The score was 21-19 in favor of North Carolina at the
half and 22-21 Duke after three quarters. Then came the
frantic fourth period, when Carolina had the ball three
times and scored on all possessions and Duke scored two
of the three times it had the ball.

With 2:53 left in the game, Duke quarterback Mike
Dunn scored one of his four touchdowns with a nine-yard
run. A two-point conversion on a plunge by Tony Benjamin gave the Blue Devils a 38-31 lead and subdued many
of the 48,000 fans at Kenan.

The Tar Heels, however, were going to give it that old
college try after bringing the kickoff back to their twenty-
one-yard line. The crowd shifted uneasily as the irrepressible Voight was sent up the middle twice for nine
yards. Kupec, who supplemented Voight's spectacular running with eighty-five passing yards, got the first down on a
five-yard run. Kupec then rolled to his right and hit
Delbert Powell for nineteen yards.

On the next play, the North Carolina quarterback threw

long down the right sideline toward Walker Lee. The pass was underthrown, but a Duke defender was called for interference and the Tar Heels were given a gorgeous opportunity with a first down on the Duke twelve. Needless to say, the play greatly disturbed Duke Coach Mike McGee. "I won't say anything about the interference call because it would be emotional," he was to state later in the depression of the Duke locker room. "I will wait until I see the film."

Voight, the running terror of the Atlantic Coast Conference with an ultimate total of 3,971 yards and forty-two touchdowns in his career, got four yards to the Duke eight. Then Kupec, rolling to his right, hit fullback Billy Johnson in the flat and the freshman raced into the end zone for Carolina's thirty-seventh point.

"I just read their strong safety," Kupec said later, describing the play. "He went with Mel Collins and Johnson was wide open. I hit him and I knew it would be hard to stop him."

North Carolina's two-point try was a run all the way, Kupec said. He rolled right before pitching to Voight, who went in standing up.

"I was almost ready to run it myself," Kupec said. "I was hoping someone would come up to hit me, I wanted Voight to run. They came up and I pitched back to him."

McGee, close to tears in the Duke locker room, said simply, "North Carolina's offense out-executed our defense. Our offense line blocked well but they ran inside and Voight had a great individual performance."

About Voight's performance, incidentally: his forty-seven carries in the game equaled McCauley's great day against Duke in 1970; his touchdown total helped break Carolina's career record of thirty-nine set by the inimitable Justice; and his yardage figure boosted his career total into fifth place on the all-time NCAA rushing list.

Dunn was equally as heroic for Duke. Along with his four touchdowns, the sophomore quarterback racked up 130 yards on the ground and 109 in the air. "A tremendous performance," said Dooley. "He put pressure on us all day."

Dunn would have liked one more crack at Carolina, though. As it was, he would have to wait a year and that's a lot of time to think about revenge, especially when your enemy lives practically next door.'

5
PITT—PENN STATE
Lions and Panthers

As a senior, Tom Donchez was well acquainted with the bitterness of the Penn State–Pitt football rivalry. However, he was not prepared for the intensity of emotion that poured out of western Pennsylvania in 1974.

"An unbelievable amount of bad stuff was written," said the Penn State fullback. "Little quotes here and there. After a while it really got to us."

The quotes attributed to Pitt players in the newspapers were spiced with venom directed at the Penn State team. As a matter of motivation, Nittany Lion coach Joe Paterno made sure his players saw the quotes, pinning up the newspaper clippings in the locker room just before the big game between the traditional intrastate rivals.

"After I read the articles, I realized this wasn't just a regular football game," said flanker Jimmy Cefalo. "They really, truly wanted to beat us. It was something they lived for."

The "Hate State" credo became even more palpable when the Nittany Lion players entered Three Rivers Stadium in Pittsburgh. Recalls Donchez:

"We were walking in Three Rivers Stadium and they were laughing at us, spitting at us, calling us chumps, turkeys. . . . Maybe you can do that in pro ball. College is a little different, isn't it?"

Penn State receiver Jim Eaise remembers, "They were doing a lot of bush things before the game. A couple of our players were walking in and they spit on the ground in front of them. It's disgusting. Things were getting a little out of hand. . . ."

If the conduct by the Pittsburgh football team could not be condoned, it could certainly be understood. The Panthers were acting out of frustration, for Pitt had lost eight straight times to Penn State, never having beaten a Paterno-coached team. In the meantime, Penn State had enjoyed astounding success with the perplexed Panthers, winning by outrageous margins that reached as high as fifty-six points. It did not help Pitt's inferiority complex, either, when preseason estimates in 1974 once again put Penn State at the head of the class of Eastern football.

Observers might see a psychotic overkill in the Pitt behavior, but where these two ferocious rivals are concerned, it's understandable. They have been going at it since 1893 in one of the nation's most enduring rivalries, one in which state pride has often overshadowed national status. The Penn State–Pitt rivalry is all the more dramatic because of the stature of these two football teams through the years. While both have hit long depressions in certain eras, rarely will one find two teams that have so dominated a state such as Pitt and Penn State.

The series has been one of dramatic cycles. In the twenties and thirties, when Jock Sutherland ruled Pitt, the Panthers won fourteen straight games from their neighbor to the east. In fact, owing to scoreless ties in 1920 and 1921 and three years of interruption from 1932 through 1934, Penn State was unable to beat Pitt for nineteen years at one point. Paterno later made up for it in the sixties and seventies, when Penn State became not only the dominating team in the series but the Number-One team in Eastern football.

Ironically, as strong as Penn State has been in modern times, it has never won a mythical national championship —something that Pitt has done several times. Owing to the poor image of Eastern football in modern times and a supposedly weak schedule, Penn State has had to take a back seat in this regard, even in 1969 when Paterno produced possibly his best team and finished Number Two to Texas in the national poll. Circumstances opened the door to a national title for Pitt in 1976, giving Penn State good cause for jealousy. "It probably has to be grating to the people at Penn State that Pitt was able to win a national championship in 1976 while Penn State hasn't with possibly better teams in the past," said one sportswriter close to the Penn State scene, Ronnie Christ of the *Harrisburg Patriot-News*.

Pitt, in fact, earned its national title by climbing over Penn State's body. In one of the most emotional games of the series, the Panthers beat the Nittany Lions 24-7 as FBI agents guarded Paterno and some of his players from death threats by a crank caller.

This bitter series started on a note of good will in 1893, but didn't take long to develop into an intrastate war. This was instigated by George W. Hoskins, a turncoat who first played for Penn State and then jumped to Pitt.

When the Nittany Lions first played Pitt (then Western University of Pennsylvania), Hoskins was the center for Penn State, as well as the first instructor of physical education at the mountain-bound school and a trainer for the athletic teams. The initial Pitt–Penn State game was scheduled for a Saturday afternoon, but bad weather forced postponement until Monday. Meanwhile, a spirit of brotherhood was fostered by the Penn State players, who welcomed the boys from Pitt into their fraternity houses for the weekend and "treated them royally," according to one oldtimer.

"The game on Monday was a model of sportsmanship," recalled the oldtimer, "possibly because of the warm glow of fellowship engendered over the weekend."

A story of football nobility unfolded after the cleanly played game. Noted the Penn State newspaper, *Free Lance:* "We must compliment the players on the marked absence of slugging [obviously then a hallmark of the day]. Both teams behaved like gentlemen. . . . We want the Western boys to come again and come often."

The second game in the series, in 1896, however, provided a different atmosphere. This time, Hoskins was

playing center for Pitt and triggered one of the biggest
brawls ever seen at State College as Penn State won 10-4.
Again the *Free Lance* had something to say, but this time
it was uncomplimentary:

"The second game of the season on Beaver Field with
Western University of Pennsylvania did more injury to the
prestige of the game of football than its promoter can repair in many years."

Penn State could erase its bitterness with the sweet taste of
victory and would continue to enjoy that fruit in the Pitt
series for several more years. After a three-year interruption, the rivalry took hold in 1900, when Penn State won
12-0 and established an early superiority. The Nittany
Lions won the first six games from Pitt and, inspired by
such players as "Pop" Golden, "Mother" Dunn, Bill
Hollenback, "Shorty" Miller and Pete Mauthe, held a 12-3
edge over the Panthers through the 1912 season.

As trainer-coach and Penn State's first athletic director,
Golden was the architect of an unprecedented rise in football society for the Nittany Lions. When Golden first made
his appearance at Penn State in 1900, the Nittany Lions
had finished an unimpressive era. But by 1912, Penn State
was not only rubbing elbows with some of the nation's best
teams but beating them as well. Included among the victories during his tenure were four straight shutouts of Pitt
from 1900 through 1903.

William T. Dunn was regarded as one of Penn State's
greatest linemen—"a powerful charger on offense . . . a terror to opponents on defense," according to one writer.
From his moment of arrival at Penn State in 1903, Dunn
took charge of things. He had never played football, but
had read somewhere about the "flying tackle." On the first
day of practice, the sinewy freshman used it with such dexterity that he was immediately made a regular. He earned
his unusual nickname as freshman class president leading
his classmates across campus to challenge the cocky
sophomores in one of the school "rushes." A sophomore
yelled, "There goes Mother Dunn and all her baby chicks,"

and the appellation stayed with him.

If little respect was intended in that upper classman's sarcastic remark, Dunn got plenty of it from Penn State's opposition. With Dunn keying the Nittany Lions as one of football's first roving centers, Penn State became one of the best defensive teams in the country. This was dramatically reflected by the squad of 1906, which shut out nine opponents and allowed but ten points all season. One of those shutouts was a 6-0 victory over Pitt, marking the end of Dunn's college career. The lead in a Pittsburgh newspaper read:

"Six to nothing against our own WUP, a coterie of gentlemanly football players from Bellefonte [sic], a village in the almost exact center of the Commonwealth, yesterday scored as above. The winning touchdown and goal were made by (Bull) McLeary just thirty seconds before the game ended."

Hollenback brought the vigors of youth and the value of leadership to Penn State in 1909, when he became head coach at the extremely young age of twenty-two. Hollenback, an All-American at Penn, proved that he was as good a coach as he was a player, leading Penn State to undefeated seasons in his first three years at State College. The Nittany Lions capped their 1909 season with a 5-0 victory over Pitt, fashioned on McLeary's touchdown run and a tough defense that held the Panthers without a first down in the first half. Penn State students who heard the play-by-play of the game via telephone line did not wait too long after it was over to round up all available wood and build a mammoth bonfire.

After a one-year hiatus at Missouri, Hollenback returned to Penn State to produce some of the most powerful Nittany Lion teams of that era, with the help of Miller at quarterback and Mauthe at fullback. The 1912 team, which demolished Pitt 38-0 among eight victories, was considered Hollenback's best, and one of the best of all time in Penn State history.

That 1912 Pitt game not only produced a conclusive victory for Penn State but also a humorous Hollenback story. Leading 31-0 in the fourth quarter, Penn State had the ball on its own twenty-yard line and lined up in an appropriate kick formation. But apparently Miller diagnosed a perfect opportunity for an end run, so he switched signals as Hollenback watched intently. Once more taking in the defensive alignment, Miller decided that another change was in order—a pass play over the center of the line. Hollenback didn't like that at all.

"Give me a gun! Oh, give me a gun, so I can shoot him!" Hollenback exploded in a fit of anger on the sidelines. "He's trying to hand them a touchdown on a platter!"

By the time Hollenback got through screaming, the pass had already been made to Dexter Very, and the Nittany Lion receiver ran seventy yards to the Pitt ten-yard line before he was downed. Hollenback watched the play to completion and then turned back to his bench with a big grin and remarked without batting an eyelash: "There, by gosh! That's brains and how to use 'em!"

Things involving Miller—and Penn State in general— always seemed to turn out all right during that era. Except for momentary disenchantments, as in the Hollenback story, Penn State's coach had a love affair with his little star. Miller was worthy of Hollenback's admiration. His unlikely football size—five-foot-five and 140 pounds— made him even more potent than king-size heroes.

"Shorty was one of the greatest broken-field runners ever seen at Penn State," recalls Dutch Herman, a teammate of Miller's in 1911. "He was a little fellow, but he was quick and fast. Because of his short legs he could stop and start on a dime without losing speed, and was so small that bigger fellows had a hard time stopping him. I can remember times when he'd get tripped up and would be almost running on his hands before he'd regain his balance."

Mauthe was the other half of Penn State's "M Squad" in 1912. A sportswriter characterized the stocky fullback as a "plunger who could rip a line to shreds. . . . He always got his distance under pressure. As an inspirational leader of men, Mauthe never could be surpassed. He was always out front, setting the pace. Mauthe could pass fifty yards and hit a moving target. Here was a football player!"

The ubiquitous Mauthe won games with his kicking as well as his irrepressible running. Penn State especially needed his toe in the 1911 Pitt game, when Mauthe kicked a thirty-five-yard field goal. The Nittany Lions had approached that game on Thanksgiving Day with supreme nonchalance, highly confident of an undefeated season. The Pitt "jinx," later to become almost a tradition, had not yet emerged, and Hollenback warned his team of overconfidence but to no avail. The heavily favored Nittany Lions refused to listen to their coach, even though Pitt, approaching its first golden era, had emerged with one of its strongest teams in its young history.

Mauthe's field goal had given Penn State a 3-0 lead in the first quarter, and it turned out to be the only score of the game, because Miller's touchdown—pushed across the final period—was disallowed by an official's ruling. After Dick Harlow had blocked a punt for Penn State, Miller carried the ball over the Pitt six-yard line and was piled up at the goal line. When the mountain of players unfolded, Miller appeared to be over the line, but it was ruled that the quarterback had pushed the ball across after he was downed. Very and Hube Wagner, a famous Pitt player of the day, each had excellent games at end for his team and the *Pittsburgh Gazette-Times* reported:

"Nearly half of the spectators were women. They came from all over western Pennsylvania to see their annual game of football and then go back home with memories of a Wagner or the flaxen top of a Very, their football idols."

Mauthe's kicking was the highlight of the 1912 game with Pitt as well. Local fans were stunned by his placement kick from a yard past midfield.

"Our linemen turned around and looked at me as if I were crazy," said Miller, who amazed his teammates by calling for a field goal from that extraordinary distance.

But Miller repeated his orders, got the snap from center, and held the ball for Mauthe, who kicked it fifty-one yards for a field goal—a record that stood until Chris Bahr broke it in 1975.

"When Captain Mauthe and his men gave the college yell at Forbes Field on Thanksgiving Day, the most successful season the Blue and White has ever had became history," reported Penn State's student newspaper, the *Collegian*. "Other great teams have represented the Blue and White on the gridiron in past years, but none accomplished quite as much."

The author of that story might have savored the victory over Pitt even more, had he known the kind of trouble Penn State would have with the Panthers in subsequent years. Penn State would defeat Pitt only once during a long drought extending from 1913 through 1938. The Pitt "jinx" started in 1913 when Penn State lost 7-6 on a missed extra point by Miller and continued in 1914 when the Nittany Lions gave a 13-3 decision to the Panthers with fumbles and bad passes.

As obvious as the Penn State mistakes was the fact that this period marked the beginning of one of Pitt's finest football eras. From 1913 through the West Virginia game in 1919, the Panthers only lost one game in forty-one (to Washington & Jefferson in 1914). Most of this success was the result of the coaching of Glenn Scobey "Pop" Warner, one of the most innovative minds the football world has ever known. Pitt ran from the double-wing and single-wing formations, two original Warner ideas from which spewed forth a bewildering set of spins, reverses, double reverses, fake reverses, runs from fake passes and passes from fake runs. Besides these revolutionary formations, Warner's firsts included the rolling body block, the spiral punt, the block dummy, fiber padding and the numbering of players.

Amos Alonzo Stagg, one of football's patriarchs and quite an innovator himself, at one point stated that Warner was more responsible than any other man for the enactment of rules that improved football.

"Glenn was never active on the rules committee," Stagg said. "But we'd make a rule and Glenn would think up a way to get around it within the rules and we'd have to meet his challenge. He kept us on our toes, I can tell you."

At Pitt, Warner became probably the most talked-about coach in the country. He put together four straight unbeaten seasons, 1915-1918, and his Panthers went through thirty-one straight games before losing to Syracuse in 1919. His success continued into the twenties, when he left for Stanford.

Warner, a strangely contradictory character whose gruff exterior concealed a big heart, showed surprising exhibitions of compassion and rarely poured it on the opposition. But his teams were usually so strong, they were able to win over good opponents with surprising ease. For instance, Penn State fielded strong squads under Dick Harlow in 1915 and 1916, but was shut out those years by Pitt by 20-0 and 31-0 scores. The Nittany Lions had to take their glory in small doses in those days and be content with merely winning the freshman games from the Panthers. But even at that, they had to borrow a page from Warner's book to do it. In 1916, the Lion Cubs defeated Pitt freshmen using Warner's own single- and double-wing plays, which Harlow had picked up while scouting the Panther varsity.

Although, realistically, Penn State was not in Pitt's class in 1915, that game was touted by some observers as "the battle for the Pennsylvania championship." The Nittany Lions, beaten only by mighty Harvard, came into the Pitt game encouraged by victories over Lehigh and Lafayette, and a boost from some of the nation's football experts. Grantland Rice wrote, "Pitt had better defeat Penn State before it claims a championship," and Walter Camp called the game a tossup. "Really anybody's game," he said. "State has the stronger defense." Noting that the season had been one of many upsets, the Penn State *Collegian* prophesied victory:

"Yale has been Haughtonized [Percy Haughton, coach of Harvard in that period], Princeton has been Shevlinized

[Yale Coach Tom Shevlin], why can't Pitt be Harlowized?"

Pitt eventually showed why. Notwithstanding a line that had outplayed Harvard, Penn, Lehigh and Lafayette, the Nittany Lions were actually no match for the Panther forwards, anchored by two-time All-American Bob Peck. Andy Hastings scored fifteen of Pitt's points on two touchdowns and a field goal and with the 20-0 victory, Pitt extended its Pennsylvania championship to encompass the entire East.

The overwhelming defeat by Pitt in 1916 solidified a growing feeling among Penn State loyalists that the season should be measured by the outcome of that traditional game. Although the 31-0 beating by Pitt in 1916 was only Penn State's second in ten games, the Nittany Lions "emerged from that defeat believing that nothing of importance had been accomplished during the year," according to Penn State historian Ridge Riley. Harlow was so depressed after that loss, Riley said, that he "almost broke under the strain of the disappointment, and according to close friends, had to be talked out of resigning on the spot."

Harlow at least could console himself that he had been beaten by perhaps Warner's finest team. The 1916 Panthers included many famous names in Pitt football history—George McLaren, Red Carlson, Pat Herron, "Tiny" Thornhill, Jock Sutherland (later the Pitt coach), Dale Seis, Pud Seidel, Jimmy DeHart and Andy Hastings.

Hugo Bezdek had better success with Pitt, although it could hardly be called noteworthy. Simultaneously pictured as a savior and a dictator, Bezdek was usually controversial and innovative but never dull in his nineteen years as the power behind Penn State's athletic program—twelve of them as a coach. Bezdek's teams following the First World War included All-Americans such as Bob Higgins, Charley Way, Glenn Killinger and Joe Bedenk and were easily among the best in the country but obviously not better than Pitt. In twelve meetings with Pitt teams, first coached by Warner and then the illustrious Suther-

land, Bezdek could only manage one victory and two
scoreless ties in a three-year period from 1919 through
1921. The Pitt strength in this period was all the more ex-
emplary, considering that Penn State had a 40-12-7 record
from 1919 through 1924 and in one period was undefeated
in thirty games. The Nittany Lions as well went to a Rose
Bowl in 1922, though defeated 14-0 by the Panthers.

The 1919 game, won 20-0 by the Nittany Lions, not only
stands out as their only victory over Pitt in a long, dry
period, but as the scene for the longest pass-and-run play in
Penn State history. With the game only a couple of minutes
old and Penn State in an obvious kicking situation, the Nittany Lions pulled off a play that "will be seen perhaps once
in a hundred collegiate football games," according to one
newspaper account. Bill Hess, a fullback who had never
thrown a pass in his life and never would again, took the
snap from center in his own end zone and threw a short
screen pass to Bob Higgins and Penn State's All-American
end ran ninety yards for a touchdown.

Rarely out-coached, Warner took good-natured jibes
from writers. Said one: "Taking liberties with Glenn
Warner is almost as common as razzing Willie Hoppe into
scratching at a critical moment of a billiard match. It is
done about as often as Mississippi goes Republican or a
landlord reduces the rent." Although Bezdek was applauded for his "air wizardries" by observers, actually the
credit for that backbreaking pass play at the start should
have gone to assistant coach Dick Harlow. He had scouted
the Panthers for weeks and noticed that they continually
rushed from nine to ten men whenever they had an opponent with their backs to the goal line. Penn State had practiced the fake kick play all week leading up to the game.
Bezdek, who had not been told about the play, went along
with it hesitatingly when he finally learned what was afoot.
"It sounds okay," he growled, "but next time let me know
what's going on around here."

As Penn State coaches had before and would afterward,
Bezdek learned what a victory over Pitt meant. He was

lionized at home and given a bonus, a raise and an extended contract.

By 1920, Penn State was as good as any team in the East except perhaps undefeated Harvard. However, ties with Lehigh and Pitt forestalled claims for national honors. The 7-7 tie with Lehigh was totally unexpected, but the scoreless tie with Pitt was typical of the series in that period. Even when the Nittany-Lions appeared to have a stronger team, the Panthers always provided superhuman opposition. Again, in 1921, in a typical Forbes Field "mud bowl" where rain had smothered Thanksgiving Day, the teams fought to another scoreless tie. "Lighthorse" Harry Wilson stopped the only serious Pitt drive with a pass interception. Penn State was also unable to get untracked in the mud and failed to capitalize on its single opportunity when the Panthers' Ray Baer recovered a Nittany Lion fumble on the Pitt eighteen.

That was as close as Penn State came to beating Pitt in the ensuing seventeen years. Warner started the Pittsburgh victory string and then Sutherland continued it. Bezdek's bad luck in the Pitt series was complicated by a personal feud with Warner.

The 1923 game, Warner's last with Pittsburgh, provided a typically controversial scene. The Pitt coach instigated a psychological war before the game started by protesting Penn State's use of leather pads on the sleeves and chests. The pads were sewn there for protection, but Warner objected to the fact that they were deceptive because they gave the appearance of footballs tucked under the arm. There is no record that the objection was sustained.

Warner's complaint was just another in a long string of annoyances for Bezdek. It was said that Warner, among other things, liked to water down the field to slow Penn State runners. In an effort to counteract the alleged Pitt ploy, Bezdek forced his players to wear extra-long wooden cleats so their feet could take hold in the muddy turf.

The departure of Warner took one thorn out of Bezdek's side and the emergence of Sutherland stuck another in.

Few football teams ever demonstrated the running attack with more precision and power than did Sutherland's Golden Panthers from 1924 through 1938. Harlow, himself an outstanding single-wing innovator, could only look with admiration and awe at Sutherland's teams:

"The coach with the greatest ground attack against the strongest teams in my time was Jock Sutherland. Remember, everyone was shooting at him. . . . He ran Notre Dame right off the schedule. . . . The Pitt team could pick off, check, and destroy a shifting defense better than any team I ever saw."

Pitt's devotion to the running attack caused friends to tease that Sutherland considered the forward pass not only cowardly, but immoral. "He rehearsed every play as if it were an investment representing millions," pointed out one historian. Sutherland would trace blocking routes with a stick until the pulling linemen ran them to the inch and the split second. It was said that no other coach came closer to reducing the running game to a pure science than Sutherland.

It was this running game that literally helped to run Bezdek out of a coaching job at Penn State. A victory over Pitt in the traditional Thanksgiving Day game in 1927 would have provided Penn State with one of its best records of the decade. But when the Nittany Lions lost to the Panthers by a wider margin than usual, 30-0, some thought that Bezdek had carried his new "easy practice" schedule too far. There was only a light workout for Penn State the Monday before the game and none Tuesday and Wednesday. And the night before the contest, some players stayed up playing cards at a country club (using the thirty-five dollar allowances provided them by the Athletic Association). Penn State's lusterless performance the next afternoon further angered Penn State alumni in the Pitt area —against Bezdek. Winning no major games in 1928, and suffering another embarrassing loss to Pitt (this by a 26-0 score) did more to undermine the Bezdek image. Bezdek's analysis of that defeat was partially true, but entirely self-destructive:

"Defeat was due to lack of preparation in executing finer details of the plays. Remedy for such a situation lies in drilling the men to the maximum mastery of a limited number of promising plays. Errorless performance in scrimmage should be demanded."

In effect, he was pointing the finger of guilt at himself.

Bezdek produced a winning season in 1921, but his eighth straight loss to Pitt was too much to take. The one-time golden boy of Penn State football was kicked upstairs to the newly created position of dean of the School of Physical Education and Athletics, and Bob Higgins took Bezdek's place as coach. Higgins, once an applauded football player at Penn State, did not take over the coaching job under the most ideal conditions. The combination of Penn State's "purity" campaign against athletic scholarships and the Depression had plunged the Nittany Lions into their darkest period of football history. As a result, Higgins did not have a winning season for seven years and lost to the likes of little Waynesburg College.

"When you get licked as often as I did in those terrible thirties," Higgins once recalled, "you got over being a tough guy."

Penn State's series with Pitt had become so one-sided that it inspired fan apathy. The lack of crowds on Thanksgiving Day forced Pitt to seek another opponent for that traditional time and induced the teams to move the game back to the middle of the season for 1931. By 1932, the game was moved completely off the schedule by Penn State authorities and it stayed that way for three years.

Pitt was back on the Penn State schedule in 1935 but it wasn't until 1939 that the Nittany Lions were able to claim a victory over their top rivals. Higgins, who had suffered through the Nittany Lions' worst football period, began one of their best in the last year of the thirties. Higgins broke the long-time jinx with a 10-0 victory over Penn

State's tormentors and the rare triumph triggered a rather exuberant piece by alumni secretary Ridge Riley in his weekly *Football Letter:*

"Twenty football seasons have been played. Twenty hopeful Nittany Lions teams have taken the field against the Golden Panthers of Pittsburgh. Nineteen have left the gridiron without victory. Small wonder that Penn State's delirious student body last Saturday became so confused that it stormed out on the field and captured its own goal posts and bore them triumphantly down campus to the main gate."

After unexpectedly winning that game, Penn State was expected to win the following season against an inferior Pitt team that had been booed off the stage at its own pep rally. But the Nittany Lions lost, 20-7, and the defeat by Pitt cost them an undefeated year and a certain Bowl bid.

Reacting eloquently to the drama of the moment, one of the saddest in Higgins's tenure, this time Riley wrote:

"Within the grimness of Pitt Stadium, Penn State's visions of an undefeated season went up in the murky Pittsburgh sky, and heavy Penn State hearts finished out a weekend in the Smokey City with forced gaiety and dreams of what might have been."

Riley added some comfort at the bottom of his grim note, however: "Well, anyway, the varsity soccer team finished its eighth consecutive season without defeat."

"We were terribly overconfident in that game," recalls Leon Gajecki, the Penn State center that year who became an All-American player in 1940. "We should have never underestimated them. They deserved to beat us. They were better on that day. But on another day, we felt we could have won. We had a tremendous football team at that time."

It was a team that not only had Gajecki but also one of the best passing combinations in Penn State history, Billy Smaltz to Len Krouse, and outstanding runners in "Pepper" Petrella and Chuck Peters. They started Penn State on one of college football's greatest achievements, a record streak of non-losing seasons that has not been broken at this writing. Higgins's achievements in his final ten seasons at Penn State (1939-1948) compared favorably with that of any coach in the country, belying his unfortunate link with the Nittany Lions' darkest football period. In that time, Higgins had a 62-17-7 record, including five victories over Pitt.

When Penn State defeated Pitt for the second time in three years, in 1941, Riley recalled "an anecdote worth retelling" following the 31-7 victory:

"I was sitting next to 'Zez' [Howard W.] Cohen, an old Nittany Lion who was the drama critic for the *Pittsburgh Post-Gazette*. Next to him was Bob Lane, a young Penn State graduate. Bob was then serving as our sports information assistant. He was born and brought up in Pittsburgh and had never seen a Penn State triumph in the Pitt Stadium. As the score mounted, in youthful ecstasy, with eyes shining, Bob turned to Zez and said: 'Oh, boy, I've been waiting a long time for this.' I'll never remember the look of utter scorn and pity on Zez's face as he turned vehemently on the youth. 'You've been waiting a long time?' he said. '*You've* been waiting a long time?' "

Starting with that 1941 victory, Higgins won three straight games over Pitt, dimming memories of his early disastrous years. The significance of the Pitt game was evident after the 1943 victory, when Higgins was commended highly by the Penn State Athletic Board for an otherwise modest 5-3-1 season.

Higgins would build better teams at Penn State, including the undefeated 1947 squad that crushed Pitt 29-0 and went on to tie SMU 13-13 in the Cotton Bowl. However, that victory over Pitt was one of the rare occasions that followed form in the forties. Seldom did the favored team win during this period, as evidenced by Pitt's 7-0 victories in 1945 and 1948.

In the 1945 game, an eighty-four-yard punt return by Jimmy Robinson in the first quarter was all the Panthers needed to win. Alumni criticism caused Higgins to observe that most people think they can do three things better than anyone else—"build a fire, run a hotel, and coach a football team." Though losing to Pitt, Higgins's circumstances were still far more solid than those of Panther coach Clark Shaughnessy, who had fallen out of favor because school authorities objected to his advisory connections with pro football. During his stormy reign at Pitt, the T master also antagonized Panther alumni by dressing his team in nontraditional scarlet. Having lost six games in that color in 1945, Shaughnessy reverted to traditional gold and blue for the Penn State game and Nittany Lion supporters later claimed that this gave their rivals an insurmountable psychological edge.

Pitt was decided underdog as well in 1948, but managed to win the war despite losing the statistical battle. The end of the game showed Penn State with fourteen first downs to but four for Pitt, and 242 yards by rushing and passing to merely 79 for the Panthers. But these figures became meaningless after Elwood Petchell's pass was intercepted by Nick Bolkovac and run back for a Pitt touchdown early in the fourth period. The Panthers stopped every desperate drive by the Nittany Lions, including one on their two-yard line with twenty seconds remaining.

"We should have beaten Pitt," insists Sam Tamburo, Penn State's All-American end of that era. "We had a good ball carrier in Larry Joe, but kept running Fran Rogel up the middle. Joe, a speedster who could run outside, sat on the bench because they were afraid of his fumbling. We had the horses, we were supposed to beat them by three touchdowns."

Rogel, incidentally, gained 116 yards for the day with his line bucks but was stopped at the goal line on that last drive as the gun went off.

The end of the 1948 season signaled the departure of Higgins, who was in failing health. After a lame-duck year under Joe Bedenk, the one-time Penn State star, the Nittany Lions began their climb to Eastern leadership and widespread national recognition under Rip Engle. Engle and the college football renaissance arrived just about at the same time at Penn State. The fifties signaled a significant change in the sport. The World War II veterans who had dominated college football in the late forties eventually drained out of the system and gave way to teenagers. The "boys" had replaced the "men" and this was one of the main reasons for an unusual amount of upsets in the early fifties. The dramatic readjustments at most universities usually provided an element of chance in every game.

Along with the change of makeup in college football came a change in Penn State style. The single wing was out and the wing-T in, and Engle had Vince O'Bara to run it in his first season at Penn State and later a prize-winning quarterback in Richie Lucas.

Engle immediately made high marks with the alumni by beating Pitt in his first year, a 21-20 thriller fashioned with the help of power runner Paul Anders. The only bad thing that happened to Penn State's new coach that day was that he fell into a snow drift and lost his wallet. It was said he wore a money belt to football games after that. In 1952, Penn State's star jumped considerably with a 17-0 victory over the Panthers, a team of high stature at the time. Engle calls that victory one of his biggest thrills, and it was no doubt also one of the most significant of his career. The Panthers had national ranking and a Bowl bid in the offing, and the Nittany Lions had nothing to lose.

"A Pitt win over us would get them a bid to the Orange Bowl," says Engle, who recalls that Pitt officials were so certain of victory over Penn State that "many of their wives had already done their packing for a year-end vacation in sunny Florida."

Most of the crowd of 53,766 came out in Pittsburgh to wish the local heroes bon voyage to the Orange Bowl, but instead watched their Panthers become the goats. Intercepted passes played a big part in the Penn State victory, providing the spark for both Nittany Lion touchdowns and helping to turn back a Pitt drive in the second quarter. Engle in later years pointed to that particular victory over

Pitt as one of the most important steps in Penn State's resurgence in the fifties.

"That was the first one that got us moving," recalls Engle. "Pitt had one of its great teams that year. They had beaten Ohio State, Notre Dame, Army and a lot of fine football teams. But we went out there and broke lose for a touchdown in the first half and went on to beat them by seventeen points. At the end of the game the frustrated Pitt students started throwing oranges at their bench from the stands. I though maybe they were going to throw them at us. It was too bad. I felt sorry for the Panthers from that standpoint. But it was a great victory for Penn State."

Pitt, less potent and proud in ensuing years, dropped two more games by shutouts to Penn State and after the 1954 Nittany Lion victory, Engle escaped to the happy confusion of the locker room to find this blackboard message: "Seniors 47, Pitt 0."

By this time, Lenny Moore and Roosevelt Grier had become the proud symbols of Penn State's rise in the college football superstructure. Moore, one of the greatest of Penn State halfbacks and later a successful professional player, gave Engle the type of breakaway threat he so desperately needed. Moore's singular presence changed Penn State's offensive orientation from passing to running. Even when not carrying the ball, Moore could be an effective weapon for Engle. In the 1954 Pitt game, the Panthers were totally geared to stop Moore. But Engle used his great runner as a decoy and later apologized for not giving him a chance at some Eastern rushing records.

"Coach," said Moore, "I had a wonderful time in there today. Faking is much easier on you."

As it was, Moore still managed to set a single-season rushing record for Penn State with 1,082 yards, breaking Shorty Miller's mark set in 1912.

Grier, a splendid tackle who like Moore made it big in the pros, was perhaps Engle's favorite person. "Rosey was a great human being," Engle says. "He had a sense of humor that contributed greatly to our squad morale. He always knew when to insert a little humor into a dull practice session or give someone a lift when it was needed most."

Engle's favorite "Rosey" story happened long after the player left Penn State. The Nittany Lion coach had undergone extensive surgery and afterward, he received a get-well card from his former tackle.

"I had always insisted to the squad that you can never make the team sitting in the training room or in the whirlpool bath," Engle said. "Fifteen year later, I got his version of my statement of facts on a telegram after the surgery. It read: 'Dear Rip, you can't make the club sitting in the tub. Get Well. Signed, Rosey.' "

With players the caliber of Moore and Grier, Engle had continued success through the fifties and into the sixties, leading Penn State into four Bowl games. During this period, the Nittany Lions built up their intersectional schedule, playing and beating many of the country's top teams. No victories, however, could be sweeter than the ones over Pitt —and the silver-haired Engle had more of these than any of his predecessors at Penn State. His record over Pitt was 9-6-1 and even some of the losses to his bitter rival were considered memorable.

Losing to Pitt was never easy for Penn State, but the 1963 and 1965 games were so exciting and well played that the pain was eased a bit. Quarterback Fred Mazurek was the difference for Pitt in 1963. He ran for 137 yards against the Nittany Lions, who had led 21-15 after three quarters, and engineered the winning touchdown on a seventy-seven-yard drive, scoring himself on a seventeen-yard rollout. Penn State had time to win, but Ron Coates just missed two field goals against a strong wind.

In 1965, a victory was a necessity for Pitt coach Johnny Michelosen, whose job was reported to be in a precarious position. He got the game he needed, but not without some apprehensive moments.

The contest started as a nightmare for Penn State. Three devastating Nittany Lion fumbles set up three touchdowns for Pitt in the first half, which ended 20-0 in the Panthers' favor. It seemed that the lead would hold after Pitt went up 27-7 at the end of the third quarter. But then in a span of sixteen minutes, the Nittany Lions completed drives measuring fifty-nine, sixty-eight and eighty-eight yards, largely on the running of Dave McNaughton and Don Kunit. Making up for his first-half fumbles, Kunit scored all three fourth-quarter touchdowns for Penn State, to pull the Nittany Lions into a 27-27 tie.

After kickoff, Pitt now had the ball on its own forty with merely fifty seconds left in the game. Kenny Lucas, whose brother, Richie, had been an All-American quarterback for Penn State in 1959, lead the Panthers on an inexorable drive downfield as sophomore Bob Longo helped by making three difficult catches on passes. Finally on the one-yard line, Lucas called a timeout with three seconds to go. Coach Michelosen then called on a substitute whose two years on the squad had been spent mostly sitting on the bench, Frank Clark. Clark took a half-dozen practice swings with his leg and went in to kick the winning field goal for a 30-27 Pitt decision.

Michelosen, hero for a day and among the most respected Eastern coaches, was not rewarded for his spectacular victory over Penn State, or for his 5-5-1 record in the tough series. Not long thereafter, Michelosen was fired as the Pitt coach and his job given to Dave Hart. The next time Pitt beat Penn State was in 1976.

In the interim, Penn State won ten straight games with clinical ease, except for a one-point decision in 1975. The Nittany Lions' compelling domination of Pitt began with their spectacular rise in football circles under dynamic Joe Paterno, an Engle protégé. Paterno, who played quarterback for Engle at Brown and followed him to Penn State as an assistant to help with the installation of the wing-T offense, finally replaced him as a coach in 1966. Engle's retirement apparently left the coaching job in good hands.

"I knew that Joe would become an outstanding coach," Engle said in later years. "I knew even when I came here that he had a keen football mind. His leadership and competitive attitude made him a fine quarterback, and when I came to Penn State in 1950 he was the one person I brought along even though he had just graduated from college. I was aware even then of his potential as a coach."

A sportswriter once said of Paterno, the player: "He can't run and he can't pass. All he can do is think—and win!" The same might be said of Paterno, the coach. He is renowned as a gridiron gambler, never afraid to take chances or to be innovative. After an inauspicious start in 1966 (5-5), Paterno's teams became shooting stars, reaching the giddiest heights in Penn State history. Every year meant not only a winning season, but a ranking in the Top Twenty and usually an invitation to a major Bowl.

Even in the inconsistent 1966 season, Paterno showed he meant business with a 48-24 rout of Pitt, a type of score that soon became the norm in the series. Both teams were trying to salvage mediocre seasons in that game by winning, according to one observer, "the championship of Route 22." The Nittany Lions were accused of running up the score, but Paterno's players were merely reacting to the guidelines set by their new coach. "We will play every play as if we were behind," became one of Paterno's most-quoted aphorisms.

Under Paterno, the Nittany Lions obliterated memories of past humiliations suffered at Pitt's hands. En route to an undefeated season and the Orange Bowl in 1968, the Lions handed the Panthers their biggest thrashing in the series, 65-9. It was the worst defeat suffered by either team in the rivalry since Dan Reed's Penn State squad crushed the Panthers 59-0 in 1903. Penn State almost duplicated that feat with a 55-18 beating of Pitt on the way to the Cotton Bowl in 1971. John Hufnagel, Penn State's all-time passing leader, led a Nittany Lion offense that totaled 530 yards, with Lydell Mitchell running for 180 of them.

By 1973, Pitt began building toward the top with a new coach in Johnny Majors and one of the nation's most exciting runners in Tony Dorsett. After years of compiling los-

ing records, the Panthers were justifiably proud of their
1973 season, when they had a 6-3-1 mark and a bid to the
Fiesta Bowl prior to the Penn State game. Confidence in
the Pitt camp, mingled with bitterness over Penn State's
recent domination of the series and perhaps some jealousy
over their undefeated season and Orange Bowl bid, made
this an extraordinarily tough assignment for the Nittany
Lions. This was evident when Carson Long kicked a fifty-
yard field goal on the last play of the half to give Pitt a 13-3
lead, then turned toward the Penn State bench and raised
his arm, fist clenched in triumph. At Long's signal, the entire Pitt squad came on the field and surrounded the
freshman kicking sensation in an exuberant celebration.
The Nittany Lions contemplated their perilous position as
they ran soberly to their dressing room for the halftime rest
period, but later got a lift from the crowd as they came out
for the second half. If ever a home-field advantage existed
in college football, here it was.

"You know, at Penn State you're expected to win all the
time," says Ed O'Neil, the excellent Nittany Lion linebacker from that period. "If you don't win by the expected
point margin, the fans let you know how unhappy they are.
Sometimes we'd go into a locker room winning by two
touchdowns and we were supposed to be winning by four,
and the kids would boo us and tell us that we're playing
lousy. So that's why we were so surprised at what happened. When we came out after the halftime break losing
13-3, I never heard Beaver Stadium go so crazy over us. We
didn't expect it. Everything we did, they loved, and I never
heard people scream and holler so intently in the whole
second half and this really spurred us on."

Thus inspired by the emphatic hometown crowd, the
Nittany Lions cut the Pitt lead to 13-11 with eight points in
the third quarter, holding the Panthers and the explosive
Dorsett to a net yardage of minus fifteen. In the fourth
period, John Cappelletti's running and Tom Shuman's
passing led Penn State to score twenty-four points and a
remarkable 35-13 victory. Penn State's defense was as po-

tent as the offense, holding the sensational Dorsett to a meager eighty-nine yards—a figure he was capable of breaking off at a moment's notice. Prior to the game, Paterno's mail had been heavy with concern about Pitt's exceptional runner who was the second best rusher in the country with an average of over 150 yards a game.

"We had, and still have, a great respect for Tony Dorsett's ability," said Paterno after the game. "But you'd think we never played a great runner before. We didn't change our normal defense to stop Tony; we were just determined to execute better, and we did."

The 1974 game was on national television at Pittsburgh's Three Rivers Stadium under the lights, and there an almost duplicate scenario was played out. Emotions were exceptionally high at Pitt, partially due to the fact that they had been ignored by Bowl selectors and Penn State had received a premature, if unofficial, bid to the Cotton Bowl. The week before, Paterno had made an off-the-record statement to some newspaper friends that he would let the Pitt–Penn State game decide the East's representative to the Cotton Bowl, assuming that school and Bowl officials would consent and because both teams had 8-2 records going into the contest. Both Pitt and Penn State would have had to win games beforehand to set up such a possibility, the Panthers with Notre Dame and the Nittany Lions with Ohio University. Paterno's unprecedented remark drew an astonished reaction from one reporter. "You mean to say you'd take a chance of giving up a Cotton Bowl net of over $400,000?" the reporter asked. Paterno smiled and said, "What makes you think I expect to lose to Pitt?"

Pitt's loss to Notre Dame negated any such showdown behind the East's best two teams, but the Panthers still had something at stake—pride. Majors had made big strides at Pitt in his two years there and was confident that Dorsett could run with brilliance against Penn State as he had against everyone else that year. The Nittany Lions, meanwhile, had to defend their selection as the Bowl team in an inflammable Pittsburgh atmosphere.

Penn State's emotional level was clearly equal to that of Pitt's. Before the game, the Nittany Lions had a private meeting, a Paterno custom where the seniors speak their minds before the coaches, trainers and doctors join them for the pregame prayer. Mike Hartenstine, usually the tamest Lion, surprised his teammates with an opening inspirational talk. Tom Donchez, in stronger and more emotional language, reminded everyone how devastating a defeat would be and got so carried away in his talk that he heaved his helmet against a locker. It bounced off and hit linebacker Greg Buttle between the eyes, knocking him cold. Paterno, overhearing the commotion as he ran by, grumbled, "Oh, God, can't we even get through the team prayer without an injury?"

Patched up, revived and taped, Buttle later was ready to take his place in the starting lineup, wobbly and a trifle pale. He reported afterward that the first quarter seemed to be in slow motion, like a bad dream, and at the half had six stitches put in a gash over his eye. "But he never missed a signal," assistant coach Jim O'Hora said proudly.

The first half must have seemed like a bad dream to the rest of the Penn State players as well. They trailed 7-6 at halftime. But both Buttle and Penn State got better after that. Repeating their 1973 second-half comeback, the Nittany Lions wore down Pitt with the help of Chris Bahr's field goals and won going away, 31-10. Bahr's four field goals in the game set a Penn State record.

The Nittany Lions continued their domination of Pitt in 1975, but it was hardly an overwhelming victory. Long had an extra-point try blocked and missed three field-goal attempts, allowing Penn State to escape with a 7-6 victory and the Eastern championship. Long was inconsolable afterwards. "He changed and left the locker room real fast," recalls teammate Al Romano.

Before the game, Long had other things on his mind. In the morning, his wife had given birth to a girl. When his extra-point try after a Pitt touchdown was blocked by Penn State defensive back Tom Odell, that gave him something else to think about. He had made sixty straight extra points before that.

"We noticed on the films that Pitt's center didn't come up after the snap, so Tom just lined up about seven yards back and jumped," recalls Buttle. "And I think that blocked kick might have been the reason he missed the other three. It had to be in the back of his mind."

Observed Majors: "We weren't playing for money, but I'm sure Carson Long would pay $5,000 a year for the rest of his life to have made one of those field goals."

Long didn't have to wait long, though, to beat Penn State and wipe out the memories of that bitterly frustrating game. The next year, Pitt's supreme kicker had a forty-seven-yard field goal and three letter-perfect extra points in the Panthers' 24-7 romp en route to the national championship. Dorsett scored two touchdowns and rushed for 244 yards en route to the Heisman Trophy.

The Penn State defense plan was to keep Dorsett running laterally as long as possible and then belt him when he turned upfield. Just as important, the Nittany Lions' coaches urged that the defense work as a unit and not allow any cracks through which the great runner could slip because of his ability to accelerate. This worked all right for the first half, when Penn State held Dorsett to fifty-one yards and Pitt to a 7-7 tie. But there was an uneasy calm in the Penn State dressing room at intermission. Said Penn State defensive coach Gregg Ducatte: "There can be a 'we've got 'em' kind of quiet or a 'we don't have 'em' kind of quiet. There's a fine line between them."

It turned out to be the latter in the second half as Dorsett led the Pitt charge with 173 rushing yards, some gained on quick-opening plays as a fullback, and his second touchdown run of the day on a 40-yard burst. Dorsett's bruising runs left Paterno a bit stunned in the gloomy Penn State locker room.

"Dorsett didn't beat us," said Paterno, "the whole team did."

Then he paused.

"Ah, heck, I don't know what happened."

The Panthers' conclusive victory enhanced their stature as the nation's Number-One team. They certified that position by beating Georgia in the Sugar Bowl, but the national championship couldn't have been any sweeter for them than the championship of Pennsylvania.

6
SOUTHERN CAL—UCLA
More Important Than Life And Death

Red Sanders put the ultimate value on a UCLA–Southern Cal football game.

"It's not a matter of life and death," said the onetime UCLA coach, "it's more important than that."

If the intensity of the fabled rivalry has outstripped most normal judgment, it's no wonder. Considering the proximity of the schools and the stakes usually involved, the atmosphere surrounding these games has reached an emotional pinnacle every season for both teams.

They have often decided a Rose Bowl berth, sometimes a national title—but most importantly, the championship of Los Angeles.

As one Southern Cal official says, "You hve to beat UCLA. It's better for us to live in this town if we do."

There is no question that no intracity rivalry in America transcends the UCLA–Southern Cal war. Hollywood itself could not have come up with a better script. And, as with most Hollywood productions, this bittersweet association has had all the accompanying hoopla through the seasons.

The fierceness of this unique competition is mirrored in creative campus pranks, usually dealing with revered school objects. Pricelesss possessions have been heisted by overzealous students, bombs set off, shrines molested and devious traps set. The series has also evoked horrific tales of barbarism.

Even the fans are a breed set apart. Says one writer, whimsically: "They are physically normal except for their mouths. Their mouths and what comes out of them defy description. The only thing known for sure about a USC–

UCLA fan's mouth is that it is some kind of a cross between that of an army drill instructor and a circus barker."

There is the story of the ecstatic fan who poured green confetti on his hot dog and threw pickle relish into the air when his team scored. And a fellow who dislocated his shoulder trying to hurl a roll of toilet paper from one end of the field to the fifty-yard line. And another who shaved the letters "USC" on his chest and wore them proudly until the temperature dropped to forty-five degrees and he turned a shade of fine UCLA blue.

Notes an observer of these unruly fans: "They have supplies of confetti, toilet paper, signs, buttons, original cheers and, of course, heartening beverages. . . . The eccentric fan might even have a pair of binoculars and a program to follow the game with."

The Southern Cal–UCLA games normally are reserved for the end of the schedule, more often than not lending a towering drama to the season. During one abnormal period of the Second World War, the Trojans and Bruins uniquely played two games a season—one at the start and one at the end. But the appeal of the game even then was hardly lessened by overexposure. Monster crowds witnessed the event each season from 1943 through 1945, and the last year was especially successful in terms of crowd lure. In the first game of 1945, 81,000 fans attended the game and in the second, there were more than 100,000 witnesses at the Los Angeles Coliseum.

The ready-made box office appeal of two Los Angeles schools made both eager to get a rivalry going in the twenties. But at that point, Southern Cal was ranked far above UCLA in football stature. The Trojans had already established themselves as a power, having beaten Penn State in the 1923 Rose Bowl. At that juncture, UCLA had had only four graduated classes and it would take the Bruins years to catch up with the Trojans in organization and effective recruiting. This was vividly apparent after opening games in 1929 and 1930, when Southern Cal won by 76-0 and 52-0 scores. The series was aborted and renewed six years later when the teams were more evenly matched.

In 1936, they played to a 7-7 tie. In 1937, Southern Cal beat UCLA 19-13—but not before some very anxious moments. Attached to that 1937 game is a classic story involving Southern Cal coach Howard Jones and Bill Spaulding, the coach of UCLA.

Kenny Washington, UCLA's All-American halfback, drove Southern Cal to distraction in the fourth period. Washington's passing helped the Bruins score two touchdowns and brought them to the fringe of another. The Bruin rally threw the Coliseum crowd into a frenzy and had Jones on the edge of nervous exhaustion.

After the game Spaulding paid his customary visit to the Trojan locker room and found the door closed. He knocked.

"Who's there?" a voice asked.

"Bill Spaulding," the coach said.

"What do you want?" the voice responded.

"Tell Howard he can come out now," Spaulding answered without missing a beat. "We've stopped passing."

The foundation for this exquisite series was laid by Jones and Spaulding through a close friendship that found them together for card games and golf matches despite their fierce football duels. Though his teams were usually beaten by the Trojans, Spaulding revered Jones as "the finest friend I ever had."

The 1939 game was the first to be played with any national implications. By then, UCLA not only had the ubiquitous Washington but another fine runner who would eventually make his mark in baseball, Jackie Robinson. Washington and Robinson created problems for the Southern Cal defense all day. In the fading minutes, it was these two who spearheaded a UCLA drive deep into Trojan territory. But, ironically, neither got the call to run in the last ten seconds, when UCLA needed them the most, and it cost the Bruins a spot in the Rose Bowl.

Neither team had scored in the tough defensive game,

but the Bruins had every expectation of winning at the end after quarterback Ned Matthews had driven them seventy-six yards and placed the ball inside the Southern Cal ten-yard line. However, the UCLA quarterback who had played such a brilliant game all day made the wrong decisions at the end.

With first down and goal to go on the Southern Cal four, Matthews called for Washington to dive into the middle of the Trojan line. The halfback got nowhere.

On second down, Matthews ordered Leo Cantor to slant over right tackle. He got two yards.

On third down Matthews called the same play. This time Cantor was thrown for a three-yard loss back to the five.

In the huddle for the fourth down, Matthews called for a vote on the next play. Five players wanted to try a field goal, and five others opted for a touchdown. It was up to Matthews to cast the tie-breaking vote, and he decided on a pass from Washington to Bob MacPherson. As the Bruins came out of the huddle, the roars of 103,000 passionate fans filled the Los Angeles Coliseum. The noise from the UCLA side quickly died after Southern Cal defensive back Bobby Robertson flashed in front of Mac-Pherson and knocked the ball to the ground, salvaging a scoreless tie for the Trojans.

The Trojans were instantly selected for the Rose Bowl by the Pacific Coast Conference members. Their record of 8-0-2 to UCLA's 6-0-4 clinched the invitation.

Southern Cal's goal-line stand was a poetic finish to a game of building excitement. The Trojans themselves missed several golden scoring chances. On one play in particular, quarterback Grenville Lansdell fumbled the ball while going over the UCLA goal line in the first period. That gave the ball to the Bruins. The Trojans also had the ball on the UCLA twenty-two when Lansdell fumbled again. Another time they got as far as the twenty-five before dying.

"It was one of the cleanest, yet most bitter struggles in Coliseum history," wrote Paul Zimmerman of the *Los An-*

geles Times. "In the dressing rooms, Bruins and Trojans were mingling after the contest to congratulate each other on fine play, which is the finest display of sportsmanship anyone could ask of this torrid crosstown rivalry. In the final analysis, there was nothing wrong with the ballgame —but the final score."

If the score did not please Zimmerman, think how the gamblers must have felt. That fraternity had thought glowingly of Southern Cal and made the Trojans a big favorite over UCLA. The results shattered some illusions about Southern Cal, but Howard Jones was quick to explain afterward:

"UCLA was a much-improved football team over its showing in the previous games in which I saw them, and the Trojans seemingly were not up to their physical peak, so the result was a scoreless tie."

And UCLA of course had Washington, a player of enormous talents.

"You just can't get a clear shot at Washington when you try to tackle him," said a Southern Cal player in the postgame discussions. "Just when you think you've got him cornered, he does a lot of hip-wiggling and gets away."

Suffering from shoulder and thumb injuries, Lansdell could not hold the ball with his customary strength. He apologized for fumbling away a sure touchdown in that first quarter.

"I'm sorry, Coach," he said to Jones.

Jones took his hand and reacted warmly: "Forget it. You played a fine game."

When Howard Jones died on July 27, 1941, it not only signaled the end of a monarch's reign but the finish of a school's monopoly. During Jones' intelligent administration, the Trojans had won two national championships, five Rose Bowl games and eight Pacific Coast Conference titles. UCLA could scarcely be mentioned in the same breath with Southern Cal during the time of the "Head Man" but in the forties was finally able to claim parity with its bitter rival.

Beaten for the first time in 1942 by the Bruins, 14-7, the Jeff Cravath-led Trojans came to the stark realization that the city of Los Angeles no longer belonged to them. Forever the king of Southern California, the Trojans now shared the reign with another team. This new coexistence was punctuated by a fabled campus prank that seemed to symbolize a fresh fighting spirit between the schools.

A group of courageous Southern Cal fraternity members made off with UCLA's Victory Bell after one game in 1941 and the theft of the 295-pound locomotive clanger and subsequent search stirred a great amount of excitement on both campuses. For more than a year it was hidden, first in the Hollywood Hills and then in a Santa Ana haystack. The police were called in on the search, but were just as frustrated as UCLA students in finding the object. After a series of crosstown raids, the student body presidents of both schools met to negotiate an end to the search. Southern Cal agreed to return the bell—on the condition that it would remain a permanent game trophy.

The year of the "Victory Bell Caper," the Trojans and Bruins played to a 7-7 tie and the students had a vicious scrimmage as well the week after. When four Southern Cal students toured the UCLA campus by truck in a display of sheer arrogance, they were pulled before the student body and had their heads shaved. Later in the day, Southern Cal students got even for the UCLA indignities. When twenty carloads of UCLA students invaded the Trojan campus with the taunt, "Rose Bowl, here we come! Ex-Trojans, we're sorry for you!" they paid for it.

Irate Southern Cal students dragged their UCLA counterparts through a series of humiliations. They shaved their heads and painted "SC" on their skulls. They dumped them into a fish pond with the chant, "Fish Bowl, here we come!" UCLA females were treated with disdain, although not as harshly molested as the males. They had their heads dunked. "Automobile sparkplugs were pulled, motor hoods were ripped off, tires were deflated, and a jeep was pushed squarely in the middle of the fish pond," reported a newspaper. As they limped past police riot cars, UCLA students promised: "We'll be back tomorrow—wait."

Although the Bruins proved that they could play with the Trojans, that did not mean that they could always beat them. The games in the late thirties and forties were competitive but usually ended in Southern Cal's favor. The Trojans visited the Rose Bowl six times in the period from 1938 to 1947, while the Bruins fiddled and the vengeful Bruin disciples created small excitements off the field. In bitter frustration, UCLA students once kidnapped Tirebiter, Southern Cal's famous dog. When finally rescued, the mascot had the letters U-C-L-A shaved on his back. Tirebiter went to the game that day with a Trojan blanket over him.

The 1946 season was the year of the Great Water Hoax. Prior to the USC–UCLA game, Los Angeles newspapers published stories about how Southern Cal students, using fire hoses, had flooded the field of the Los Angeles Coliseum the night before to slow the Bruins' fine runners. Reports from self-styled "witnesses" had told newspapers of the flooding and a subsequent "bloody battle" that ensued between UCLA and USC students. Wire services picked up the story and sent it out nationwide, only to find that it was a phony. Both schools and the Los Angeles police force later denied that such an incident had taken place —and the newspapers printed an apology.

Since then, pranks have reached innovative heights. Head-shaving was cut out after a while, giving way to more sophisticated hazing. In later years mice were released in the UCLA library, a bomb went off in the UCLA rooting section, and the Trojan horse, Traveler, was painted blue. Tommy Trojan, the campus statue that is the proud symbol of Southern Cal athletics, was another victim. UCLA students painted him and welded his own sword into his back, among other things.

"One time they came in with a helicopter and dropped something on the statue that really smelled," recalls Nick Pappas, in charge of Southern Cal's athletic support groups. "It was the worst thing I ever smelled—some kind of chemical, just rotten, rotten. And we couldn't wash it off. But the payoff was, we get to the ballgame, and some UCLA kids have a banner right up in the Coliseum. It said, 'Didn't Tommy Stink?'"

Guerrilla warfare on campus became icily scientific. Southern Cal "spies" infiltrated UCLA one season and schemed to disrupt the Bruins' card stunts at football games. A red-and-gold "SC" appeared in each corner of each card stunt picture, much to the puzzlement of UCLA students.

Another time, Southern Cal students pulled off an imaginative electronic job.

"How they did it, I don't know," says Pappas. "But they somehow got into the classroom speaker system at UCLA. These guys wired into several of the buildings. Then, every fifteen minutes or so, they'd play tapes of the Southern Cal fight song. At intervals, 'Fight On For Old SC' would blare through the UCLA campus. Oh, it just drove them crazy."

Pappas, a one-time star runner at Southern Cal, also recalls when football players had to fight strange wars:

"Once I was told to go to sleep early one night so I could get up early in the morning to go on a raiding mission and burn out a UCLA bonfire site," notes Pappas. "They had telephone poles and things stacked up forty feet in the air on the field. Some guy in our fraternity house had this chemical and made a bomb out of it. So they got us out of bed about 3:30 in the morning, and we went up Sunset Boulevard, sneaking on our hands and knees. It was dark as hell, no moon out. Geez, we're finally going across this playing field on our hands and knees and all of a sudden I see feet. I looked up and here are these guys from UCLA. They said, 'What are you doing?' I said, 'Ah, nothing.' So this guy from UCLA says, 'If you've come to burn the thing down, you're too late. It was burned down this afternoon."

Dan Berger, a sportswriter in Los Angeles, remembers another devious Southern Cal plot:

"The shop that printed the *Daily Bruin* at UCLA was invaded, stories were stolen and rewritten, pictures and captions were changed, and a bogus edition was printed by Southern Cal students," Berger says. "Then the Trojan pranksters kidnapped the truck driver who delivered the UCLA papers and replaced the genuine newspapers with the phonies. When UCLA students opened their daily paper the next day, they read this quote from their star quarterback, 'I'd feel much better about our chances against those terrific Trojans if we had a couple of players who understood the game.' The coach added, 'I can't see any hope for our team.' "

The arrival of Sanders at UCLA in 1949 put the series into an entirely new perspective and established unprecedented prestige for the Bruins. Seemingly an old-fashioned sort of coach with his single-wing offense, Sanders was chided for being a horse-and-buggy football man by some. But the witty, guileful Sanders had a symbolic answer for his critics. "Maybe it's a horse-and-buggy offense," he said, "but there's a TV set in the dashboard."

Sanders' second UCLA team crushed Southern Cal 35-0 and the Bruins built on their new-found respectibility by defeating the Trojans three straight seasons, 1953-55. Suddenly, Sanders was the most respected man in town. A popularity poll, conducted by the *Los Angeles Mirror*, established Sanders as the most admired man in Los Angeles, giving him the edge over such luminaries as Bob Hope and Walt Disney. UCLA students were so enthralled that they presented Sanders with a certificate applauding him as "the finest, most beloved and respected coach in the nation." When the undergraduates appeared at Sanders' home demanding a speech from their hero, he was pleased but somewhat skeptical. "Which one's got the rope?" he whispered to his wife, Anne.

Later, John McKay would bring a similarly compelling wit to Southern Cal and gain as much, if not more, adoration from the masses for his giant strides. Called by many the "spiritual heir" to Howard Jones, McKay seemed a positive reincarnation as well, echoing and then surpassing the proud successes of the once-idolized "Head Man." McKay joined Southern Cal in 1960 and guided the Trojans to four national championships and eight Rose Bowl appearances in sixteen seasons, much to the bitter consternation of crosstown rival UCLA. The Bruins during this period had exceptionally good teams as well, owing to the all-around excellence of Heisman Trophy–winning quarterback Gary Beban and the guidance of coach Tommy Prothro. The Bruins were compared favorably to the Sanders-coached powerhouses of the mid-fifties, but if they were good, Southern Cal was usually a little better.

The reason in part for this Trojan domination was an exotic new offensive maneuver conjured up by McKay called the I-Formation and an exquisite halfback to run out of it called O. J. Simpson. Simpson combined a halfback's speed with a fullback's power to gain an herculean total of 3,124 yards in two seasons, and it's probable that UCLA will especially remember sixty-four of them. That was the amount of yardage Simpson stepped off in one touchdown dash in 1967, to give Southern Cal a 21-20 victory over UCLA, wrap up the Pacific-8 title and send the Trojans into the Rose Bowl. In effect, it decided the national championship as well, because Southern Cal went on to win that with a 14-3 victory over Indiana at Pasadena.

"Of the remarkable 1,415 yards Simpson gained this season, those sixty-four were the most impressive of all," said one writer, "for they came after two hours of the toughest punishment he had endured—and they stretched all the way from Pasadena to Number Onesville."

It was fitting that Simpson himself should settle the score with UCLA. The important game blended a myriad of surrealistic implications. It was improbable enough that Simpson and Beban should emerge in the same city as Heisman Trophy candidates. Furthermore, here were two schools in a divided city fighting not only for the championship of

Los Angeles but the championship of their conference, a Rose Bowl berth, and top national ranking all in one splendid afternoon.

"It is so garishly theatrical that it really should have started at a soda fountain in a Hollywood drug store," noted one whimsical sportswriter. "It is strictly from the studio lots."

As with most Hollywood productions, this one had the accompanying tinsel. There was Marvin Goux, the stern-looking assistant coach at Southern Cal, playing the part of inspiration man. Perhaps he was not in the class of, say, a Knute Rockne, but Goux had done some bit-acting in films and prepared the Trojans by delivering fiery, college spirit-soaked speeches. In a small dressing room jammed with players and the Southern Cal band, Goux begged the Trojans to "win one for John." Then he held up a photograph of coach John McKay, looking dejected after the previous year's loss to UCLA. Raising his fist, Goux said: "Listen, listen. The worst thing in life is to be a prisoner. Never. I would rather die. We've been prisoners to those indecencies over there for two years. Today's the day we go free." Everyone cheered.

Over at UCLA, coach Tommy Prothro and others stressed the virtues of Beban. Prothro emphasized that his quarterback could beat them in a number of ways—with a run, pass, fake or call. "And this ability to change plays at the line of scrimmage is perhaps his greatest asset," Prothro pointed out. UCLA's award-winning quarterback was a familiar sight, all right—his fierce royal figure bobbing behind the center, as he shifted his backs, checked, raised his head to survey the defense, contemplating last-second changes.

"There's something about the way he manages things out there that gives everyone confidence," said UCLA fullback Rick Purdy.

Beban had been the class college quarterback of the country for three years but denied any association with greatness. "I suppose I'm rather ordinary," he said. Others would have to disagree, particularly Simpson, who insisted: "Gary's the greatest."

Poise, Beban's supreme quality, was singled out by one professional scout: "He's about the most self-assured player I've ever seen. He knows exactly what he is going to do, and he will spot things out there, file them away mentally, and use them on you later. You don't judge Beban on how much he does, not on his statistics. He beats you with the 'when' he does something. Invariably, it's the perfect time."

Similarly acclaimed for his poise, Simpson had endurance and strength to match. When he first came to Southern Cal from a junior college, Simpson was prized for his startling speed. But McKay also discovered something about his bullishness. "We wanted to see if he could take it inside," McKay said. "We ran him seven straight times in one scrimmage, and that was it. He busted people backward."

Simpson never imagined that he would be carrying the ball as much as he did in 1967, like the thirty-eight times against Notre Dame, thirty-six against Michigan State and thirty against both Texas and Washington. Still, he rarely tripped. "I don't get real tired," Simpson said at one point of the season. "Maybe it's because I'm anticipating that on the next carry I'll break clear. I feel like I can go all the way every time, mainly because we've got such a good line."

Before the game, McKay was particularly vexed that Prothro supposedly "had his number." Prothro had beaten McKay the previous two years, and there were feelings, whether warranted or not, that the UCLA coach had won with guile, rather than talent. Responding to this criticism, McKay suddenly lost his sense of humor. "Well, we pushed 'em all over the field in 1965, but we fumbled on their one, seven, and seventeen. I guess he planned that."

The teams' styles were as different as their campuses, as far removed as their coaches' styles. Along with the presence of the superb Beban on offense, the Bruins were also a fanatical defensive team.

"UCLA swarms on its foe, sticks him, prods him and buzzes around him," pointed out one pregame analyst. "It stunts and squirms, hits and slides, penetrates and scrambles and forces mistakes." Although they played an excellent defense, the Trojans were an offense-oriented team.

Distinctly contrasting in personality, UCLA and Southern Cal were perfectly matched in talent. Using a special grading system, McKay had weighed the value of the teams, player by player, and came up with the arithmetical equation that UCLA and Southern Cal were exactly equal. "It's going to be a helluva game," McKay decided in the most unscientific terms.

Southern Cal was installed as a three-point favorite, although ranked second in the country to Number-One UCLA. Analysts figured that the Trojans had faced a tougher schedule than the Bruins.

Emotionally, the UCLA players seemed higher than Southern Cal's. Prothro kept his charges in a demonstrative state of frenzy before the game. He encouraged them to "hop around on the sidelines like thieves trapped in a corridor," pointed out one sportswriter. The Trojans were more businesslike by comparison. In the team meeting before the game, McKay told his players that they would be coming back to the locker room in two hours or so. "It'll be the shortest walk of your life," the coach said quietly, "or it'll be the longest."

It turned out to be the shortest, but not without some apprehension on the part of the Trojans. As if sanctified by some Hollywood movie mogul, the teams battled toward an engrossing finish before an audience of more than 90,000 in the Los Angeles Coliseum and millions more on national television.

The teams were tied at 14-14 when UCLA scored on a typical Beban-inspired scheme. The star quarterback completed four passes in a seven-play drive covering sixty-five yards, the last one to Dave Nuttall for a touchdown. A subtle, calculating move by McKay then provided the Trojans with a key play. When the Bruins lined up for the extra-point kick, McKay inserted six-foot-eight Bill Hayhoe into the defensive line. "We knew that Zenon Andrusyshyn [the UCLA kicker] kicked the ball low so we just put the tallest guy we had in there on defense. We told the kids it wasn't so important that they bust through and make him rush the kick as it was just getting to the scrimmage line and raising their arms high."

Hayhoe got his arms high enough to put a finger on the ball and deflect it. The kick was no good and McKay said afterward with a wink, "I call that brilliant coaching."

Simpson, of course, made McKay look like a genius after that with his game-winning touchdown run.

Toby Page had taken over for Steve Sogge at quarterback and repeatedly sent Simpson whirling through the Bruin defenders. On this particular series of downs, Simpson had appeared winded after carrying the ball two straight times.

"Page looked at me as if I couldn't carry the ball a third straight time," Simpson recalls. "I looked at him as if I could."

Originally, Page decided not to use Simpson as the Trojans lined up. It was third down on the Southern Cal thirty-six. Then Page noticed that UCLA's linebackers had anticipated the play he had ordered and changed signals at the line of scrimmage.

"I was bent over there, and I heard him call the 23-Blast," Simpson remembers. "I said to myself, the 23-Blast —oh, oh, that's me."

Simpson got the ball from Page and headed for the left side of the line. Guard Steve Lehmer and tackle Mike Taylor cleared the runner through a huge hole.

"As it unfolded it looked like a five-yard gain," noted one writer. "Then Simpson veered toward the left sideline. Oh, well, a fifteen-yard gain and first down."

But suddenly there was Southern Cal end Ron Drake blocking out UCLA's halfback, and the safety was out of the way, too. Simpson turned toward the middle of the field, going to his right, and open land appeared before him. Soon he was exerting his famous 9.4 speed, accelerating toward the goal line despite a sore foot and despite having played a complete afternoon of torturous football. After that spectacular run, Rikki Aldridge kicked the crucial tie-breaking extra point for the Trojans, to give USC the 21-20 victory.

Although neither Simpson nor Beban was in perfect physical condition, each star responded to the high stakes with efficacy. Beban, whose rib cage "looked like an abstract painting in purples and pinks," according to one observer, passed for more than 300 yards. Simpson, whose swollen right foot was described by another as something that should be "in a museum of natural history," drove for 177 yards. And Jim Murray of the *Los Angeles Times* suggested, "They should send the Heisman out here with two straws."

Beban won the Heisman Trophy that year, but undoubtedly, he would have given his right arm to go to the Rose Bowl. After all, he had given everything else that brilliant autumn afternoon.

7

LSU—MISSISSIPPI

"Go to Hell, Ole Miss"
"Go to Hell, LSU"

For years, football fans had been enjoying spirited games between Mississippi and Louisiana State University, but it took an extraordinary run by Billy Cannon in 1959 to really make them sit up and take notice.

On a sultry Halloween night at LSU's Tiger Stadium that year, the bowlegged halfback in white and gold plucked a bouncing punt out of the air on his eleven-yard line and set out for glory. Cannon shrugged off one red-jerseyed tackler, ran through another, and at midfield surprised Mississippi fullback Charlie Flowers with a neat cut. "It was like a high-school player trying to tackle an All-American." Flowers said later. "He went through my hands like nothing." Cannon was all by himself when he hit the end zone at the end of his eighty-nine-yard touchdown dash and LSU was alone in the winner's circle with an epic 7-3 triumph.

Although forty-six games had been played before, many of them memorable, some say this is where the Mississippi –LSU rivalry really got off the ground.

The late fifties and early sixties provided some of the most meaningful and titillating games in the series, with Conference championships and sometimes national titles hinging in a large measure on their outcome. During this dramatic cycle, both Southeastern Conference teams were at the height of their power, Mississippi under the guiding genius of Johnny Vaught, and LSU, the pride of Paul Dietzel and later, Charlie McClendon.

It was Dietzel's team that had won a national championship in 1958, counting Mississippi among its victims

for the first time since 1950. The flamboyant Dietzel always
seemed to enjoy meeting Ole Miss, possibly because it allowed him the opportunity to exercise his imagination in
pregame gimmickery and psychological preparation. He
missed no tricks for the 1959 game, which featured a nationally heralded battle between his top-ranked team and
Mississippi, rated Number Six in the land at the time. First,
a newspaper story that quoted Rebel fullback Flowers as
declaring he would "outgain Billy Cannon" became mandatory reading in the LSU dressing room. Then, the LSU
campus was bombed by "Go To Hell LSU" leaflets and
there were some suspicions that Dietzel himself was at the
control of the plane. Taking note that the LSU coach was
a B-29 pilot during World War II, Vaught remarked, "I
thought his flying days were over."

On the Friday before the game, LSU players were
greeted by a gigantic mural of a hairy gorilla, done in vivid
color by Dietzel and wearing, of course, Flowers' No. 41.
That evening, as was the custom before home games, the
team attended a movie in the projection room at Tiger Stadium. Dietzel's choice that night was, *Kiss Me Deadly,* the
blood-and-bullets saga of Mickey Spillane's tough anti-
hero, detective Mike Hammer.

All through the week, it seemed, Dietzel was more concerned about the psychological rather than the tactical
aspect of the Ole Miss game. "You have to build toward a
peak and not reach it too soon," he explained.

While Dietzel was meditating on a couch in his office
two hours before the eight p.m. kickoff, Vaught was applying some last-minute psychological strokes himself for
Mississippi. Trying a new experiment to acclimate his team
to LSU's intimidating Tiger Stadium, a chamber of horrors
for visitors, Vaught brought his Rebels onto the field at
6:30 p.m. in street clothes. They inspected the field, then
strolled over to their bench where they sat for twenty
minutes listening to LSU students chanting, "We're
Number One."

The full evening was warm to the point of discomfort—

seventy-three degrees and 100 percent humidity. A thick
mist hung in the air, giving the stadium a dramatic, unearthly quality. But the LSU fans quickly returned to reality when Cannon, the ultimate campus hero, fumbled the
ball away early in the game and gave Mississippi
possession on the Tiger twenty-one-yard line. A few plays
later, Bob Khayat kicked a field goal to give Mississippi a
3-0 lead. Cannon's fumble was to be the first of four by
LSU that night and each one either killed a Tiger drive or
gave Ole Miss a golden scoring opportunity. On one of
these chances, Mississippi had a first down on the LSU
seven-yard line. But Andy Bourgeois, one of Dietzel's
famed "Chinese Bandit" defenders, stopped quarterback
Bobby Franklin on a rollout on the last play of the first
half and the score remained 3-0 in favor of Mississippi.

The insolent Rebels continued to twist the Tigers' tails in
the third period. So confident was Vaught of his team's
defense that he had the Rebels kicking on first down, hoping that tired LSU would fumble the ball deep in its own
territory. The total ineptness of the Tigers during the first
three periods seemed like the symbolic last gasps from a
national champion. Meanwhile, the faces in the crowd
echoed their frustration, as the fans chanted plaintively and
profanely, "Go to hell, Ole Miss, go to hell."

As the last quarter began, Vaught saw no reason to
change his punting strategy. Jake Gibbs, who later went
on to a successful pro baseball career as a catcher, had been
kicking skyscrapers all night, one punt traveling fifty-two
yards. So on a third-and-seventeen from the Ole Miss
forty-two, Vaught ordered his team into another punt formation. Cannon, battle-weary by now but still rankled by
that first-quarter fumble that helped give Mississippi the
early lead, dropped back to his five-yard line to await another long kick from the inimitable Gibbs. This one was a
forty-seven-yarder, skidding inside the twenty until it took
a high bounce into Cannon's arms on the eleven.

Cannon looked up field and saw a treacherous course
before him, a flood of redshirts closing in. At the nineteen,

the LSU back was hit on the knees by Richard Price, but Cannon struggled loose. Jerry Daniels had a clear shot at Cannon at the twenty, grabbing Billy near the shoulders, but by the thirty the Mississippi tackler slipped off. Mickey Mangham threw a terrific block at the forty and all of a sudden Cannon was at midfield—running so close to the Mississippi bench that Vaught could almost reach out and touch him. Gibbs was not entirely out of the picture at this point. He eluded a block and then made a lunge at Cannon at the forty-five. For a moment the Mississippi punter held on, but Cannon finally shook free and all he could see before him was open land. "When I saw Johnny Robinson looking back for someone to block," Cannon said later, "I felt this was it. Just don't stub your toe, I told myself."

Oblivious to the terrific noise in the stadium during his brilliant runback, Cannon became vividly aware of it as soon as he crossed the goal line. "I seemed to hear everyone at once," he said. "I don't think I got hit much harder in the game than I did by my teammates in the end zone. I was lucky to get out alive."

Cannon later insured the immortality of his superhuman effort when he helped stop a Mississippi drive in the last minute. Doug Elmore, a third-string quarterback, led the Rebels to the doorstep of the LSU goal line before he was tackled by Cannon and Warren Rabb on the one-yard line, with eighteen seconds left. That suspenseful conclusion led Fred Russell, a veteran sportswriter in Nashville, Tennessee, to echo the majority opinion: "For its fury, suspense, and competitive team performance, Louisiana State's 7-3 heartthrobber over Ole Miss was the fullest and finest football game I've witnessed in thirty-one years of sports reporting."

The LSU dressing room was a "cross between a Turkish bath and the tunnel of love," pointed out Peter Finney in his fine book on LSU football, *The Fighting Tigers*. The most appropriate quote of that throbbing room came from guard Mike Stupka, who put his arm around an exhausted Cannon and said simply, "Thank you, Billy." Dietzel voiced the sentiments of just about everyone there when he called Cannon's run "the greatest I have ever seen on a football field." Ironically, Cannon almost didn't make the most famous run in the LSU–Mississippi series because, as he later stated, the decision to return the punt wasn't made until the last second. "I wasn't going to field it," Cannon noted. "I was going to let it roll. Gibbs didn't kick this one as long as the others and it was sort of dribbling toward me. Ole Miss was covering well and I didn't feel like taking chances—but right at the end, it took a high bounce and came right to me."

As always, LSU had played just well enough to win. As usual, the man who supplied the clutch play for the Tigers was Billy Abb Cannon, twenty-two, one of the most remarkable athletes in college football during the late fifties. As LSU tackle Bo Strange said: "When you need it, that animal is there. Cannon won't get 100 touchdowns against Podunk. But he'll get the big one against someone like Mississippi." As Cannon said, "Man, I don't like to get beat." Cannon, whose father worked as a custodian in a Louisiana State University dormitory, sold soda and peanuts at LSU football games as a kid and was predestined to enroll at the university despite the fifty offers he drew as a high school All-American. A national magazine called Cannon "possibly the strongest fast man ... or the fastest strong man in the world." Square and solid at six-one and 207 pounds, he was able to put the shot at fifty-four feet, 4½ inches and rip off the 100-yard dash in 9.4 seconds, both achievements close to world record levels. What was more, Cannon could block with power and was at his best under pressure.

Cannon's performance in the 1959 game with Mississippi highlighted one of the most exciting contests in the series and, for that matter, in the history of college football. But the LSU–Ole Miss rivalry has never had a shortage of towering moments. In one of the golden chapters of this superb series, Mississippi defeated LSU 20-18 in 1947 in a pivotal battle involving the Rebels' Charlie Conerly and the

Tigers' Y.A. Tittle, two of the more storied names in football. The 1952 game resulted in a tingling 14-12 victory for Mississippi, despite the presence of Cannon and the brilliant Jimmy Taylor in LSU's backfield. The Rebels prevented defeat in the 1960 game when Allen Green's forty-one-yard field goal with six seconds remaining gave them a breathtaking 6-6 tie.

LSU came from behind in 1961 for a 10-7 victory to deprive Mississippi of the national-poll lead at that juncture and possibly a national crown. The Tigers made another great comeback in 1964, this one in the last five minutes, to win an 11-10 decision on a late two-point conversion. The 1968-69-71 games were characteristic of the rivalry, epic thrillers won by Mississippi, 27-24, 26-23 and 24-22 respectively. A Hollywood finish was in the stars for LSU in 1972, when the Tigers edged Mississippi 17-16 before 70,502 howling fans in Baton Rouge. Bert Jones calmly drove LSU to its winning score as time was running out, and he actually threw the tying touchdown pass after time had expired. Rusty Jackson's extra point conversion came several minutes after the game had ended. In another typically frenzied battle in 1975, two Mississippi races against the clock—one just before the half and the other at the finish— resulted in a pulsating 17-13 victory for the Rebels.

This distinguished rivalry, one of the oldest in the South, has produced some of the most illustrious names in football history. In 1947, his first season at Oxford, Vaught had Charley Conerly, who later became a great quarterback in the pros, and Barney Poole, an outstanding end during this period. The battery of Conerly and Poole enabled Vaught to win the Southeastern Conference championship as a rookie coach. Winning became a habit with Mississippi's most successful coach, who won two national titles, six League championships and went to seventeen Bowls in his quarter-century of administration. Forced into retirement because of a heart condition in 1960, Vaught qualified for the College Football Hall of Fame with a record of

185-58-12. Including such stars as Conerly, Poole and the recently celebrated Archie Manning, Vaught coached twenty All-Americans.

Preceding Vaught was another successful, if not as long-lasting, Mississippi coach, Harry Mehre. He had a winning record and made many points with alumni by defeating LSU four straight seasons. Conerly and Poole also played some football under Mehre, along with Frank "Bruiser" Kinard, a famous tackle of the thirties who became Mississippi's first bona fide All-American. Mehre, a noted humorist, once said of his eight seasons at Oxford: "I was lucky to get out of there alive, but Vaught became a living legend. Vaught should have won with all the material he had. . . . I had to play such people as Charley Conerly and all those Pooles [there were four under Mehre] and Kinards."

Few Southern colleges have had a longer honor role of stars than LSU. Starting with LSU's first All-American in 1935, Gaynell Tinsley, the Tigers have produced such fine players as Y.A. Tittle, Steve Van Buren, Jimmy Taylor, Billy Cannon, Alvin Dark, Johnny Robinson, Fred Miller, Wendell Harris and Tommy Casanova. There haven't been many teams, either, that have had the enthusiastic support the Tigers have had through the years. "You have not fully experienced college football until you have seen a football game in Baton Rouge on a Saturday night," says Jesse Outlar, sports Editor of the *Atlanta Constitution*. Tiger Stadium seats 67,510 and from the moment the football Tigers follow their live Tiger mascot out onto the field, just about every voice in the place erupts with the roar, "Go Tigers! Go Tigers!"

One of LSU's most renowned fans was Huey Long, the long-time governor and "kingfish" of Louisiana politics. Long, it seemed, was as interested in the Tigers winning as he was in becoming President of the United States. He embraced the team with an alarming intensity, stalked the sidelines, took a hand in the coaching and even brought players to live at the governor's mansion for a strict diet of sour milk, cornbread and turnip greens. The Tigers were Long's pride and joy during the thirties, when Bernie Moore, the school's first truly long-term football coach, was in his heyday.

In later years, LSU football did not need a gubernatorial boost to forge ahead. The Tigers won a national championship in 1958 with a virtually unknown coach, Paul Dietzel. Dietzel captivated Dixie fans with his unique three-team plan: the White Team, the Go Team and the Chinese Bandits. When Dietzel left for West Point after the 1961 season, LSU athletic director Jim Corbett wisely imported Charlie McClendon, a former Kentucky star. McClendon became the longest-lasting and most successful coach in LSU history.

LSU and Mississippi began their series in Baton Rouge in 1894, the second year of intercollegiate competition for both schools, with a more experienced Ole Miss team winning 26-6. The first game had a unique twist. When it was apparent that Ole Miss had sewn up the game, A.P. Simmonds, the LSU coach, asked for, and received, permission to play in the Tiger backfield. Simmonds, an end on Yale's 1893 team who was hired as LSU's first professional coach in 1894, proceeded to climax an eighty-yard drive with a brilliant forty-five-yard run for the Tigers' only touchdown that day. The run brought applause from Mississippi players as well as LSU fans. The teams were evenly matched during the formative years of the rivalry, each winning six times in the first dozen games. It was to Mississippi's credit that the Rebels managed to keep abreast of the Tigers, since eight of the first twelve games were played in Baton Rouge and two others in New Orleans, which must certainly be counted as home territory for LSU.

In the second of three distinctive cycles in the series, LSU thoroughly dominated Mississippi in the period from 1915 through 1937. Despite an instability in the coaching ranks—three changes in one season and nine interchangeable faces in the twenty-three years—the Tigers won fourteen of fifteen games from the Rebels in this time. They developed six- and eight-game winning streaks broken by a lone Rebel triumph in 1927 by Homer Hazel's team. Hazel was one of the early saviors of Ole Miss football. Mississippi athletics had experienced a decade of indifferent support and results; when Hazel took over in 1925 and revitalized Rebel football, he produced winners through four of five seasons and, just as notably, ended the drought against Mississippi.

No one counted on Mississippi winning in 1938, but in the first game under coach Harry Mehre, All-American Parker Hall ran and passed the Rebels to a 20-7 victory that was considered one of the biggest upsets in the series. That not only stopped another drought against LSU but started a unique string for Mississippi—four victories in a row at Baton Rouge. This was the beginning of the third cycle in the series—Mississippi holding the edge in the highest level of competition ever between these two magnificent rivals.

Mississippi's triumph in 1947 will long be remembered as the launching pad for Vaught's trip to the top of the Southeastern Conference that year, and the legendary Rebel coach can thank Y.A. Tittle's falling pants for it. Tiger Stadium, as usual, was packed that night for the Ole Miss game when Tittle picked off a Conerly pass and headed for the end zone. One Ole Miss player swiped at Tittle and managed to catch hold of his belt, snapping it off. Tittle's gold pants began a slow descent as he was running and guard Charley Cusimano, who was in front of Y.A. looking for someone to block, heard Tittle yell, "Hold it, hold it." Cusimano looked back to see his teammate trying to pull up his trousers and run at the same time. The aborted run cost LSU the game. Mississippi wound up a 20-18 winner and Vaught was en route to his first SEC title.

Except for games in 1949 and 1950, Vaught's spell over LSU lasted into the late fifties as the successful Mississippi coach won eight and tied one of their first eleven meetings. The Rebel domination included six straight victories from 1952 through 1957, including four straight on LSU's home grounds. In 1958, however, Dietzel had made tigers out of LSU after three mediocre seasons, with the help of one of the finest backfields in the country, including the ultimate breakaway threat in Billy Cannon. Both LSU and Mississippi were undefeated in their first six games and both were ranked in the Top Ten of both wire service polls in 1958, setting the stage for Dixie's biggest game of the season. For the first time in history, 67,510-seat Tiger Stadium was sold out. A week before the game, some 15,000 end-zone seats were put on sale and gobbled up in two hours. The early sellout, of course, increased the demand for ducats and some people were willing to trade television sets for tickets. One fan reportedly offered $800 for eight good sideline seats. By midweek, pranks came into play. An Ole Miss plane flew over the Baton Rouge campus, bombarding it with "Go to Hell, LSU" leaflets. Undiscouraged by this maneuver, some 3,000 students marched into practice to cheer the team.

They had more to cheer about during the game, when their Tigers lived up to their tough nickname with a superhuman goal-line stand early in the second quarter. Mississippi had advanced the ball to the LSU two-yard line and had four shots at a touchdown. On the first play, Mississippi quarterback Bobby Franklin jabbed to the one-foot line. On second down, Franklin sent Kent Lovelace up the middle, but he was stopped just short of the goal. On third down, Franklin called on fullback Charley Flowers, but he barely made it to the line of scrimmage. On fourth down, with just about everyone in the roaring stadium on their feet, Lovelace again tried to go off-tackle, but he was snowed under at the two-yard line. Incredibly, LSU had held and when Dietzel graded the movies the next day, he was still finding it hard to believe.

"When you get shoulder-to-shoulder in an eight-man line defense, you can't afford to make a mistake," he said. "We didn't make one. Max Fugler made key tackles on two downs. When they sent Flowers up the middle, the line held and Cannon met him head on and knocked him back. Another time [Warren] Rabb came up after the initial stop was made and halted progress. It was an incredible effort."

After running into that explosive goal-line reception, Mississippi was never the same. The Rebels lost their early fire and soon provided a costly fumble that resulted in an LSU touchdown run by Rabb. The final score was 14-0 in favor of LSU and proved to be a key victory on the Tigers' high road to the national championship that season. Losing to Dietzel for the first time in four years, Vaught noted: "We played better in this game than we did in beating Texas 39-7 in last season's Sugar Bowl. LSU took advantage of the breaks, which is what you're supposed to do."

Cannon's legendary run, of course, pulled the 1959 game out of the fire for LSU as the Tigers beat the Rebels for the second straight time. But Mississippi had a measure of atonement that season, beating LSU 21-0 in a celebrated Sugar Bowl rematch behind the touchdown passing of Franklin and Jake Gibbs. Dietzel had voiced disapproval of a return game with Mississippi because of the obvious psychological factor in the Rebels' favor but was overruled.

LSU more than made up for that Sugar Bowl humiliation in the next two years, spoiling two perfectly wonderful seasons for Mississippi in 1960 and 1961. A 6-6 tie in 1960 was the only blemish on an otherwise perfect season for the Sugar Bowl-bound Rebels. Mississippi was a confident three-touchdown favorite in that game and staved off defeat only by a last-minute, forty-one-yard field goal by Allen Green. For the third time in four years, an Ole Miss –LSU game had national implications when the teams met in 1961 in their traditional Halloween Night game in Baton Rouge, and Vaught made the contest a virtual crusade. "We're going to Baton Rouge with every bit of determination and energy we can muster," he said. "This team believes in itself and the boys don't believe anyone can whip 'em. It makes no difference that we've won six games so far this season. It's what we do next Saturday that counts." If any coach had a cause to crusade against LSU, it was Vaught. His Rebels had not crossed LSU's goal line in regular season play since 1957 and Vaught, who had never had a perfect season, would have had two had it not been for the marks left by the Tigers in 1959 and 1960. The hostile climate had been further spiced by a recruiting coup that Vaught made over Dietzel for quarterback Perry Lee Dunn.

Ole Miss didn't need any last-minute incentive, but they were given one when the Rebel players were greeted by a group of inhospitable LSU students upon their arrival for a Friday afternoon warmup. The students surrounded the Mississippi bus and chanted, "Go to Hell, Ole Miss, Go to Hell!" and further antagonized the Rebels by holding up their progress to the dressing room at Tiger Stadium.

Some melodrama was added to the occasion when Minnesota upset top-ranked Michigan State in an afternoon game, leaving the road to Number One open for undefeated, unchallenged Mississippi. Rebel backers in the stands flashed banners certifying their team as Number One and it took sixty minutes of almost unbearable drama and a proficient effort by LSU to change the expressions on the faces of smug Mississippians.

Overall, it was the best Mississippi team that Vaught had sent against LSU, to that time, one better than the Tiger staff anticipated. But the Tigers, beaten in just about every important offensive category, managed to win the game nevertheless. The consensus opinion was that LSU beat a superior team 10-7 that night because of a series of clutch performances and with a trap that caught the Rebels going the wrong way. Ole Miss was able to score only once in the six times that it crossed midfield while LSU made better use of its opportunities, scoring a touchdown and a field goal while crossing the fifty-yard line merely three times.

"I hope the boys on the 1958 and 1959 teams forgive me," said Dietzel in the glow of the winning moment, "but this is the greatest victory I've ever been associated with."

It was a fifty-seven-yard run by Jerry Stovall, reminiscent of Cannon's famous Halloween Night dash two years before, that turned the game in LSU's favor. Until Stovall broke loose and carried the ball down to the Ole Miss twenty-three-yard line, it looked as if Mississippi had deflated the Tigers with a touchdown seconds before the half that gave the Rebels a 7-3 lead. But then LSU sent Wendell Harris in motion to the right. Jimmy Field started out the same way but handed off to Stovall who was coming to the left and a couple of good blocks sprang him loose. The drive seemed destined to die, but Billy Truax made a remarkable catch of a fourth-down-and-five pass from Lynn Amedee at the Ole Miss twelve. "I barely got my fingers under it," the six-five Truax said later. "As I stumbled forward, I pulled the ball into my chest." It turned out to be LSU's only pass reception of the night. Two plays later Harris raced into the end zone untouched. It was the same play, run to a different side, that Stovall used to change the momentum in LSU's favor and Dietzel said later, "Both times, we caught them going the wrong way." The margin of victory was actually a thirty-seven-yard field goal by Harris on LSU's first possession.

More often than not, the LSU–Mississippi series had scenes of similar melodrama in subsequent years. As typical of any of these exciting games was the breathtaking 1964 contest. The Rebels that year were one of Vaught's poorer teams and installed as six-point underdogs to the Tigers, a swaggering, Bowl-bound team. LSU looked every bit the favorite in the early going, dominating play in the first period as Pat Screen seemed to have forgotten all about a heavily taped knee. The LSU quarterback took his team seventy-seven yards before settling for a field goal. However, Ole Miss came alive with a sixty-nine-yard touchdown drive for a 7-3 lead. Then all the air seemed to go out of LSU's football when Screen, who had completed nine of ten passes in the first quarter, hobbled to the sidelines in the second period.

When the Rebels added a fourth-period field goal, the situation looked quite hopeless for LSU. Many of the 68,000 fans in Tiger Stadium began to leave when Buster Brown stood on the LSU goal line and punted the ball to Doug Cunningham on the Mississippi forty-seven. Suddenly, good fortune blessed LSU in the appearance of Don Ellen, who knocked an Ole Miss blocker into Cunningham, forcing the ball carrier to lose control of the football. John Aaron claimed the loose ball for the Tigers with seven minutes left. Six plays later, they were camped on the Mississippi nineteen, facing a second-and-ten situation, and the exodus of the crowd had suddenly stopped. "I called a 'flanker circle route,' " explained LSU reserve quarterback Billy Ezell, "which called for Billy Masters to go downfield ten yards and buttonhook." Masters didn't exactly follow orders. "I started downfield," he said, "but when I noticed the Ole Miss defensive man running in, I took a sudden notion to keep running." Master's "notion" produced a wide-open field for him behind the Ole Miss defender. Ezell spotted him and suddenly, incredibly, it was 10-9 Ole Miss, with three and a half minutes remaining. "If there had been more time I might have kicked the extra point," said LSU coach Charlie McClendon, "but I knew no one would have been satisfied with a tie." He had certainly read the mood of his players. "I believe if someone had thrown a kicking tee on the field, I would have thrown it back," said George Rice.

Actually, the only thing thrown in the next few seconds was a pass from Ezell to Doug Moreau. The ball was tipped by defender Tommy Luke, but Moreau caught the deflected pass on his fingertips and planted both feet six inches inside the boundary line before his momentum carried him out. LSU had a two-point conversion and an extraordinary 11-10 victory.

"I didn't know we had it until I heard the roar of the crowd," said McClendon, slapping backs and patting heads all around in the celebrating Tiger locker room. Moreau was off sailing on his personal cloud nine. "Before the game," he said, "Pat Screen and I were talking about heaven, wondering what a 'vision' is like. Now I think I have an idea. When I was leaving the field, I closed my eyes and I think I had one."

The best vision of the night was for the LSU fans, of course—the one of Moreau catching a pass to beat a hated rival.

8

OKLAHOMA—NEBRASKA

Seeing Red

When you play for Oklahoma or Nebraska, you don't feel like you're playing just for the school. The atmosphere makes you think you're playing for the whole state.

—A former Big Eight player

Oklahoma's school colors are crimson and cream and Nebraska wears scarlet and cream, a subtle nuance perhaps recognized by some purists, but not the average fan—whenever Oklahoma plays Nebraska, he only sees red.

When the Sooners began moving up in college football circles under Bud Wilkinson in the forties, it was only natural that their charge be spurred on by cries of, "Go, Big Red!" When Nebraska did the same under Bob Devaney in the sixties, the Cornhuskers heard the same clarion call.

So the Big Eight suddenly had two "Big Reds" and a lot of friendly furor over a little distinction in color. It was settled in that manner in which most lighthearted college football feuds are. Nebraska became the "Big Red of the North" and Oklahoma the "Big Red of the South."

Although there have been isolated cases of bitterness between the two football powers over the years, theirs has generally been a good-natured rivalry, spawning more goodwill than contempt.

"There is no hate involved in this rivalry," notes Volney Meece, sports editor of the *Oklahoma City Times*. "These teams have a great deal of respect for each other. A Nebraska player once told me that he always liked to play in the Oklahoma game because it was a tough, hard-hitting game, very few penalties, no dirty play. It's an intense rivalry, because it has meant so much over the years, but it's cleanly played."

In the land of table-flat terrain, oil wells, pickup trucks and chicken-fried steak, Oklahomans get psyched to madness each year for the Nebraska game. The feeling is mutual throughout the rural farmlands and hamlets of Nebraska, where football is a statewide ritual each fall. It has been that way for many years but especially since 1970, when the game took on new national status. Since the 1970 season, the Big Eight championship or a share of it has hinged on the Nebraska–Oklahoma game. And the 1971 contest, "The Big Shootout" or "The Game of the Decade," was a battle not only for the Big Eight title but the national championship as well. Whenever classic college football games are replayed in bars or living rooms, this is among the ones they always cuss and discuss.

Nebraska and Oklahoma have usually been the Big Two of their conference, whether it has been called in varying degrees the Big Six, Big Seven or Big Eight, so their games have a sense of significant history attached to them. Through 1977, Nebraska had won or shared thirty Conference championships and Oklahoma twenty-eight, counting their participation in the old Missouri Valley Conference and Oklahoma's brief appearance in the Southwest Conference.

Even more significantly, Oklahoma and Nebraska have given college football two of its most impressive success stories on a national level. The Cornhuskers were a power in the twenties and thirties and have produced national championship teams in the seventies. Wilkinson led Oklahoma to three national titles in the fifties with teams that created college football's all-time winning streak of forty-seven games and the Sooners rose to power again in the seventies under Chuck Fairbanks and Barry Switzer, realizing still another national championship.

But strangely enough, until the Sizzling Seventies, the successes of Nebraska and Oklahoma rarely paralleled and as a result their series has been one of enormous power changes. Ironically, one of these changes made the rivalry what it is today. It was generally felt that Wilkinson's long domination of the conference that embraces Middle America's flowing fields and plains served as an inspiration for Nebraska to reestablish its once formidable program.

"Wilkinson started a revolution at Oklahoma in the forties," points out Meece. "He went into Texas and recruited some lean, fast kids and the rest of the Big Six Conference [as it was known in 1947] wasn't ready for that. He forced other schools to make the decision—build up or lag behind. Nebraska did a better job than any others."

But it took time. While at the zenith of their football history, the Sooners beat Nebraska sixteen straight years from 1943 through 1958. During that period, Oklahoma was beating everyone else as well in the Conference (now the Big Seven with the admission of Colorado in the late forties) and had run up an incredible seventy-two-game unbeaten streak in league play. As if ordained by some grand design, it was none other than Nebraska that ended Oklahoma's mammoth streak with a 25-21 victory in 1959. That tight game set the tempo for things to come.

It became a burning rivalry after that. Oklahoma–Nebraska games in the sixties and particularly in the seventies became the type of competition expected from two of college football's superpowers. In the 1959–1972 period, each team won seven games and neither won more than three in a row. Although Oklahoma won six straight times from 1972 through 1977, most of the meetings were fiercely competitive.

The Nebraska–Oklahoma series, although begun in 1912, was not a yearly fixture until the 1928 season when both became part of the newly formed Big Six Conference, along with Kansas, Missouri, Kansas State and Iowa State. Led by such indomitable spirits as Fred Dawson, Dana X. Bible and Biff Jones, Nebraska's football teams plowed through the Plains with great zeal. Among those to continually go down under the Cornhuskers' haymakers were the Sooners, who were able to beat them only three times in their first twenty-two meetings from 1912 through 1942. During this period, Nebraska won sixteen times and three games were tied. Typical of this Nebraska domination was a 44-0 victory in 1921 where the Huskers used their heads as much as their feet to beat Oklahoma. The game was played in a field of mud "that would have stuck a hog," according to one writer, and the reason that Nebraska was able to beat Oklahoma so handily was because Dawson had outsmarted Bennie Owen, the first of Oklahoma's great coaches. Explained one newspaper account:

"The Owen men bogged up to their ankles in the mire, for their football shoes did not have the mud cleats that Dawson had provided for his eleven. The Huskers had specially designed conical mud spikes, three inches in length on their shoes, which prevented them from sinking in and gave them a fairly firm hold in the mud. . . . Rubber soles kept the mud from sticking to their shoes."

Bible, a fundamentalist whose teams were schooled hardest in defense and the kicking game, brought continuing success to Nebraska in the thirties with such stars as fullbacks George Sauer and Sam Francis and tackles Ray Richards and Hugh Rhea. From 1929 through 1936, Bible's teams failed to win the Big Six title only in 1930 and 1934 and lost only three Conference games. Later, it was Jones, an Oklahoma expatriate, who built on Bible's work. Jones, in fact, was the center of a small controversy that lent some spice to the growing rivalry with Oklahoma. Jones, an organizational genius, coached at Oklahoma in 1935 and 1936, building a foundation for Tom Stidham's Orange Bowl team later in the decade. No sooner had he settled in at Norman, however, than it seemed he was wooed and won by Nebraska. "There was a charge by Oklahoma that Nebraska raided their campus and stole Biff Jones away from them," recalls Meece. "This caused some bitterness between the schools for a while."

Oklahomans were partially assuaged with a brief flurry

of success against Nebraska immediately after Jones' departure for Cornhusker country. For the first time in seven years, the Sooners could claim parity with Nebraska when the 1937 game resulted in a scoreless tie. In 1938, Oklahoma enjoyed its first victory over a Nebraska team since 1930 with a 14-0 decision. However, it turned out that Oklahoma's flash of success against Nebraska would be just an aberration and dissolve as quickly as it came. By 1939, Jones started a three-game winning streak against Oklahoma in the midst of which would be a Big Six Conference title (his second at Nebraska) and a berth in the Rose Bowl. His 1940 Nebraska team, after losing its opener to Minnesota 13-7, won eight other regular-season games and became the first Cornhusker team to play in a Bowl. (As it turned out, Nebraska also became the only member of the Big Eight family to ever play in Pasadena). Although a 21-13 loser to Stanford, Jones took a special pride in his Rose Bowl team because thirty-eight of the thirty-nine men on the roster came from within the state. When the Bowl bid came to Lincoln, the state went berserk and Gregg McBride, veteran newspaperman and sports publicist at Nebraska, said: "It was the greatest thing that happened to Nebraska since William Jennings Bryan ran for the presidency." Among the All-Americans developed by Jones at Nebraska were center Charlie Brock, tackles Fred Shirey and Forrest Behm and guard Warren Alfson.

After serving in the Second World War, Jones was undercut by a common circumstantial irony associated with the times. A West Pointer and former coach at Army with a deeply rooted militaristic approach to football, Jones was a virtual outcast after the war because of his style. "Jones was a military-type guy and they didn't do very well after the war," explains Wally Provost, a columnist for the *Omaha World-Herald.* "There were a lot of Army veterans on those postwar teams who didn't want to be ordered around after what they'd been through. So this might have been part of the thinking of the Nebraska administrators when they refused to offer him the coaching job again." Jones was instead offered the position as athletic director, but this was seen as a token gesture.

With loyalties divided and morale down in the wake of the Jones debacle, circumstances were hardly conducive to continued success at Nebraska. Historians later saw it as a contributing factor to a period of decline at Lincoln that lasted until the late fifties.

It was Nebraska's further misfortune, and that of other teams in the league, to have Wilkinson as a bedfellow during this period. A blond, dashing thirty-year-old not that far removed from some of his veteran players, Wilkinson came to Oklahoma in 1947 and shaped one of college football's all-time great dynasties. Few teams in the history of the sport bullied a league or dominated an age as did Wilkinson's near-perfect Sooners. In 1946 under coach Jim Tatum, and then in 1947 under Wilkinson, the Sooners shared the Big Six championship with Kansas. Then from 1948 through 1957, Wilkinson's Sooners won all ten championships of the Big Seven Conference. And when the Conference expanded to eight members, Oklahoma won in 1958 and 1959, Wilkinson's thirteenth and fourteenth straight titles. "Not even the musical *Oklahoma* could match that run," pointed out one writer. Such dynamic players as halfbacks Billy Vessels and Tommy McDonald, centers Jerry Tubbs and Kurt Burris, tackle Jim Weatherall, guard J. D. Roberts and end Max Boydston played for Wilkinson and helped bring national championships to Oklahoma in 1950, 1955 and 1956.

En route to the national title in 1950, Oklahoma defeated Nebraska 49-35 in one of the most memorable games of their series as Vessels and Nebraska's heralded sophomore star, Bobby Reynolds, put on an exciting running show. Reynolds gained eighty-one yards in the first half to lead Nebraska to a 21-14 lead at intermission. Then Vessels took over, gaining much of his team-record 208 yards rushing, to lead the Sooners to victory. In the process, Vessels averaged 11.4 yards per carry and scored three touchdowns.

Oklahoma continued to run up basketball-size scores on Nebraska through most of the fifties, compiling anywhere from twenty-seven to fifty-five points a game, depending on the Sooners' surliness. By 1959, however, the cyclic phenomenon so indigenous to college football teams caught up with Oklahoma and the Sooners experienced their worst season in Wilkinson's regime. Oklahoma still managed to win the Big Seven title but lost three games that season, including a 25-21 decision to Nebraska that broke the Sooners' thirteen-year spell over their Conference colleagues. In a game played before an ecstatic and sometimes disbelieving homecoming crowd of 34,000 at Lincoln, the Cornhuskers took advantage of a blocked punt, two field goals and a sixty-one-yard punt return for a touchdown by Pat Fischer to upset the mighty Sooners. Nebraska's Ron Meade intercepted an Oklahoma pass in the Cornhusker end zone with only twenty-five seconds remaining to secure one of the most critical victories in his school's history. It served as a symbol of the times and an omen of things to come. Three short years later, Nebraska's star would be on the ascendancy under Devaney's guiding genius, rivaling and very often surpassing Oklahoma's in the sixties.

Wilkinson's loss to Nebraska in 1959 was doubly painful, owing to bad blood that had developed between him and Cornhusker coach Bill Jennings. There was a recruiting spat over one player in particular who eventually wound up at Nebraska, but the deeper cut was a claim by Wilkinson that Jennings turned him in to the NCAA for an illegal recruiting or slush fund that he kept at Oklahoma. Wilkinson was penalized for this transgression and long harbored a vindictive feeling toward Jennings for allegedly blowing the whistle on him. Jennings, of course, claimed innocence to the very end of his Nebraska tenure, at times becoming totally paranoid about it.

If Jennings was disliked by Wilkinson, he wasn't too popular with Nebraska fans, either. He had five straight losing seasons at Lincoln from 1957 through 1961 and

when he was finally dumped in favor of Devaney, the feeling was that things could only improve for the Cornhuskers. But they didn't realize how much Devaney would
improve them. Jennings's last team had a 3-6-1 record and
a king-size inferiority complex. Devaney's first team had a
9-2 mark and a Bowl bid. Devaney's powers, in fact,
earned five straight Bowl invitations at the start of his administration and nine overall in his last eleven years. All of
his seasons at Nebraska were winning ones, and some of
them were stunning ones. When he finally moved up to the
athletic director's chair after 1972, Devaney had recorded
an extravagant 101-20-2 record and heard more than his
share of hurrahs.

The loudest of these hurrahs came in 1970 and 1971,
when he won consecutive national championships with undefeated teams. In 1971, the Cornhuskers' thirteen victories included their famous "Game of the Decade" battle
with Oklahoma that became one of the most treasured in
the school's history. Nebraska was ranked Number One
nationally and Chuck Fairbanks' Oklahoma team Number
Two—a match-up truly made in TV heaven. The meeting
had been arranged for national television on Thanksgiving
afternoon at Norman and because of the Thursday date,
neither team had played the previous Saturday. This layoff
left their followers with more time to writhe in suspense
and left sportswriters more space to fill with hyperbole.
The most cautious writer called the game "a classic" and
the boldest described it as "the game of the century." Few
games live up to such superlative billing, but this one did.
By the time the struggle had ended with Nebraska in front
35-31, only more superlatives could describe it and both
sides had good reason to be emotionally and physically
spent.

Oklahoma gained 467 yards in total offense and Nebraska 362. Both teams scored in every quarter. Oklahoma led
twice, each time by three precarious points. Although there
were sixty-six points scored in the contest, it featured some
heroic defense. The hallmark of the day, however, was the

big play, and there were plenty of these in the fourth quarter, Nebraska, ultimately, had the last one and, as a result, had the game. With 7:10 to play, Jack Mildren moved the Sooners into a 31-28 lead with a sixteen-yard touchdown pass to Jon Harrison, at 150 pounds, the smallest figure on the field. Sensing Oklahoma's fourth national championship, the jubilant Sooner fans in the packed, freezing stadium allowed themselves to forget for the moment that Nebraska still had time to score.

The frenzied Oklahoma fans could sing "Boomer Sooner" and scream "Defense, defense" all they wanted but Jerry Tagge knew it had come down to his game to win. "Nobody said a word in the huddle but me," said the Nebraska quarterback. "We all just knew what had to be done."

It took the Cornhuskers twelve plays to cross the Oklahoma goal line, and on two of them Tagge came up with his most crucial work of the day. First, with third down and a yard to go, he spotted the Oklahoma defense stacked against a plunge, and he switched his call to send halfback Jeff Kinney wide for seventeen yards. Then, on third down and eight near midfield, he scrambled away from a tackler and passed to slotback Johnny Rodgers, who made a diving catch for a first down at the Sooner thirty-five-yard line. Four plays and two minutes later, it was second down at the Oklahoma six and Tagge, who had been constantly glancing at the clock, called timeout to talk it over with Devaney. As the quarterback remembers it, their conversation went something like this:

> Tagge: I know we can score, coach, but I've been worried about eating up time.
> Devaney: We're going for the touchdown. There won't be any ties.
> Tagge: We'll get it.
> Devaney: What's your best play?
> Tagge: I think it's the off-tackle with Jeff [Kinney].
> Devaney: O.K. Let's run it without any mistakes.

Tagge and Company did exactly that. Kinney ripped into the left side behind tackle Daryl White, knocked down someone else, and made four yards. On the next play, Kinney, who had already rushed for 169 yards, sliced into the end zone through a tiny hole for the game-winning touchdown.

Devaney, understandably enough, called it the greatest victory of his career, and more objective observers suggested that it might have been the greatest victory of anybody's career. In the saddened Oklahoma locker room, there was more praise for Nebraska than bitterness for the game. "If Nebraska doesn't give Tagge its most valuable player award," exclaimed Oklahoma defensive coach Larry Lacewell, "then the vote's fixed." Other Oklahomans expressed the opinion that Devaney should be made Coach of the Year, an indication of their appreciation of the moment. Even the losers in this game understood that they had been a part of something special. It was a victory for college football as much as for Nebraska.

The atmosphere had been enhanced by the presence of the governors of both states and assorted civic leaders, but it was the emotionalism of the ordinary fan that gave the day its special flavor. Nebraskans told frequent tales of the Oklahomans' legendary lust for points. During the record-breaking fifties, for example, Sooner fans left the stadium dissatisfied if their team won by less than three touchdowns. But in 1971, the Sooners had scored enough to satisfy the greediest of their flock with a marvelous triple-option attack that was the focal point of all the pregame analysis and hysteria. Jack Mildren, one of the country's best college quarterbacks, had directed that devastating offense with precision and poise all season and that was precisely the challenge facing Bob Devaney and his vaunted Nebraska defense. The game didn't turn out to be all that simple, of course, and it was the unexpected complexity of the affair that made it such an intriguing spectacle.

Nebraska didn't stop the Wishbone, and Oklahoma

didn't hold back the Huskers' pro-style attack. But as the game unfolded, each defense did take away certain weapons of the rivals' offense and the quarterbacks had to react with boldness and brilliance. "When you recruit a boy to play quarterback for us," said Oklahoma coach Chuck Fairbanks, "you don't take a guy who's milking a cow and worrying about tipping over the pail." Both Mildren and Tagge illustrated that metaphor in a duel of fast thinking under pressurized conditions.

When it became obvious, for instance, that Nebraska's defense was geared to stop mercurial Greg Pruitt, Mildren abandoned the pitchout to his star runner and picked apart the Cornhuskers with his own running and passing. And when Tagge realized that the Oklahoma defense was mobilized to discourage his passing, he made a radical second-half adjustment to Nebraska's offensive style. "Our trouble was that we weren't going out and sticking it to them," said Kinney. "I was hoping at halftime that we would decide to run it down their throats."

They did—and made Oklahoma choke on it.

9
LAFAYETTE—LEHIGH
The Most-Played Series

No other college teams have met more times on the football field than Lehigh and Lafayette. The rivalry has been intense, sometimes bitter, but always one of good, hard football.
— The New York Times, *November 22, 1959*

A sportswriter once said of college football that "it is a game of ancient rivalries that inspires genuine loathing, not for a weekend but for a lifetime. It is traditional games, whose meaning is deep ... there is a spirit about it, a drawing together." He might have been thinking of the Lehigh–Lafayette football series when he made that pertinent statement.

College football's most-played rivalry has had all of those elements, and some the writer never thought of. After all, it has had a lot of time and space to produce a lot of "loathing" and tradition.

The Lehigh–Lafayette series is the only collegiate football rivalry to have reached the century mark in games played. That 100th anniversary took place on November 21, 1964, and if there were a heavenly football council sitting somewhere, it, no doubt, would have decreed a tie for that historic game. And indeed it was, 6-6.

The seeds of football's most enduring series were planted on October 25, 1884, and though his team lost 50-0, a Lehigh man wrote of that first game: "We did not win ... but we gave Lafayette the worst licking she ever had in her existence and many, many a sore head went back to Easton that night."

The Leopards of Lehigh and Engineers of Lafayette have been giving each other sore heads, among other things, ever since—with the exception of 1896, when there was a squabble over a player's eligibility. The disputed player, George Barclay, had invented the first football helmet for the game that year with Penn—but it was his professional status, not his unique new headgear that caused the lone rift in the Lafayette–Lehigh series. The rivalry has been uninterrupted since, enhanced by the proximity of the schools in eastern Pennsylvania and the fervor of the flock.

Spirits run especially high in this remarkable series and the two campuses, located just fifteen miles apart in Pennsylvania's Lehigh Valley, seventy miles west of New York, are always the scene of wild, pregame antics. Years ago, conscripted freshmen would patrol each campus to keep a lookout for mischief-makers and saboteurs, such as the ones who once chemically treated Lafayette's carefully manicured field to produce the word "Lehigh" in a huge burnt patch. In the thirties, Lehigh partisans pried loose the sword from the beloved statue of the Marquis of Lafayette, leaving the proud campus symbol embarrassingly empty-handed. Now wiser, Lafayette's staff constructs a sturdy, all-encompassing crate around the famous landmark before the Lehigh game each year.

The pranks became more sophisticated as the decades wore on. Enterprising Lafayette students once printed and distributed fake copies of Lehigh's campus newspaper. The bogus edition contained a spirit-dampening story describing a State Liquor Board effort to enforce the twenty-one-year-old minimum drinking age. This fictional campaign was obviously aimed at Lehigh's hard-drinking fraternities.

Engineering students at both colleges have utilized their classroom experience in devising complex fraternity and dormitory displays that express their respective loyalties, and these "Go Team" floats or banners compete for prizes on the weekend of the game. One of the most ingenious inventions came to light in the fifties, when the all-consuming prank was to preignite the opposing school's bonfire. A Lehigh student designed a remote-controlled model airplane with an exploding device that would burst into flames upon contact. An engineering marvel, the electronically homed missile lurched off the ground and found its target—but its warhead fizzled and failed to ignite.

Going back to basics, Lafayette students reciprocated by assembling outside the Lehigh campus, locating the rival woodpile and shooting off flaming arrows. Lehigh's defenders were well prepared for such a contingency and put out the flames with blankets and buckets of sand.

Even in the seventies, some of the more positive pregame traditions have proved as resilient as the rivalry itself, with both campuses enflamed by monstrous pep rallies, marching bands, cheerleaders, banners and floats in a colorful montage not unlike a surrealistic movie.

When Lehigh's first football team traveled to Easton to play Lafayette in 1884, spirits were no less fierce. Richard Harding Davis, a husky halfback on that original Lehigh team, suffered the notable disadvantage of being a visiting player. "My chief recollections of that first game consist of my personal encounters with the spectators and Easton policemen, who had an instinctive prejudice to Lehigh men which they expressed by kicking them on the head whenever one of them went under the ropes for the ball," Davis once wrote.

Davis and his teammates got out of town bloodied and bowed. On top of the physical pain, there was that further humiliation of the 50-0 score.

Though humbled in their first game, the Engineers nevertheless made their contribution to football history in this one. No less a football authority than Walter Camp credited Lehigh with the development of the "V-trick," an innovation by J. S. Ginson, Lehigh Class of '86. The "V-trick" was the forerunner of the famous flying wedge of early American football.

There was no grass on the Lafayette athletic grounds then, nothing but rocks, tin cans and a soft quicksand of mud," according to Davis. "It was so muddy that the players' feet actually became fast in it, and 'Bish' Howe . . . the other halfback, called pathetically every few minutes,

'Don't pass that ball to me, Jake; I'm stuck in the mud and I can't get out.' "

When Lehigh first took the field in 1884 and challenged all comers, only three undergraduates had played the game before, Davis said, "and in the first match with Lafayette the other men had learned what little they knew of it in three weeks practice with the class elevens."

Lafayette, however, was better prepared. Theodore L. Welles, a successful mining engineer after graduation, had introduced football at the Easton school four years before. Welles had played with the Wilkes-Barre Academy and the Princeton freshmen and was very enthusiastic before showing up at Lafayette in 1880. About that first season, Welles once wrote: "There were no regular games played, but it was the custom of the class of '84 to play teams selected from the rest of the college during the fall seasons of '80 and '81 . . ."

The first college game that Lafayette played was with Rutgers and the historic team from New Brunswick, New Jersey, dealt the Leopards a loss. But Lafayette later made up for it in a game on November 10, 1883, which Welles called "one of the most laughable ones I have ever experienced. There was three to four inches of slushy snow on the field, and we were averse to playing the game, although the Rutgers team arrived on time. They insisted, however, that the game should be played, and so upon my orders the Lafayette team appeared on the field in all the old suits they could muster, carefully refraining from wearing the jersey suits which we had secured for that season. The ball became speedily waterlogged and it was impossible to kick it, but we succeeded in making four touchdowns to Rutgers' none. After the game the reason for their determination to play came out in the statement that, as they had been beaten every game that year, they thought they could come up and beat Lafayette anyway."

The following year, Lehigh's tyros were no match for this swaggering, seasoned Lafayette team. The Leopards left no doubt as to their superiority over the Engineers in

the first year of their meeting, beating them twice by overwhelming scores. After their rousing victory in the series
icebreaker, the Leopards won a conclusive 34-4 decision at
Bethlehem in a game that marked Lehigh's first touchdown
in history, that by the irrepressible Davis (described by one
writer as "hard as nails, a cracker-jack dodger, fast on his
feet.") Fan interest in the game was apparent even in the
first year of the series. "Everyone at Lafayette was pleased
that more than fifty students accompanied the team to the
game," said one observer. This Lafayette flock was
"treated courteously," according to the observer, but it
was one of the few times that a friendly spirit was engendered by these early Lafayette–Lehigh games. The next
year, squabbling broke out over the honesty and integrity
of the officials after the first of the annual two-game series
ended in a 6-0 victory for Lafayette. Lafayette students
called Lehigh students "sore losers" and it is assumed that
caustic remarks were returned in kind. The second game of
1886 kept Lafayette's unbeaten string going over Lehigh
and provided more fuel for antagonism. A touchdown by a
Lafayette player named Williams was the only scoring in a
game called in the second half because of rain. According
to Lafayette's school newspaper, "Lehigh . . . asked that
time be called. The referee gave the game to Lafayette.
Now after thinking about the matter for a day he wants to
change his decision and declare the game a tie. He wants to
write to Mr. [Walter] Camp about the matter." The referee, according to the *Lafayette,* was a "Mr. Knoor," a
Lehigh patriot, class of '88. Commenting on the uneasy
relationship between the schools, a reporter stated: "It is
indeed a most lamentable state of affairs when two colleges
like Lehigh and Lafayette, situated so near each other, and
whose relations ought to be of the intimate kind, can not
play a friendly game of football without causing so much ill
feeling on both sides."

It was not until 1887 that a well-seasoned Lehigh team
won its first game in the series, 10-4. In keeping with the
ingrained early bitterness of the rivalry, the Lafayette side

found cause for complaint this time. Once more, the officiating was the target even though the referees were both from Princeton and supposedly neutral. "Our team never minds a defeat when it is done in a fair game, but where we have to play a team with a blindly partial referee and an umpire who is simply a burlesque, it is discouraging," the Lafayette student newspaper editorialized.

The Lafayette students would be no happier in the ensuing years, when the series turned sharply in Lehigh's favor. The Engineers won thirteen and tied one of the subsequent sixteen games through 1894, including a victory in 1889 that ranks with the great contests in the series. In that one, Lehigh overcame a two-touchdown deficit to win 16-10 as Paul Dushiell, who became one of the country's leading football officials, scored the winning points late in the game. When the final gun went off, Lafayette was on Lehigh's fifteen-yard line. That dramatic game appeared to have inspired unusual fan interest, for in the return match at Easton that year, the largest crowd ever to see a football game at Lafayette turned up. "The windows of the halls were crowded with fair faces and the roadway was lined with carriages," reported the *Lafayette*. "The field was enclosed by ropes and a number of officers were present."

This was a distinguished Lehigh team, winning by such scores as 106-0 over Penn State and 60-0 over Haverford during an 8-3-2 season in 1889. The previous year, the Engineers had won ten games and lost but two. Led by the likes of George Hutchinson, Goodwin Ordway, Clarence Belfield and Thomas Roderick, they continued to display strong teams in the early 1890's, counting Lafayette among the most treasured of their victims. No less than three games were played between the teams in 1891, a unique college football tripleheader, rare even in those times when schools occasionally scheduled each other more than once during a season. Lehigh proved conclusively to be the better team that year, winning all three games, including the only contest in the series played outside of Bethlehem or Easton. The last game of 1891 was held in Wilkes-Barre and attracted 3,000 spectators, and according to a report of the day, it was "by far the largest crowd that ever witnessed a football game in Wilkes-Barre." It might have been the loudest crowd as well, the report indicated: "The cheering of the students seemed to startle the natives."

George Barclay soon became a significant figure in the Lehigh–Lafayette rivalry, not to mention the impact he made on college football in general. George Oliver Barclay, of Milton, Pennsylvania, who had learned his football at Bucknell Academy, was both tiny and quick. At five-foot-nine and 160 pounds, he was usually the smallest man on any field but undoubtedly had to be the smartest because he often questioned the sanity of stoicism that allowed no protection for football players during the 1890s. Admittedly "pretty" in looks, as his nickname "Rose" implied, and with a self-professed love for girls, Barclay openly detested the cauliflower ears sported by burly linemen of the day. Approaching a local harnessmaker, Barclay had a headgear constructed of padded straps to shield his ears like a boxer. He thus became the originator of the football helmet.

Barclay made starting halfback at Lafayette in his first year and ran for seventeen touchdowns. His headharness attracted as much attention as his running and the idea spread rapidly to other schools. In his junior year, 1896, Lafayette tied Princeton for the national championship and became the first small college to break into the top ranks of football power (then dominated by the "Big Four"— Princeton, Penn, Yale and Harvard). Barclay was given the lion's share of the credit for this startling ascendancy. However, it was also during this year that Barclay became embroiled in a controversy that eventually caused him to quit school.

Lehigh had seen enough of Barclay in the prior two years. In an 1894 game, he scored twenty-four points to lead Lafayette's 28-0 victory. And in 1895, he scored three touchdowns, one a record-breaking eighty-yard run from scrimmage, to key two more Lafayette triumphs. He would do no more damage against the Engineers, however, for Lehigh announced refusal to play against Barclay in the two games scheduled for 1896, owing to his professional attachments. Barclay was found to have received no more than expense money for playing baseball for Chambersburg, but Lehigh felt it was sufficient grounds to cancel that year's games, against Lafayette's loud protests. Caspar Whitney, a football authority of the day, felt that Lehigh was entirely justified and 1896 became a landmark year in the Lehigh–Lafayette series, eventually becoming known in campus lore as "The Year They Didn't Play."

Barclay dropped out of school in 1897 and began to play professional football. Within a few years a commercial model of his leather head-harness was on the market and his concept was readily accepted everywhere. Various rubber and hard leather protectors were in style until the late thirties when the internal suspension plastic helmet, now universally recognized, gained popularity.

The premature departure of the great Barclay did not hurt the Lafayette program, which continued to rise in football society with powerful Leopard teams led by such dynamic runners as George Walbridge, Gus Wiedenmayer, Harry Trout, Russell Knight, James Platt and John Ernst. The 1897 team helped swing the balance of power back to Lafayette in the Lehigh series. The Leopards won sixteen games of the ensuing twenty meetings through 1911 and at one point (1899 through 1901) scored six straight shutouts over the Engineers.

During this time, some "firsts" were established in this venerable series. In 1906, Lafayette's Edward Flad threw the first forward pass in a Lehigh–Lafayette game as the Leopards trimmed the Engineers 33-0. In 1909, the first scoring pass was witnessed in a 21-0 Lafayette triumph. The trick play came late in the game and was accomplished by having William Dannehower, the quarterback, pass to Aaron Crane, the left tackle, who was lined up eighteen yards behind the line. Crane threw a forward pass to Frank Irmschler, the left halfback, who scored. The play covered forty-seven yards from scrimmage and was used only one time all season. Also during this period, the first of two Lehigh–Lafayette games was postponed, owing to the death of Dr. Henry S. Drown, the Lehigh president. One of the few Lehigh victories during this period, a 22-0 decision in the first game of 1898, was distinguished by the first— and only—100-yard punt return in the series, an extraordinary runback by the Engineers' James Ross (fields at this time were 110 yards long).

It wasn't until an Ivy Leaguer, Tom Keady of Dartmouth, emerged to coach at Lehigh and give some stability to the Engineers' program that they were able to compete on equal footing with Lafayette. In fact, they were a step ahead of the Leopards for most of Keady's 1912-1920 term during which he posted a 55-22-3 record overall. From 1912 through 1918, Keady's teams took six out of seven games from Lafayette and it was in 1917 when Lehigh ran up the largest point production in the series, 78-0. The 1918 game, won 17-0 by Lehigh, produced a legendary run by "Snooks" Dowd. As recorded by various observers, the Lehigh halfback completed a 115-yard touchdown run, but the embellishment of time has added as many as 45 yards to that fabled figure. According to the original story, Dowd ran the wrong way, circled his own goalposts, and went the right way 100 yards for a score.

While other schools were cutting down programs and canceling games wholesale because of World War I, Lehigh and Lafayette plowed straight ahead, unperturbed by explosive global events, into the Roaring Twenties. The Leopards roared louder at this time, however, with the help of the soon-to-be famous Jock Sutherland. Sutherland, whose teams at the University of Pittsburgh would eventually rocket to the top of the college football world, applied his magic touch at Lafayette after the war and in the early twenties. His appearance at Easton symbolically gave the ball back to Lafayette in the topsy-turvy series with Lehigh, which has produced as many distinct and long-lived power changes as any in America.

Sutherland, a virtual novice in a nation of coaching giants when he arrived at Lafayette in 1919, made a big splash his first year. He had begun his college coaching with good material, although the players were inexperienced and completely unfamiliar with his system, and he made a remarkable showing against strong teams of great repute. A couple of years later, he was not only rubbing elbows with the best but beating them as well. His undefeated 1921 squad, scored on but slightly, was widely recognized as the top team in the country. After developing his fifth straight excellent team at Lehigh in 1923, Sutherland was heralded as the greatest young coach in America.

From the viewpoint of Lafayette and its alumni, Sutherland's greatest achievement in his years there was the string of five successive victories over Lehigh, a feat which never had been accomplished in all their years of competition. "While they were proud of their team and its coach for bringing Lafayette through hard schedule after hard schedule with flying colors, still the persistent victories over the time-honored opponent was the most gratifying accomplishment of all," said Harry G. Scott in his book, *Jock Sutherland, Architect of Men.* "Revenge in this instance was particularly sweet, for the Lafayette Leopards had been defeated by Lehigh in six of the seven years preceding the advent of Sutherland as coach."

Sutherland's career-long hallmark, the overbearing defensive team, was never more in evidence than during his games against Lehigh in this period. In the five meetings, the Engineers were shut out twice and scored no more than seven points in any game. Even when Lehigh had similar defensive heavyweights, such as in 1922, Lafayette usually found a way to win. That year, Leonard "Bots" Brunner, the only man to star for both Lafayette and Lehigh, kicked a twenty-five-yard field goal with forty-five seconds left to bring the Leopards a 3-0 victory in the lowest scoring game, and one of the most dramatic, of the series.

Sutherland's successor, Herb McCracken, continued to

give Lafayette the whip hand over Lehigh, even in seasons when the Engineers theoretically had stronger teams. In 1924, Lafayette had entered the Lehigh game with a 6-2 record, but the losses included an inexplicable 42-7 defeat at the hands of Rutgers. The Leopards had been an inconsistent team, while Lehigh, meanwhile, was undefeated and heavily favored. Nevertheless, the game, played "on a most unpleasant day for football" according to the *Easton Express,* ended in Lafayette's favor, 7-0. Reporting in the gaudy language of the day, the *Express* said in overstatement:

"Kicked about from top to bottom in the cauldron of football in the most varied season a Lafayette eleven has ever experienced, the Leopards made their last stand Saturday, made it under circumstances that were anything but safe for standing but they made it in a manner that convinced the most skeptical that a really great eleven, previously drubbed in the mire of defeat, was still able to rise and strike a worthy opponent a strong blow."

Lafayette added five more victories on to Sutherland's original five-game string and it wasn't until 1929 that Lehigh finally beat a Lafayette team. Then, it wasn't until five years later that the Engineers could do it again. No wonder, then, that the lead of the game story in the *Express* after Lehigh's 13-7 victory in 1934 read: "Everybody took their hats off to Lehigh." And no wonder, also, that the Lehigh contingent at Easton walked off not only with the game but the goal posts and the Lafayette College flag as well. The Lafayette people had wisely removed the sideline markers before the game was over. Noted the *Express:* "Ten minutes before the game ended, the latter were carried to a point where Lehigh celebrators could not lay hands on them."

Lehigh's victory that day was one of the few the Engineers could relish over a Herb McCracken team. In the twelve years he was coach at Lafayette, he defeated Lehigh nine times during one of the most successful coaching administrations at the Easton school. McCracken had a solid football foundation when he first came to Lafayette as a young coach in 1924, having played for one of the best-known coaching names at the time, Pop Warner. McCracken inherited a veteran team from Sutherland, including one of Lafayette's legendary players in Charley Berry, and won fifty-nine games during his stay at Easton against some of the nation's stiffest competition.

Meanwhile, Lehigh's fortunes steadily declined after Tom Keady's departure in 1921. The Engineers were led by a succession of coaches, none of whom met much success or stayed too long until William B. Leckonby, a one time professional football star, brought an athletic Renaissance to Lehigh in 1946. Before Leckonby's highly successful sixteen-year tenure, the most familiar coaching name at Lehigh was Glen Harmeson, a product of Purdue who stayed from 1934 to 1941 and produced some modestly strong teams. It was Harmeson's misfortune, however, to be coaching in roughly the same period that Edward "Hook" Mylin rose to power at Lafayette. Mylin produced some of Lafayette's strongest teams in history, including perfect records in 1937 and 1940, a year the Leopards counted mighty Army among their cherished victims. Walt Zirinisky, an indefatigable back for Lafayette during the late thirties and early forties, helped the Leopards rout Lehigh on three straight occasions and nourish a long undefeated string in the series. From 1937 through 1949, Lehigh could not beat Lafayette, losing fourteen games and tying one in that span. In fact, the 7-7 tie in 1942 was highly suspect, since the game ended in a storm of confusion with Lafayette on the brink of scoring the winning touchdown. Lafayette drove to the Lehigh one-yard line with less than a minute to play when the Leopards' John Maddock was hurt. According to a report in the *Lafayette*, "Ralph Hackett went in to replace the injured Maddock and Maddock came out. However, the referee ruled that as soon as the substitution was completed, the clock was to start again. With only two seconds remaining there was naturally not enough time left for Lafayette to get in another play."

During the 1943 and 1944 war years, Lehigh and Lafayette played twice each season for the first time since 1901. Predictably, Lafayette won all four games, including an overwhelming 64-0 decision in 1944 that featured a series record five-touchdown performance by Fred Robbins.

Lehigh served as a whipping boy for Lafayette right through the end of the forties, as Ivan Williamson and "Chipper" Smith followed Mylin as Leopard coaches, but anyone with a discernible eye could see that the whippings were getting lighter. Lehigh became more competitive with Lafayette during this period and the reason was the emergence of William Leckonby as coach in 1946. Leckonby's appointment, at the age of twenty-eight, made him the youngest football coach in Lehigh's history. He was also the most successful, posting an 85-53-5 record in sixteen years at the school in Bethlehem. Included among Leckonby's achievements was Lehigh's first unbeaten, untied season, in 1950, and possession in 1957 and 1961 of the Lambert Cup, symbolic of the outstanding medium-sized college team in the East. Prior to assuming the coaching job at Lehigh, Leckonby's individual accomplishments were admirable. He was one of the finest triple-threat halfbacks in the history of St. Lawrence University and played for three years with the Brooklyn Dodgers of the National Football League, a tailback in Jock Sutherland's famous single-wing attack.

Leckonby gave Lehigh its first victory over Lafayette in fourteen years with a 38-0 rout in 1950 that started a string of three Engineer triumphs. Leckonby's victories in 1952, and 1961, his farewell game, were considered among the best in this rich series. In 1952, Lehigh beat Lafayette 14-7 in the closing minutes when John Conti, a sophomore reserve quarterback who weighed about 165 pounds, threw a twenty-three-yard touchdown pass to Tom Gunn. In this game, Lafayette was stopped three times inside Lehigh's five-yard line, and Lehigh was stopped once after getting a first down at the Lafayette two. In the 1961 game, considered one of the great Lehigh–Lafayette thrillers of all time, the Engineers defeated the Leopards 17-14 on a twenty-yard field goal by Andy Larko with six seconds to play. Lehigh got the ball at the Lafayette forty-seven with thirty seconds left. John DeNoia then passed forty-four yards to Pat Clark to move the ball to the three-yard line. Lehigh failed to score in two running plays, but Larko came in to kick the first field goal of his career to win the game.

Though both teams were having poor seasons in 1964 (their combined record was 1-14-1 going into the game), the historic 100th contest was a magnet for one of the largest crowds in the history of the series. Lafayette's Fisher Field overflowed with 19,000 people, although its standard seating capacity was only 13,500. From an artistic standpoint, the game had little to offer, ending in a hardly memorable 6-6 tie. The only excitement came at the end when the stubborn Engineers dug in and held Lafayette for four downs with the ball inches away from their goal line.

Despite the unsatisfactory conclusion for both sides, the day was accorded its rightful place in college football history. Immediately after the opening kickoff, the ball used to start the game was given to the National Football Foundation and Hall of Fame in a special ceremony. The Lehigh band played "Happy Birthday" and legendary alumni from both sides were in view. Among those in attendance was Howard Foering of Bethlehem, a Lehigh graduate of 1890 who was watching his ninety-first Lehigh–Lafayette game, a remarkable achievement in any world record book. This, of course, did not go unnoticed in the press box. Upon hearing of Foering's dazzling attendance record, a sportswriter remarked with a straight face:

"I wonder where he was the other nine games."

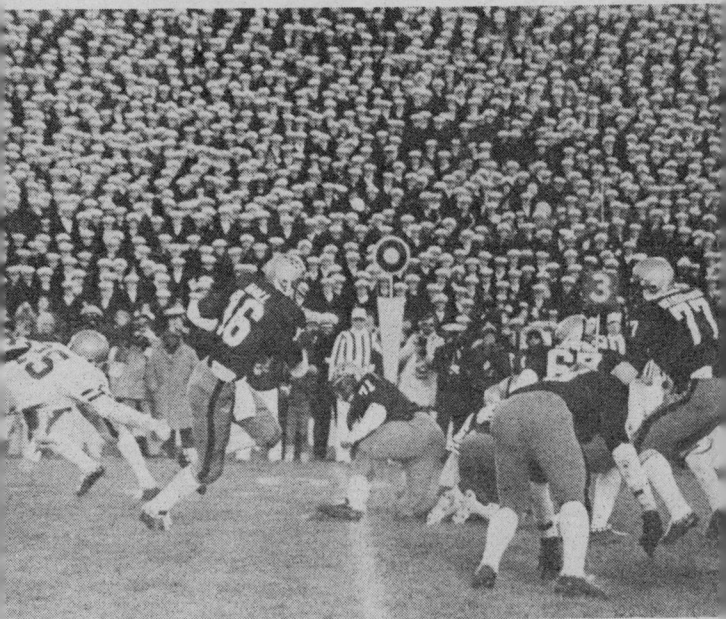

Army-Navy action—the competitive urgency of an armed skirmish and the flaming color of a Roman circus. *Military Academy photo*

Navy's Heisman Trophy winner Joe Bellino skirts around end against Army in 1959. He scored three touchdowns as Navy enjoyed a 43-12 victory. *Navy photo*

Army's Rollie Stichweh asks for silence from 102,000 cheering fans in final moments of historic 1963 game. He failed to get off the play from the two and Navy had a controversial 21-15 win. *Naval Academy photo*

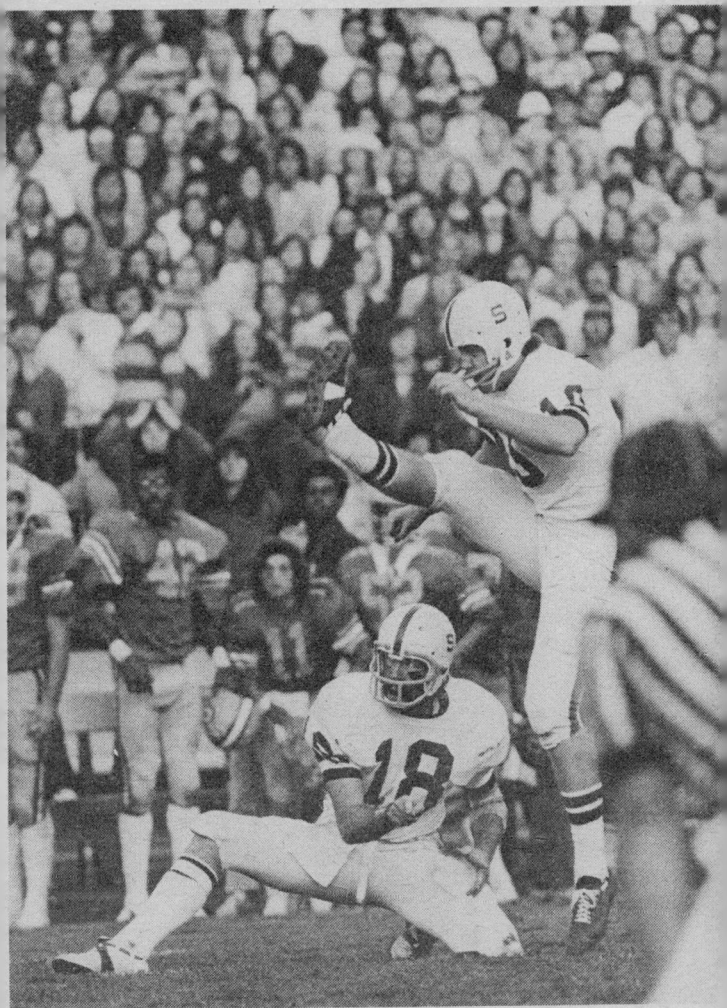

One of the biggest plays in the Stanford-California series—Mike Langford's field goal in 1974 that gave Stanford a pulsating 22-20 victory. *Stanford University photo*

UCLA quarterback Gary Beban has a convoy of blockers during Bruins' 20-16 win over USC in 1965 en route to the Rose Bowl. *UCLA photo*

Southern Cal's O.J. Simpson rushing against UCLA in 1967. The Trojans beat the Bruins 21-20 in a showdown that decided the national championship. *USC photo*

Southern Cal's Pat Haden passes against Notre Dame in 1973. The Irish snapped USC's 23-game unbeaten streak, 23-14. *USC photo*

Rod Sherman pulls in a Craig Fertig pass for a TD with 1:33 left as USC upsets Notre Dame in 1964, 20-17. The play cost the Irish a national championship. *USC photo*

LSU's Billy Cannon is off against Ole Miss in 1959, headed for an 89-yard touchdown jaunt and a 7-3 Tiger triumph. *LSU photo*

Tennessee's Johnny Butler picks up steam on historic 56-yard TD run against Alabama in 1939. The Vols won 21-0. *Univ. of Tenn. photo*

Gene McEver of Tennessee. His 98-yard touchdown run in 1928 really set the series with Alabama in motion. *Univ. of Tenn. photo*

Tennessee coach Robert Neyland—a tough nut for Alabama to crack. *Univ. of Tenn. photo*

The game that started it all between Lafayette and Lehigh. The year was 1884, the dress of the day was knee socks and caps, the score was 50-0, Lafayette. *Lafayette College photo*

Pitt battles Penn State for "the championship of Route 22" in the mud at Forbes Field. This one ended 0-0, in 1921. *Penn State photo*

Oklahoma's Duanne Baccus (88) and David Smith (44) halt a Nebraska runner for no gain in the 1973 game that decided the Big Eight championship. Oklahoma won, 27-0. *Univ. of Okla. photo*

Earl Campbell scores in Texas' 13-6 victory over Oklahoma in 1977 behind Steve Hall's block. *Univ. of Texas photo*

North Carolina's Ken Willard reaches for goal line against Duke in one of their great battles. *Univ. of North Carolina photo*

Happiness is beating Ohio State! And the Michigan sideline explodes with joy after a big 21-12 victory in 1969. *Univ. of Michigan photo*

One of college football's most cherished trophies, the Old Oaken Bucket. Indiana and Purdue play for it, and spare no passion doing so. *Univ. of Indiana photo*

Missouri's Don Faurot winds up his coaching career on a high note after his Tigers beat Kansas 15-13, in 1956. *Univ. of Missouri photo*

A full house for Kansas and Missouri in the feverish 1930's. Note "Beat MU" scrawled on the gridiron. *Univ. of Kansas photo*

10
INDIANA—PURDUE
Battle for a Bucket

It is just a bucket, a physically clumsy object about the size of a nail keg, its curve misshapen, its oaken staves dark with use. Bound round with iron, it is appropriately leaky. In itself, the thing isn't worth fifty cents. But no sum of money could buy it these days.

The Old Oaken Bucket, one of the nation's most famous football victory symbols, is hotter than the Hope Diamond and just as desirable as far as Purdue and Indiana are concerned.

The 100-year-old bucket has been the treasured prize of every Purdue–Indiana football game since 1925, symbolic crown jewels to either school. To the victor goes the privilege of affixing his "I" or "P" to the clanking chain of initials that dangles from the bucket and the honor of possessing the prize for a year until the next game. In the event of a tie, each school gets to keep it six months.

Normally the letters are brass, but in the case of an extraordinary season such as a Big Ten championship, they sparkle with gold plate—and in one instance, a diamond from the undefeated 1943 Purdue team, which won a piece of the league championship.

How this weathered, decayed, moss- and mold-covered bucket got to be the ultimate goal of football players, fans and coaches in the state of Indiana is the result of some imaginative thought. Both schools had been meeting on the football field since 1891 when the Indiana and Purdue Alumni Clubs of Chicago held a joint meeting in 1925 to "discuss the possibility of undertaking worthy joint enterprises in the behalf of the two schools." The thought occurred to the assemblage that an enduring trophy was needed to symbolize the ancient, honorable rivalry. One alumnus from each school was assigned the job of finding one genuine, old, oaken bucket from an authentic, damp Indiana well "as the most typically Hoosier form of trophy."

Fritz Ernst of Purdue and Indiana's Wiley J. Huddle, the two given the task of finding such a bucket, finally uncovered the object on the Old Bruner Farm near Hanover, in southern Indiana. The region had been settled by the Bruner family in the 1840s, making the bucket well over a century old. It was no ordinary bucket, though, for it had been touched by some magical American history. It is known that at least one prominent person drank out of the bucket—Civil War General Morgan, head of the famous Morgan Raiders. The Confederate officer and his men once camped near the Bruner farm, visiting the well frequently to drink cold, clear water from the now noted receptacle.

More romanticism was added to the glorified utensil from Bruner's well upon its acceptance as a trophy for the Indiana–Purdue series. Boys being boys and trophies being trophies, the Old Oaken Bucket has constantly been threatened by student pranksters over the years and more than once has mysteriously disappeared around game time. One of the cleverest plans of kidnapping the trophy was devised in 1930 when Indiana pulled off a 7-6 upset. Charley Hoover, Indiana class of 1932, had been delegated to accept the trophy but, upon being confronted by an angry mob of Purdue students, decided to leave it in the care of the Purdue Union, to be sent later.

The bucket started to Indiana University by railway express, to be picked up in Indianapolis. On the night of its arrival, however, a rainstorm prevented Hoover from getting to Indianapolis. In desperation, Hoover called a friend, John Bookwater of Indianapolis, and asked him to pick up the trophy. Bookwater promised he would and said he would send it on to Bloomington by bus. But when the bus arrived, there was no bucket in it. After a frantic call to

Indianapolis, Hoover was assured by Bookwater that the trophy was resting safely with some Indiana University students.

"I gave the bucket to a bunch of IU students last night," he said cheerfully.

Hoover almost suffered a heart attack. A group of undercover agents from Purdue, passing themselves off as Indiana students, had cleverly relieved Bookwater of the trophy.

The disappearance of the bucket sparked a turmoil on the Indiana campus. "Charges and counter-charges rocked every whistle stop between Bloomington and Lafayette," the Indiana student newspaper reported. Detectives were hired and students paused daily to mourn the missing trophy. Then, just as strangely as it had disappeared, it reappeared in the middle of Lafayette, resting unmolested on a loading platform. It was then safely relayed to Bloomington.

Not long after that incident, special care was taken to guard the bucket. At Purdue, it was kept locked in a glass trophy case and at Indiana, the president himself kept it in his vault. When it was put on open display anywhere, usually armed guards and plainclothed student detectives hovered about. The bucket became a hot potato that aroused uncommon apprehension. Once when it was sent from the Indiana campus to a football dinner in Indianapolis, athletic director Zora G. Clevenger turned it over to trustee J. Dwight Peterson with these solemn words: "Unto you I entrust this sacred symbol."

"Not me," Peterson hastily replied, and had the bucket taken from his office to the Indianapolis Athletic Club—four blocks away—in an armored car, under guard.

Tom Miller, the Indiana sports information director, was similarly uneasy when he first met the bucket. This happened in 1947 when Miller came back to his alma mater as assistant to Sports Information Director Bob Cook.

"In 1947, we had beaten Purdue 16-14 on a field goal by Rex Grossman," Miller recalls. "Well, when we got to

Indianapolis for our annual banquet following the game, Bob Cook had entrusted the bucket to me, and here I was a first year assistant carrying this case containing the bucket.

"As I lifted the bucket out of the case, it fell apart in my hands. Fortunately, a couple of us were able to put the staves back within the four rings, but the next year we lost it to Purdue. I always told everyone afterwards that Purdue took it back to have their engineers put it back together. They misunderstood and kept it for ten years."

One of the pranks closest to Indiana hearts regarding the trophy occurred in 1967, the year of the Hoosiers' "Cardiac Kids" with their never-ending string of surprise victories. Both Purdue and Indiana were in the running for the Big Ten championship along with Minnesota. The bid to the Rose Bowl hinged on the final game between the two state rivals. If Indiana won, it would make the trip (and eventually did), or if Purdue won, then the Golden Gophers would play in Pasedena on New Year's Day. Purdue was ineligible for the trip because the Boilermakers had gone the year before.

Before the Indiana–Purdue game, a group of Indiana students removed the bucket from a locked glass case in the Purdue Union and brought it back to their Bloomington campus. Through a series of handoffs, the bucket was passed among fraternity houses during the frenzied week leading up to the game. After the contest had resulted in a thrilling 19-14 victory for Indiana, the bucket suddenly appeared filled with a dozen red roses.

Until 1925, the Indiana–Purdue meeting was a normally heated rivalry of state teams. But with the inception of the sacred bucket as contest trophy, temperatures rose considerably and the game took on the intensity of a Holy War.

The bucket has been such a significant element in the series that coaches sometimes use it as a recruiting tool. "Lee Corso never fails to show prospective players the bucket whenever they come to Indiana," notes Bruce

Ramey, sports editor of the *Lafayette Journal and Courier*.

Ramey has seen Purdue–Indiana games since the forties from his vantage point in the press box and his privileged accessibility to the locker room; in his mind there are few rivalries in the country to equal it.

"The rivalry is wild—almost unreal," he says. "There's a lot of animosity built up. Perhaps a lot of it is manufactured, but it's real, all right."

The night before the game, Purdue students make up a dummy called "Miss Indiana," stretch her out in a coffin and throw her on a bonfire. The Indiana people do the same thing with a dummy called, "Jawn Purdue." They dress this dummy like a hayseed country bumpkin and treat him most inhospitably. Planes drop leaflets saying, "Indiana 40, Cow College 0." (Indiana students call Purdue the "Cow College.") They've climbed over fences and burned "IU" in the sod at Purdue with chemicals. "Police now patrol the field the night before a game, it's gotten so bad," Ramey explains.

For a while during the early seventies, animosity was visibly discernible among the players.

"There was a period of brawls for three to four years in a row, with players coming off the bench and swinging their helmets," Ramey recalls. "But Corso has put a stop to this vicious kind of feeling. There is more bench control now since Corso has become head coach at Indiana."

Corso has injected life into the series in other ways, with his friendly jibes and glib one-liners. He calls the annual meeting with Purdue his "J.S." game. "J. S.," he explains, stands for "Job-Saver." "I learned a long time ago you can lose to other Big Ten teams and still be coach at Indiana as long as you beat Purdue," Corso emphasizes.

Some think that is perhaps an overstatement, but in reality, the result of the Purdue–Indiana game has indeed had an influence on making or breaking a coach. "It did cost Alex Agase his job at Purdue, not being able to beat Indiana in 1976 and 1977," says Ramey. "The university president [Dr. Arthur G. Hansen] made the decision in that case. He was under great pressure to fire him."

Other coaches may not have been fired over the Purdue
–Indiana game but certainly have suffered a lot for it. Stu
Holcomb lost his first game to Indiana in his rookie season
at Purdue in 1947 and never lived it down. As one observer
put it, "he carried that scar with him to the grave."

"No matter what you do the rest of the year," notes
Ramey, "people always want to know how you did in the
Indiana–Purdue game."

George Taliaferro, a star halfback for Indiana in the forties, said he found out about the Boilermaker–Hoosier rivalry when "most of the Army veterans got back from the
war. Prior to that, we just had freshmen who had not par-
ticipated in it before. But then when guys like Pete Pihos
came back from the war, we really got to know what it was
about."

Taliaferro later found the rivalry to be "like war . . . It's
unlike any experience you could ever imagine. Even the
second and third time, it's different. Listen, we *had* to beat
Purdue."

Anti-Purdue feeling at Indiana runs deep. As Taliaferro
notes whimsically, "We never call them Purdue, only Pur-
Don't." A deceased friend of Taliaferro's, Howard Brown,
perhaps epitomized the Indiana thought in this regard.
"Howard was captain of our team in 1946 and 1947 and
was the freshman football coach at Indiana when I first
took the job of special assistant to the president,"
Taliaferro recalls. "One day Howard and I went to lunch
and he in all seriousness suggested that something be done
to change the name of one of our combined campus
schools with Purdue. There was one in Indianapolis called
Purdue University-Indiana University at Indianapolis
[PUIUI]. It galled him to see Indiana linked with Purdue in
any way, even academically. That's how the feelings are in
this rivalry."

Taliaferro has been one of many good players produced
by Indiana over the years and could be joined on an all-
Hoosier team that includes halfback Bill Hillenbrand and

end Pete Pihos from the forties and defensive end Earl
Faison and backs Marv Woodson and Tom Nowatzke of
the early sixties.

The Hoosiers' first Big Ten title came in 1945 when
Alvin "Bo" McMillin arrived from Kansas State and
brought with him victory rains that alleviated the drought
of fourteen losing seasons. A white-haired captivator who
dispensed solid fundamentals with Southern charm at Indiana, McMillin quickly gained three first-division finishes
and his so-called "Pore Li'l Boys" won the 1945 title outright, bringing him the Big Ten's first ten-year coaching
contract, which he rejected for a professional football job.

In 1965, John Pont rectified a situation that was possibly
worse than the one faced by McMillin in the forties. When
Pont took over as Hoosier coach, Indiana had had only
one winning season in its previous seventeen. Pont quickly
breathed new life into the Hoosiers and in two years had
them standing on their feet fully recovered from the
sickness of losing. Finally, three jaunty sophomores—
quarterback Harry Gonso, tailback John Isenbarger and
wide receiver Jade Butcher—led a blend of rookies and veterans to a tie for the 1967 Big Ten title and a Rose Bowl
berth, winning fame as "the Cardiac Kids" and "the Happy Hooligans." Because Isenbarger had a persistent habit
of running when he was supposed to be punting, "Punt,
John, punt," soon became a happy war cry at Bloomington. Volatile, exuberant Lee Corso later came in as Pont's
replacement and soon turned into the life of the party in
the Big Ten with his breezy, colorful style, both on and off
the field. No conservative, he takes such calculated risks as
running on fourth down deep in his own territory and coming up with a gimmick play on occasion. Philosophically,
Corso appears to be a winner—taking intermittent drives
past cemeteries to remind himself that "things could be
worse."

Among Purdue's attributes are its "Golden Girl" (a coed
whose title is transferred when she graduates), its self-pro-
claimed "World's Largest Bass Drum" and its colorful

nickname, "The Boilermakers" (which is sometimes amended to "Spoilermakers" when the occasion demands it). More than anything else, however, Purdue football has been known for its great run of quarterbacks, starting with Bob DeMoss in 1945, who was eligible as a freshman and had four glittering years. Since then, Len Dawson, Dale Samuels, Ron DiGravio, Bob Griese and Mike Phipps have earned high grades, most of them under Jack Mollenkopf. DeMoss was head coach for only a few undistinguished seasons in the seventies, but his contribution as a handler of quarterbacks through the years was invaluable to Purdue. Griese, the great professional player, for one blossomed under DeMoss's hand. "Griese always said that Mollenkopf taught him how to win, but that De-Moss taught him how to win and how to throw," notes Ramey.

Stu Holcomb coached Purdue to a tie for the Big Ten crown in 1952 and Mollenkopf repeated in 1967, but for the most part the Boilermakers have had a legacy of "almosts." For instance, a Boilermaker has never won a Heisman Trophy, although three players have finished second in the voting—Griese in 1966, flanker LeRoy Keyes in 1968 and Phipps in 1969. When the earthy Mollenkopf retired after 1969, DeMoss took over and lasted three years before yielding to Alex Agase, a stocky, cigar-chewing Assyrian who had been an All-American guard at Purdue in the early forties. He wasn't as successful at coaching as he was at playing, and Agase in turn gave way after the 1976 season to vibrant Jim Young, a Midwestern product who had been coach at Arizona. Otis Armstrong, a Big Ten rushing champion, and Dave Butz, one of the league's biggest and best tackles, were two of Purdue's better-known football products of the seventies.

Until the late forties, Purdue and Indiana had waged a reasonably close series, with distinct power changes and innumerable streaks marking the rivalry. With a 132-0 scoring margin in the first three years, Purdue took a quick lead in the series which began in 1891. The streak included a 68-0 victory in 1892, the Boilermakers' biggest over Indiana. It wasn't until the sixth game of the series that Indiana was able to beat Purdue and that 17-5 victory in 1899 started a three-game streak for the Hoosiers. A halfback by the name of Hawley reeled off 248 yards for Indiana in that game, a remarkable figure for the day.

Purdue's longest winless period of the rivalry came from 1916 through 1923, when the Boilermakers lost four games and tied two, and it took the dedication of their Ross-Ade Stadium to end the winless streak. Tudy Bahr and Harold Harmeson formed an excellent passing team in the 1924 game to provide Purdue with a 26-7 victory. The Old Oaken Bucket, officially introduced into the series with a midfield presentation at the 1925 game, played no favorites its first time out. The teams obliged on this harmonious occasion to play to a scoreless tie.

"Cotton" Wilcox and "Pest" Welsh, two of the more colorful names in the series, led Purdue to a 24-14 upset in 1926 that started a four-game winning streak for the Boilermakers. Indiana subsequently scored two big upsets of its own in the thirties, beating Purdue 7-6 in 1930 as Ed Hughes kicked the extra point and winning 17-6 in 1934 to cost the Boilermakers a share of the Conference championship. A long pass from Wendell Walker to Vern Huffman was good for another Indiana victory in 1935 and then came the spectacular 20-20 tie of 1936 that is known as the classic of the series. Purdue's Cecil Isbell, later a Boilermaker coach, and Huffman took turns throwing touchdown passes in a brilliant afternoon of aerial football.

Indiana dominated the series, losing only once in an eight-game span from 1940 through 1947. Of the Hoosiers' seven victories during this period, the one in 1945 was clearly the biggest, giving them the Big Ten championship and a lot to yell about after forty-six fruitless years. Indiana smashed Purdue 26-0 with four tcuchdowns in the second half. Noted Jesse Ambramson in the *New York Herald Tribune:* "The Old Oaken Bucket was filled to the brim today with joy such as Indiana University never had known before."

The adage of "turning boys into men" has been used in many an Indiana–Purdue game, but it was never truer for Taliaferro that day. He remembers:

"I made a mistake that I felt was the most gross thing that could happen. I allowed a guy to catch a pass in my area that netted them a first down, I think, on our thirty-yard line. I recall saying, 'I'm sorry,' to Pete Pihos. He said to me, 'Shut up and play football!' That made me so angry I really wanted to show the guy what I could do, how I could really play. The game was a scoreless tie at the time and we went on to win big. Pihos didn't have time to listen to an eighteen-year-old crying about a mistake. I guess I grew up a little that day."

McMillin had the greatest success of any Indiana coach against Purdue, winning nine games and tying one in fourteen attempts, and this record became all the more sacred in Bloomington after Purdue's incredible domination of the series after he left in the late forties. From 1948 through 1975, the Hoosiers were able to beat the Boilermakers only three times. In that period, Purdue managed to roll up a two-to-one edge in the overall series with its dominating chapter of 24-3-1. The period included fourteen straight winless years for Indiana until 1961, which caused the team to develop a terrible inferiority complex. But even with Purdue's consistency in modern times, the series has been artistically pleasing, with many of the games winding up "ding-dong affairs," according to DeMoss: "A lot of games have hinged on the last play. In 1973, one of Indiana's players fumbled on the last play near our goal line, otherwise they might have had a touchdown. [Purdue won 28-23]. There was the 9-7 game in 1975. And back in 1952, they just missed a first down on our three or four yard line and we held on to win [21-16]. Of course, they thought they were cheated on that first-down measurement. We played on a field of ice in 1950 and won 13-0 in the most ridiculous of conditions. We were slipping and sliding all over the place."

Len Dawson remembers a 6-4 "baseball score" for Purdue in 1955, and for good reason. "It was a terrific battle and I scored all four points—for Indiana," says the one-time Purdue quarterback. "Twice I was tackled in the end zone."

Although Purdue has built up a top-heavy margin in the series in the modern age, Indiana has considerably upgraded its program under the ebullient Corso and figures to stop playing whipping boy to the Boilermakers in the years to come. Dramatic Hoosier victories in 1976 and 1977 are evidence of the Indiana shift and leave DeMoss disconcerted.

Said he: "It's a long, cold winter when you lose to Indiana."

11
GEORGIA—GEORGIA TECH
Civil War

While he was having dinner at a boardinghouse in Athens, Georgia, Morgan Blake was introduced to the unbridled spirit of the Georgia–Georgia Tech series. The diners were, of course, all strong for Georgia, and Blake, a sportswriter on assignment from Atlanta, decided to "have a little fun" by boosting a Georgia Tech star.

"Immediately," remembered Blake, "a very nice young lady arose from the table indignantly and said with high scorn: 'I can't eat anymore! It takes my appetite every time I see a Tech booster!' And she really left the table. I felt like a fool. But I learned a lesson."

That incident occurred in 1919, and things haven't changed much since. The state of Georgia is still in a state of frenzy where these two rivals are concerned. As predictable as fried chicken on Sunday, the Georgia–Georgia Tech series makes tempers boil and starts civil wars brewing all over again.

The longevity of the rivalry (one of a relatively few pairings with seventy or more meetings to their credit), the proximity of the schools (seventy miles apart), and the fierce state pride are some of the magical elements that have made this series one of the most charismatic and colorful in the country.

Significantly, both of these schools have contributed important chapters to American football history. Georgia Tech is the only college that has produced three coaches with 100 victories or more: John Heisman (102-29-6), William Alexander (134-95-15) and Bobby Dodd (165-64-8).

Alexander succeeded Heisman in 1920 and became as

prominent in Dixie as his well-known predecessor, whose name adorns the most prestigious individual trophy in college football. The first of Alexander's twenty-five teams at Georgia Tech was acclaimed national champion with the help of such players as tackle Bill Fincher, quarterback Buck Flowers and halfbacks Red Baron and Judy Harlan. Alexander subsequently had many distinctive teams but perhaps his most famous was the 1928 edition of the "Ramblin' Wreck" that won the Rose Bowl over California in the game best remembered for the "wrong-way run" of the Golden Bears' Roy Reigels. Three All-Americans—halfback Warner Mizell, center Peter Pund and tackle Frank Speer—led Georgia Tech to the national title with an 8-7 victory over Cal in that renowned Rose Bowl game. Before retiring to the athletic director's chair, Alexander had earned virtually every conceivable honor of his profession.

Alexander's successor, Dodd, eventually surpassed his achievements, becoming Georgia Tech's winningest coach and one of the top all-time winners in college football history. As an All-American player under General Robert Neyland at Tennessee, Dodd was often unorthodox and always daring. He carried these attributes over to his coaching style. Preparations for games took on a country-club atmosphere at times, with Dodd permitting his players to play volleyball and take it easy during the week instead of going through the time-honored practice of the scrimmage. This off-beat approach worked for Dodd, if it didn't for anyone else, and he became the only coach to win six straight Bowl games. Along the way, he produced twenty-two All-Americans, including such superior players as centers Larry Morris, George Morris and Maxie Baughan, quarterback Billy Lothridge and halfbacks Leon Harderman and Paul Rotenberry.

Georgia's football heritage has been just as rich, thanks to coaches such as Dr. Charles Herty, Pop Warner, Alex Cunningham, Harry Mehre and Wally Butts. The Bulldogs reached their peak during the twenty-two-year tenure of

Butts, whose teams were noted for wide-open offensive football. Called "an offensive genius" by no less than Notre Dame's Frank Leahy, Butts had his Georgia players running pro-type patterns long before many of the pros were using them.

The best of the Butts teams surfaced in 1942, with Heisman Trophy winner Frank Sinkwich, along with Charlie Trippi in the same backfield. The Bulldogs capped an 11-1 season that year with a victory over UCLA in the Rose Bowl. The gallant Trippi returned to Georgia after World War II and sparked the undefeated 1946 Sugar Bowl champions, who defeated North Carolina and Charlie "Choo Choo" Justice in an explosive contest in New Orleans. John Rauch, who later coached in the pros, quarterbacked four straight Bowl teams for Butts.

The Georgia–Georgia Tech series had an appropriately boisterous beginning, with Georgia Tech winning 28-6 in 1893 amid charges and counter-charges of professionalism and mob rule. Both schools had begun playing football on an abbreviated schedule one year earlier and their first meeting was more or less set up as a "practice" game for Georgia, who was prepping for a big contest with Vanderbilt. It was the most natural of rivalries, though, the college boys from Atlanta against the college boys from Athens, and on the day of the game, the Georgia Tech football team and an estimated 150 supporters took the "Seaboard Football Special" to the Georgia campus. The Athens natives were not especially impressed by the Georgia Tech entourage. The football team, according to one newspaper account, "was a heterogeneous collection including a U. S. Army surgeon [Leonard Wood], a medical student [Park Howell], a lawyer [John Kimball], and an insurance agent [who was never identified.]"

When they arrived at old Herty Field, it was hate at first sight. The players faced an antagonistic mob and were forced to elbow and shove their way through a crowd of belligerent Georgia fans to get to the sidelines. Once there, they hoped to hear the cheers of their admirers, but instead drums and cowbells from the Georgia side drowned out any shouts of encouragement. Supporters of Georgia nursed an immediate instinctive dislike for the "Techity Techs," as they called the visitors from Altanta, and disliked them even more after losing to them.

Wood, a guard on defense and a fullback on offense, ran every four of five plays for Georgia Tech and scored three touchdowns. Howell, who had played for Georgia in 1892 and was living in Atlanta, kicked four field goals for the winners in a game described as "intense from start to finish" by a reporter for the *Atlanta Constitution.* The Georgia fans were far from gracious losers, harassing the Tech players during the second half by bouncing epithets off their ears and rocks off their heads. A stone propelled by a slingshot struck Wood over the right eye and left a wide gash that brought forth a gusher of blood. But the acknowledged Father of Georgia Tech Football wiped the blood from his eyes and delivered it to the faces of his would-be tacklers with straight arms.

Other Georgia Tech players, not to mention an official accused of partiality, were threatened with knives, poked and gouged with canes by Athenians. The vicious Georgia crowd also showered the umpire with a barage of unkind language. Reported the *Constitution:*

After three or four decisions by the Atlanta umpire, which they deemed unfair, about 140 University students bunched and gave the following cry whenever his decision struck them as being unfair:
"Well, well, well,
Who can tell,
The Tech's umpire has cheated like hell."

The Georgia captain suggested three cheers for the victors, but the natives were not so magnanimous. Recreating that parting scene, Georgia Tech halfback W. W. Hunter said, "After the game we were greeted by a shower of rocks, sticks and missiles. Most of us were badly scared, but Wood calmly walked off the field and made his way to the station." Finally underway, the football entourage had a joyous, uneventful ride until ramming into the rear of a freight train in Lawrenceville, "putting our train out of commission," according to Hunter. "There was no serious disaster and no lives were lost," reported the *Constitution,* and the Georgia Tech party climbed aboard the freight train and continued the journey home to Atlanta. According to legend, the accident was the basis for Georgia Tech's colorful athletic appellation, "The Ramblin' Wreck."

Following the game, each school accused the other of using professional athletes among their personnel. Athenians complained that Wood was not a bona fide student and therefore ineligible to play, and from the Georgia Tech side came the accusation that Georgia played a ringer at halfback.

The second meeting of the teams, held in 1898 after a four-year cooling-off period, was almost serene by comparison. "A few words were passed by Tichenor of the Varsity team and Newman of the Techs," reported the *Atlanta Constitution,* "but no trouble resulted. . . . Hart, of the Techs, had one of his eyeteeth knocked out on a hard tackle by Moore." That smashing defensive play by Georgia characterized the tenor of the rivalry through the late 1890s and early 1900s. Georgia was consistently forceful on defense, holding Georgia Tech scoreless during a six-game period from 1897 through 1903. This overbearing defensive effort resulted in five victories for Georgia and a scoreless tie in 1902.

The Georgia monopoly in the series ended as quickly as one could say, "John Heisman." One of the early shapers of modern football, Heisman was brought to The Flats in 1904 as Georgia Tech's first professional coach and immediately proceeded to do a professional-like job. With Heisman's innovative ideas and great tactical skills, Georgia Tech rose to the forefront of Southern football and gained national recognition for the first time.

At the time he arrived in Atlanta, Heisman was well into his coaching career, having made stops at four Northern schools and two in the South. He would coach at other schools as well, but Georgia Tech was to be his longest—and most illustrious—stop on the football circuit. During Heisman's sixteen years there, he produced some of the strongest teams in Georgia Tech history, including a national championship club in 1917 that placed six players on the All-Southern team.

Heisman's contributions to football included virtually every important change in the early game. He introduced the first shift, the hidden-ball play, the center snap, the "hike" or "hut" vocal signal for the starting play, the alignment that put the quarterback at safety on defense, and scoreboards listing downs and yardage. He is regarded as the father of the forward pass and fought for its legalization. Heisman was instrumental in the campaign to divide the game into quarters instead of halves.

A flair for the dramatic enhanced Heisman's coaching abilities. A part-time actor, whose decision to join Georgia Tech was influenced by the availability of theater outlets in Atlanta, Heisman made a grand entrance on the practice field his first season. His words to the Ramblin' Wreck players have become an oft-quoted part of football lore.

Speaking to his new football class, Heisman held up a football with the theatrical aura of Hamlet holding up Yorick's skull.

"Gentlemen," he said, "what is this?"

The question was, of course, rhetorical, and Heisman provided his own answer.

"This," he said, "is a prolate spheroid, an elongated sphere in which the outer leathern casing is drawn tightly over a somewhat smaller rubber tubing."

Some of the players nodded knowingly but probably thought they had wandered by mistake into English class instead of a football meeting. Others might have thought, "what a nut." Heisman let the words sink in, then with all the dramatic ability at his command, delivered the never-to-be forgotten punch line:

"Better to have died as a small boy than to fumble this football."

Not many did fumble that ball during Heisman's administration and as a result, the Ramblin' Wreck turned into a slick new model overnight. Heisman's first Georgia Tech team won as many games (eight) and scored more points (287) than all the previous eleven seasons had produced at the Flats. Among the victories in Heisman's first season at Georgia Tech was the first of five straight over Georgia, a 23-6 decision that provided one of the most intriguing and unorthodox games in Southern football history.

King Sullivan, the Georgia punter, had dropped back nine yards behind the goal line to kick. He put his toe to the ball, but it struck the goal post and bounced over a sixteen-foot wooden wall ten yards behind him. For several moments, all twenty-two players stood around looking at each other, not knowing what to do. They appealed to referee George Butler and he decided that the ball was still in play. (In 1904, there were no end zones.) This triggered a mad scramble for the fence.

"Suddenly both elevens make a dash at the slippery fence," wrote a young reporter named Grantland Rice in the *Atlanta Journal*. "To climb the rain-washed wall in itself is a Herculean task, but no sooner does a begrimed athlete scramble to the top than he is yanked back by some rival on guard and the fight to scale the palisade starts all over again."

Dozier Lowndes, a Georgia substitute, was not eligible to chase the ball but came off the bench to seize a large stump near the wall, successfully defending it from two Georgia Tech men trying to take advantage of it for scaling efforts. Sullivan of Georgia, Red Wilson of Georgia Tech and referee Butler finally made it over the wall with the help of that stump. For several minutes they searched for the ball in the clumps of bushes skirting a nearby lake. Meanwhile, the crowd waited in a state of noisy expectancy.

"Suddenly," continued Rice, "Wilson reappears over the wall with the missing sphere under his arms as a storm of cheers rolls across the battlefield."

The frantic recovery gave Georgia Tech a touchdown, but alerted school officials to the inadequacies of Piedmont Park for home games. The next year, the park was discarded as Georgia Tech's home playing site and the hollow on campus, where Grant Field is presently located, was converted into an athletic field.

Georgia was not able to solve the mysteries of a Heisman team until the great Bob McWhorter surfaced at Athens in 1910. Thereafter, for the four years he played with the Bulldogs, Georgia swept Georgia Tech by scores of 11-6, 5-0, 20-0 and 14-0, giving McWhorter the distinction of being the only Georgia player in history to have performed in four varsity victories over Georgia Tech. Much of this was his own doing, of course. In 1910, he gave a rousing demonstration of why he was considered the outstanding running back in the South. McWhorter had ninety-five and fifty-yard runs nullified by penalties early in the game at Ponce de Leon Park in Atlanta, but this did not discourage him. In fact, it only made him madder. A miffed McWhorter took charge in the fourth quarter, helping Georgia wipe out a 6-0 deficit. He returned a punt thirty yards to set up a touchdown sprint from the twenty. And he capped his explosive day with a forty-five-yard dash to the Georgia Tech four, assuring Georgia's first victory in the series in five years and the first over a Heisman team in fifteen.

In 1911, McWhorter scored the game's only points with a 45-yard touchdown run in the fourth quarter and gained 122 yards on fourteen carries. In 1912, McWhorter scored two touchdowns during his 163-yard rushing day and a Georgia Tech student wrote for the school yearbook that, "Georgia came and McWhorter conquered." In 1913, McWhorter didn't score but was the leading ground-gainer of the day with forty-three yards as Georgia continued its spell over the Ramblin' Wreck.

McWhorter, first All-American to play in the Georgia–Georgia Tech series and an eventual Hall of Famer, not only helped to wreck Georgia Tech but just about everyone else on Georgia's football horizon. During his football career in Athens, the indefatigable runner never missed a game and scored sixty-one touchdowns as the Bulldogs amassed a fine 25-6-3 record. Behind this outstanding player, Georgia jumped higher than it had ever been before in Southern football circles, winning six and then seven games for the first time in its young history.

The coach of these exceptional Georgia teams was W.A. "Alex" Cunningham, who lent stability to the Bulldog football program. Prior to Cunningham's regime, Georgia employed fourteen coaches and had only seven winning seasons. But the former Vanderbilt star and successful Southern high school coach remained at Athens for eight years, experiencing a losing season only once in that time. Cunningham's edge in his meetings with Heisman (4-2-1) was among his most glittering accomplishments at Georgia, for it was during this era that the Ramblin' Wreck began to burst toward the top of the college football superstructure. Heisman fought for national recognition in 1916 with an undefeated, once-tied team that recorded football's all-time greatest rout, a 222-0 decision over little Cumberland College. That aberration, plus a 21-0 victory over Georgia, helped put Georgia Tech among the nation's football socialites. In 1917, Georgia Tech won the national championship with one of the best teams the South had ever produced. The backfield, often called the finest ever to come out of that sector, included quarterback Albert Hill and runners Everett Strupper, Indian Joe Guyon and Judy Harlan. The great line of 1917 had Cy Bell and Ray Ulrich at ends, captain Walker "Big Six" Carpenter and Bill Fincher at tackles, Dan Whelchel and Ham Dowling at guards and Pup Phillips at center.

Luckily for Georgia, it did not have to play this particular team. Georgia had canceled football during the years of the First World War and waited three years before resuming play in 1919.

Georgia and Georgia Tech had planned to resume their series at this time, but a bizarre chain of events in Atlanta and Athens strained the schools' relations to the breaking point and it wasn't until six more years that they would meet on an athletic field. Bad feelings started during a two-game baseball series between the teams in Atlanta in May of 1919. During the first game, Georgia Tech's band left the stands and gathered near the basepaths to blare forth, hoping to upset the Georgia pitcher. This stunt inspired boisterous behavior from the students of both schools during the next day's game, and the simmering furor that resulted prompted an attempted peace treaty between student leaders, who met in conferences in Athens and Atlanta later in the month. But their good intentions were exploded beyond repair by a painful incident during a parade in Athens following Georgia's third straight baseball victory over the Ramblin' Wreck. The line was led by a simulated tank inscribed, "Georgia in Argonne," and followed by a small car occupied by three students wearing Georgia Tech sweaters and labeled "1917 Tech in Atlanta." Georgia Tech officials were highly insulted. The inference was clear that while Georgia players were off fighting a war in Europe, the legions of Georgia Tech remained home in the safety of the football arena. Georgia men were somewhat resentful, it was felt, that Georgia Tech had continued to field teams during the war years and, in fact, did win the national championship in 1917, not to mention the claiming of two Southern championships.

Dr. J. B. Crenshaw, Georgia Tech's athletic director, stated that his school would demand a public apology from the senior class of Georgia, or athletic relations between the schools would be "forever severed." He got none, and thus a protracted cooling-off period began that lasted until 1925.

By the time Georgia and Georgia Tech resumed their tempestuous series, a lot had happened. Both Heisman of Tech and Cunningham of Georgia had left their respective teams, each in 1919. Heisman turned the job of coaching Georgia Tech football over to Alexander, who would prove worthy of following in the great man's footprints. Cunningham, who had won sixty-eight percent of his games at Georgia (43-18-9), meanwhile, had stepped aside for H. J. Stegeman, whose 1920 team brought the Southern Intercollegiate Athletic Association championship to Athens. George Woodruff succeeded Stegeman in 1923.

Since the last meeting of these teams, neither had suffered a losing season. The Yellowjackets (another of the many appellations for Georgia Tech) had posted a 53-13-5 record during this nine-year hiatus and the Bulldogs (the officially adopted nickname of Georgia in 1921) had recorded a 36-14-7 mark. The renewal of their spirited rivalry on November 14, 1925, inspired unusual interest and that day Grant Field held 33,000 people, the largest crowd to date to see a Southern football game.

Neither team scored a touchdown in their twentieth meeting, but Georgia Tech's Ivan Williams kicked a third-quarter field goal to give the Yellowjackets a 3-0 victory that evened the series at nine victories apiece, with two ties. While it was an obviously bitter defeat for Georgia to take, the series renewal game was generally accepted as being wholly beneficial to the rivalry. "Players on both sides declared the game was the cleanest, the hardest and the greatest battle they have ever fought in their football careers," pointed out George Congdon in the *Atlanta Constitution*.

Proving they could coexist, Georgia and Georgia Tech made up for lost time by providing the South, and the nation, with some of the most meaningful and exciting football in subsequent years. The Roaring Twenties was a justifiable appellation for the era, but it also could have embodied the type of football played at these two fine Georgia universities. George Woodruff had built a truly explosive football machine at Georgia during this period and Bill Alexander had done the same at Georgia Tech.

The "Notre Dame System," popularized by the immortal Knute Rockne, was in vogue then and Woodruff imported three Rockne pupils to help teach it at Georgia—Harry Mehre, Frank Thomas and Jim Crowley. They would all, of course, become coaching greats in their own right. In five seasons, 1923 through 1927, Woodruff and his brilliant aides compiled a 29-16-1 record and produced the renowned "Dream and Wonder Team" of 1927. In thirty-four previous seasons, Georgia football teams had produced but two All-Americans, Bob McWhorter in 1913 and Joe Bennett in 1923. But Woodruff's 1927 team which came within one game of a national championship and a Rose Bowl featured All-American ends Tom Nash and Chuck Shiver, plus All-Southern guard Gene Smith, fullback Herdis McCrary and quarterback John Broadnax.

The Bulldogs were sitting on top of the college football world most of the season but had to get by a tough Georgia Tech team to win the national championship and land a Rose Bowl berth. Undefeated, untied and ranked Number One in the country, Georgia visited Georgia Tech in a season finale that was the talk of Dixie. The pregame buildup generated an extraordinary amount of interest. Throughout the week leading up to the game, newspapers were filled with stories about the teams and their upcoming battle. Many of the nation's top journalists poured into Atlanta. The day before the game, a reporter said that Athens was completely deserted. "The whole town is in Atlanta." he wrote.

Finally, the big day dawned, and it will perhaps be remembered as the most bitter in the long history of Georgia football. Warner Mizell tossed a forty-nine yard touchdown pass to Bob Durant, and Jack "Stumpy" Thomason scored on a pass interception as Georgia Tech beat Georgia 12-0 in a sea of mud before a rain-soaked crowd of 30,000 at Grant Field. The Rose Bowl people never called Athens; Illinois was declared the 1927 national champion and the relationship between Georgia and Georgia Tech suffered a bit of a setback. After the game, embittered Athenians, obviously clutching at straws, hurled charges of unethical practices at Georgia Tech. "Although it had rained all day Friday and early Saturday, Georgia accused us of watering the field," remembers Fill Fincher, the Georgia Tech line coach whose defenders were brilliant that day. "Funny, it was wet on their side of the field and dry on ours."

Alexander put that one right up there with his brightest

victories, along with the following season's triumph over Georgia. This time, the situations were reversed. Georgia Tech was the team bound for the Rose Bowl, but the Yellowjackets didn't trip as Georgia had the previous year. As it eventually turned out, Georgia Tech defeated Georgia 20-6, traveled to Pasadena as one of the top teams in the nation and won the national championship by beating California's Golden Bears and their ill-fated runner, Roy Riegels.

Most of Alexander's big coaching years came at the beginning and the end of his twenty-five year career at Georgia Tech, and in between, Georgia was his constant nemesis. The last hurrah of the Rose Bowl was barely an echo when his football empire crumbled. In the ten-year period from 1929 through 1938, Alexander experienced only one winning season and for one six-year stretch was unable to beat Georgia. Overall, he had a 7-10-3 record against Georgia Tech's most traditional rivals until he relinquished the coaching job to Bobby Dodd after the 1944 season. However, Alexander went out in style, scoring successive 48-0 and 44-0 routs over wartime-depleted Georgia teams.

Even with his highs and lows, Alexander's prestige was so consistent throughout his career that he was offered top college coaching jobs in the midst of losing seasons. Georgia Tech's administration obviously agreed with Knute Rockne's appraisal that Alexander got more out of a little than any coach he knew. To Dodd, Alexander "had the football know-how of Knute Rockne, the sense of humor and storytelling ability of Mark Twain, the storehouse of miscellaneous information of a John Kieran or Oscar Levant and the sympathetic understanding of Dorothy Dix."

Georgia, meanwhile, had a Pied Piper of its own in Harry Mehre, a handpicked and worthy successor to George Woodruff in 1928. Mehre, a transplanted Northerner who developed a love for Georgia and the South that never went unrequited, flourished as coach amid the magnolias for a decade. His teams especially gave Georgia Tech a tough time, holding a 6-2-2 edge over Georgia's archenemies from 1928 through 1937. Among Mehre's most cherished Georgia squads was his "Whistlestop Team" of 1929, which upset mighty Yale. The Bulldog players were so nicknamed because of the small hometowns of many of the players, most of whom were Georgians.

Under Mehre's command were such fine personnel as Vernon "Catfish" Smith, Herb Maffett, Milton Leathers, Ralph Maddox, Jack Roberts, Austin Downes, Spud Chandler, Bill Hartman and Quinton Lumpkin. They made Georgia teams standouts in the South during the thirties and helped establish a dramatic trend in the series with Georgia Tech. Mehre's teams set the tempo and the beat went on under Wally Butts as Georgia held a 9-2-3 advantage over Georgia Tech from 1929 through 1942.

One of the most exciting games in the series, and another of the most significant, were played in the forties, both of them resulting in Georgia victories. The first took place in 1940, when Frank Sinkwich, the only Heisman Trophy winner in the series, led the Bulldogs to a 21-19 triumph in what the *Atlanta Constitution* headlined as a "slam-bang game." Two days before the thirty-fifth meeting between Tech and Georgia, Sinkwich was in the university infirmary with 104-degree fever. On game day, however, Georgia's nonpareil back made Georgia Tech look sick with 127 yards rushing and twelve pass completions for 106 yards, including two touchdowns. While 28,000 sunbathed fans looked on in Georgia's Sanford Stadium, Georgia Tech rushed to a 13-0 lead but fell behind, 21-13. The Yellowjackets battled back in the fourth quarter with a touchdown and had a good chance for victory with less than a minute left in the game, but a field goal try fell short. It was the second time in the series that Georgia Tech lost a 13-0 lead. In 1926, Georgia rallied for a 14-13 victory.

More was at stake in 1942 between Georgia Tech and Georgia than at any other time in the series. Both were ranked among the top five teams in the country and the winner had a chance for the national championship. To the victor also would go the Southeastern Conference title, not to mention a berth in the Rose Bowl. Georgia had been rated the country's number one team (and Tech number two) just prior to their big meeting, but an inexplicable loss to an average Auburn team had sent the Bulldogs plunging to fifth place. Butts said he was so shocked after that upset that, "I don't think I spoke to any of our players for a week."

It's likely that few number-one teams have been manhandled the way Georgia Tech was that day. Sinkwich and running mate Charlie Trippi accounted for 409 yards between them through the air and on land and end Van Davis caught two touchdown passes and scored another to highlight Georgia's spectacular 34-0 victory. The fans in jubilant Sanford Stadium chanted, "We're Number One" as they filed out, and Georgia Tech coach Dodd acclaimed Georgia as "the greatest team in the country." But apparently, the voters in the Associated Press poll were not listening, even after Georgia had beaten UCLA in the Rose Bowl. The AP made Ohio State Number One and Georgia Number Two in the final rankings.

Many viewed that 1942 Georgia–Georgia Tech game as a reincarnation of the 1927 contest, with an ironic twist of plot. Fifteen years before, the situation had been exactly reversed, with the once-beaten Yellowjackets upsetting the previously unbeaten Bulldogs, costing them a Rose Bowl berth and the national championship.

At this time Butts was coming into prominence as the Georgia coach. He eventually would establish a record for coaching longevity at the school in Athens, winning sixty-four percent of his games with a 140-86-9 mark. Butts had a 5-2-1 record in eight Bowls, including unprecedented victories in the Rose, Orange and Sugar contests, and won four Southeastern Conference championships along the way. His record at Georgia was all the more admirable, considering that the Bulldogs played more than half their games on the road to balance a thin budget.

At five-foot-six and 155 pounds Butts was theoretically too small to play college football, but sheer determination made him a star end at Mercer College. Bernie Moore, head coach at Mercer and LSU and a long-time commissioner of the SEC, called Butts the best blocking end he coached. In a decade as a prep coach in the South, Butts's teams lost a mere total of ten games. He joined Joel Hunt's staff at Georgia in 1938 and one year later was the head coach.

Bobby Dodd's success at Georgia Tech nearly paralleled that of Butts, although his football philosophy was at the other end of the field. Contrary to Butts's work ethic, Dodd admittedly ran the most relaxed practice in college football. "I never considered coaching a drudgery, and I don't want my players to think so," he had said. "There is a certain amount of boredom connected with practice. That you can't avoid. But I want my players to enjoy the game as I did as a player in high school and at Tennessee."

Dodd had a simple guideline. As a coach he used methods that he would have wanted his son exposed to. He reflected great indulgence in training rules, insisting only that his players apply themselves to studies and attend church each Sunday. It was Dodd's way and, as most everyone agreed, a unique situation in college football. Alabama's Bear Bryant used to say, "Nobody else in the country can coach like Dodd and win." Rice coach Jess Neely put it this way: "I want to find the guy who coaches like Dodd and play him. Not Dodd—just somebody like him."

The record proved Dodd's theories sound. He was called the "Bowlmaster" by many and his Yellowjackets won eight in a row before losing. Upon retirement, he had a 9-4 record in postseason play and under him, Georgia Tech became the first and only school to win six major Bowls in successive years. Dodd's teams once went thirty-one games without defeat, dating from 1950 to the sixth game of the 1953 season. He had two undefeated seasons at the height of his power in the early fifties and when he retired had become the only Georgia Tech coach outside of John Heisman to hold an edge over Georgia (12-10). Rushing toward national recognition, Dodd's Georgia Tech teams ran over Georgia for eight straight years, from 1949 through 1957, the longest winning streak by either team in the series.

When Georgia finally broke the long drought against Georgia Tech with a 7-0 victory in 1957 spearheaded by Theron Sapp, pandemonium broke loose in the Georgia section of Grant Field. "Georgians swept onto the field from everywhere," wrote Furman Bisher in the *Atlanta Journal.* "Men kissed men. Women kissed women. Red-shirted Bulldogs swept their coach Butts up onto their shoulders, and his meeting with coach Bobby Dodd of Tech was brief because his athletes would not allow him the time." In 1958, Georgia fans were just as euphoric after the Bulldogs cracked another Yellowjacket jinx of sorts, beating their top rivals for the first time in ten years in Athens. And this time Bisher reported, "Georgia lovers refused to let go this rapturous moment and clung to the stands in happy clusters long after the final score was in."

There would be other such rapturous moments for Georgia with the emergence of Vince Dooley as head coach. Many are apt to remember the 23-14 conquest of Georgia Tech in 1966 as well as any of his victories.

In 1966, Georgia Tech was ranked Number Five nationally and Georgia, with only a one-point loss to mar its record, was Number Seven when they met in their traditional season-ending game. (They had been playing the game continuously as a season-ending fixture since 1941.)

It was a homogeneous crowd of 55,000 at Sanford Stadium, typical of all Georgia–Georgia Tech games since the schools are located so close to each other. As usual, there were equal parts Bulldog and Yellowjacket in the stands. As the Georgia Tech players ran onto the field, the stadium went wild. The roar of approval from the Tech side struggled against the staccato chants of "Dog food! Dog food! Dog food!" Moments later came Georgia. The partisans for the Bulldogs were on their feet and barking for their Bulldogs but not loud enough to drown out, "To hell with

Georgia! To hell with Georgia!" Then the stadium announcer put in his two cents over the public-address system while going down the lineups. As a benefit to the Georgia Tech fans, he added this warning: "Ladies and gentlemen, you are now in Bulldog Country!" This, of course, triggered more cheers and jeers from the crowd.

They were no quieter after the game started, and the Georgia fans had considerably more to yell about than their Georgia Tech counterparts. Kent Lawrence ran back a punt seventy-one yards for a Georgia touchdown in the longest TD punt return of the series, setting the tone for the day. Brad Johnson later scored another Georgia touchdown, and Bobby Etter kicked a series record three field goals. It would have been even worse for Georgia Tech had not penalties canceled two more touchdowns scored by Lawrence.

Games such as these have made Georgia supporters eternally grateful to Dooley. Not only has he made their Bulldogs a perpetual contender for the Southeastern Conference championship and postseason Bowl games, he has handled Georgia Tech as no other coach in Georgia's history. When Dooley took over at Georgia in 1964, the Bulldogs had lost eleven of the fifteen previous games with Georgia Tech, including the last three in a row. His appearance signaled an immediate and healthy recovery for the Bulldogs. His teams beat Georgia Tech five straight times—an unprecedented accomplishment for a Georgia coach. For the first time in a series as well, Georgia scored as many as forty points in a game against Tech. This occurred in 1968, when the Bulldogs beat the Yellowjackets 47-8. During his first fourteen years at Georgia, Dooley by far had the best record of any coach in the series, 10-4.

The title of "Saint Vincent" bestowed on the Georgia coach by his flock suggests no irreverence. To many, what he has done at Athens has been nothing short of a miracle.

12
NOTRE DAME—SOUTHERN CAL
Long-Distance Hate

John McKay got off one of his more memorable lines during the opening kickoff of the 1965 Southern Cal–Notre Dame game. A light rain fell as Trojan Mike Hunter took the kickoff, slipped and sprawled heavily to the turf without a tackler within ten yards of him.

"My God, they've shot him," the Southern Cal football coach said.

To this day, nobody knows whether McKay was kidding or serious. But Southern Cal people will tell you that the series with Notre Dame has always been enflamed by lunatic emotions.

"There is no intersectional rivalry like it in college football," says McKay, now a professional coach with Tampa Bay. "Nothing even comes close."

A man who has had first-hand experience in the trenches, Nick Pappas, illuminates that seemingly universal opinion.

"There is no hitting like the hitting in a USC–Notre Dame game," says Pappas, Southern Cal alumni activity director who led the Trojans in rushing as a sophomore in 1935. "Any Trojan who ever played in a Notre Dame game remembers every tackle, every block, every call in the huddle. It's a fantastic experience."

The 1964 game perhaps best typifies the emotion, excitement and significance of this series, which leads the college football world in inspiration and bizarre turnabouts. It was in that game in the Los Angeles Coliseum that Ara Parseghian was thirty minutes away from an undefeated season and a national championship in his first year as coach of the Fighting Irish, but everything collapsed for him under a second-half stampede by the Trojans. And Southern Cal did it against a prize-winning Notre Dame team.

Notre Dame quarterback John Huarte had been named the Heisman Trophy winner three days earlier. Jack Snow was the All-American end. Bill Wolski and Nick Eddy were among the nation's best power runners. Kevin Hardy, Alan Page, Jim Lynch, Tom Regner, Ken Maglicik and Nick Rassas sparked a thunderous defense.

The exuberant Fighting Irish rushed to a 17-0 halftime lead and then took the third quarter kickoff and marched down the field for another apparent score. But Joe Kantor's plunge for a touchdown was erased by a holding penalty and then strange things began to happen. The Trojans turned the momentum upside down and narrowed the lead to 17-13. Then, with 1:33 left to play, Southern Cal quarterback Craig Fertig hit Rod Sherman with a touchdown pass that gave the Trojans a remarkable 20-17 victory.

Notre Dame's status as a fourteen-point favorite was not lost in the final counting. The underdog has taken the biggest bite in this series of shocks and surprises.

A casual gentlemen's agreement brought together two of the fiercest rivals in college football. Some time before the series started in 1926, Knute Rockne's Notre Dame team had been upset by an Iowa squad coached by Howard Jones. The two shook hands in the center of the football field after that 10-7 Iowa victory.

"Now, don't forget," Rockne said. "You owe me a game."

"You'll get it," Jones replied.

When Jones later joined Southern Cal, Rockne remembered his promise and arranged a home-and-home series with the Trojans. The first game, won by Notre Dame 13-12, set the tone for future, heady struggles. The Fighting Irish had come to California with a chip on their shoulders, put there by Carnegie Tech's shutout the week before.

"They were fighting mad and determined to avenge this unlucky reverse," said one observer.

For a while, it didn't look like they would. Southern Cal held a 12-7 lead with about a minute to go in the game. Then Rockne rushed Art Parisien into the game to put more fight into the Fighting Irish. Parisien's throws moved Notre Dame to Southern Cal's twenty-yard line, and then with just seconds left, he fired a touchdown pass to John Niemiec for the winning points. This Frank Merriwell finish was made all the more dramatic when it was discovered after the game that Parisien had come out of sick bay to rally the team.

It was as much Southern Cal's stubbed toes as Parisien's arm that beat the Trojans that day. They were unable to kick the extra points after scoring touchdowns and this inability to convert would haunt the Trojans in future games with Notre Dame. In 1927, the Irish won 7-6 when Southern Cal was unable to convert the extra point after a touchdown pass from Morley Drury to Russ Saunders. Even at that, the Trojans went home sulking about the loss because they felt they should have had two points for a safety on one particular play.

"We were robbed," said Drury upon returning to Los Angeles from the trip.

The Jones–Rockne rivalry, although short-lived because of the premature death of the Notre Dame coach in 1931, was a sunburst on the football horizon. Their association had produced a rivalry that not only was an artistic success, but a box-office bonanza as well. An estimated crowd of 120,000 (producing a record gross in excess of $250,000) had witnessed the 1927 game in Chicago's elephantine Soldier Field, and there were always legions of anecdotes about the two to inspire more public interest.

One year when Southern Cal arrived in Chicago to play Notre Dame, Jones was greeted by a newspaper headline which read, "Knute To Start Shock Troops." (Using the "Shock Troops" was one of Rockne's famous psychological ploys. They were members of the second and third teams that Rockne sometimes used to start the game, letting them go all out for a few minutes before hitting the opposition hard with his best players.)

"If he does start them," Jones said, "we'll score in the first minute of the game."

The Chicago newspapers picked up this remark and announced in the next morning's editions: "Jones Says Will Score In First Minute Of Play."

Rockne started his "Shock Troops," a band of his meanest, if not most talented, players. And, true to Jones' word, Southern Cal scored in the first minute.

Before another of their memorable meetings, this one in 1928, this laughable confrontation took place:

> Rockne: Howard, we've had a wonderful series, always close. We've lost two games and you have a weak team this year. Now, it wouldn't be right for you to humiliate us. I tell you—I'll give you a safety on the first play if you promise not to score any more. You know we couldn't score if we wanted to.
>
> Jones: What do you say we play the game and see how it comes out?

Southern Cal won, 27-14.

The usually stolid Jones engaged with Rockne in an animated pregame repartee on another occasion.

"My gosh, Howard!" Rockne said. "What are you so nervous about? You're chain-smoking!"

"Well, you're not the coolest guy out here," said Jones in one of his rare comebacks. "Your cigar looks like a shredded rope!"

In the best tradition of the series, the teams battled on even terms in the 1929 game before Rockne's inspiration gave the Irish a little push. It showed to what lengths the master psychologist would go to win a football game. Playing before another monster crowd at Soldier Field of 112,912, the Trojans and Fighting Irish struggled to a 6-6 halftime tie while Rockne was in a sick bed somewhere with leg problems. When Notre Dame's players trudged to their locker room and tumbled down at their spaces, they saw former Irish running star Paul Castner step into the center of the room to take Rockne's place as halftime orator.

"Fellows, who do you go to when you're in trouble? It's Rock, isn't it? Who do you regard as your best friend at Notre Dame? It's Rock again. Who is . . ."

At this point, Castner was interrupted by the creaking of the locker room door. It was Rockne this time, in the flesh. Two managers wheeled the sick coach into the room. He was obviously in pain from making the trip—against doctor's orders—from South Bend to Chicago, and further strained by watching that tense first half. But obviously he had enough strength to speak, for after looking around the room and giving dramatic pause, Rockne said:

"Boys, I want you to get out there and play them hard the first five minutes. They aren't going to like it, but you just play them hard! Rock will be watching you. Go ahead now, play them hard!"

The Irish "played them hard," as the beloved Rockne had suggested, and finally beat them down, 13-12. It was probably the most important victory of the season for the Fighting Irish, who went on undefeated and won the national championship.

Possibly no other game underscored Rockne's ability to inspire a team than his upset of Southern Cal in the Los Angeles Coliseum in 1930. Although Notre Dame's football team hadn't lost a game in two years and was considered one of Rockne's best, it had suffered by attrition in the last month of the season. The locomotive Joe Savoldi, Notre Dame's ranking fullback, had been ruled ineligible because of his marriage and second-string fullback Larry Moon Mullins had been injured, along with several other good players. The Irish had managed to come through nine games unbeaten, but had showed the wear and tear of the season in the last two, both tight victories over Northwestern and Army.

Southern Cal, on the other hand, had one of its strongest and healthiest teams. The Trojan backfield of Orville Mohler at quarterback, Gus Shaver and Ernie Pinckert at the halves and Jim Musick at fullback was believed unstoppable, behind a comparatively talented line. Despite an earlier 7-6 loss to Washington State, the high-powered Trojan machine had outscored nine opponents by 382 points to 39 and was considered to be perhaps the strongest team Howard Jones had turned out. Coupled with the home-field advantage, the circumstances had made Southern Cal a 5-3 favorite.

En route to Los Angeles, Rockne's public projections were gloomy. During a two-day practice stop at Tucson, Arizona, Rockne dropped a psychological bomb on his players in hopes of shaking them out of their late-season apathy. He threatened to go back to Notre Dame rather than coach a squad that "did not seem interested in the game ahead." The players begged him to stay, and of course he did.

Privately, he had every expectation of beating Southern Cal and winning a second straight national championship. The key to his game plan was a secret weapon by the name of Paul "Bucky" O'Connor, an almost unknown substitute right halfback. Rockne would use him at fullback in the game but kept his identity unknown to the press beforehand. O'Connor, in fact, during Tucson practices, wore the jersey of Dick Hanley—the apparent Notre Dame starter at fullback. While California newspapermen watched, O'Connor, in the guise of Hanley, dutifully ran short bucks into the line and avoided the outside running at which he excelled.

In the game, however, O'Connor took his mercurial running to the outside and scored two quick touchdowns, one on an eighty-yard dash, before the Trojans knew who he was. The final score was 27-0 in favor of the Fighting Irish and they had well earned their national title. "That was the greatest Notre Dame team I've ever seen," said Jones.

Rockne wasn't around to orchestrate in 1931, but the

Southern Cal–Notre Dame rivalry continued to command public attention with one of the most gripping games in the series. Notre Dame had every right to expect to win this one, according to Southern Cal scout Aubrey Devine.

"Notre Dame is so good that Hunk Anderson could lick any team he has played, Northwestern excepted, with his second team," Devine told the Trojan camp after returning to Los Angeles from a scouting mission. "It is impossible to set a foolproof defense for the Irish because they are such a versatile squad. Just when you think you have them stopped, they break out in another direction."

Jones himself expressed similar fears, enlarging his pessimism as game time grew nearer.

"There is every reason to believe that the team we buck up against Saturday is much stronger than the one which trounced us 27 to 0 last year," said the Southern Cal coach. "On the other hand, there is nothing to indicate that my boys are any better than they were that day Knute Rockne made us look bad."

In the *Los Angeles Examiner,* a whimsical Maxwell Stiles projected more gloom for the Trojans. He datelined his departure story written while he was aboard the Southern Cal train with: "ABOARD THE TROJAN SPECIAL, Bound For Heaven Knows What, November 17." The Fighting Irish, now coached by Hunk Anderson after Rockne's untimely death in an airplane crash, were generally recognized throughout the Middle West and East as the greatest American football team of the generation. "That's quite a mouthful to take in one bite," said Stiles in his story.

Ridiculed by the press and razzed by most of the fans in Notre Dame Stadium, the unnerved Trojans took the field against the Fighting Irish on November 21, 1931. And Notre Dame further upset their equilibrium with a four-yard touchdown blast by Steve Banas in the second quarter and a three-yard run by Marchy Schwartz in the third. That gave the Fighting Irish a 14-0 lead going into the fourth quarter, an advantage that "looked as big as the population of China," according to one California writer.

For the first three quarters, it had not been Southern Cal's day at all. This Trojan frustration was symbolized by an injury to fullback Phil Musick, who had his nose broken by Notre Dame's vicious gang-tackling. He was led from the field, snarling and scolding the Fighting Irish for "dirty football."

There was still a full quarter to go, however, and a classic mental fumble by the Notre Dame coach helped turn the game in an opposite direction. A minute or two into the last quarter, Anderson, sensing an easy killing, withdrew most of his regulars from the game and inserted fresh substitutes to finish off the Trojans. This was a mistake, it turned out, because the rules prevented the regulars from returning to the game in the same quarter and the Trojans were able to chip away at the lesser Notre Dame talents.

When the Fighting Irish did get the ball, the feeble offense couldn't move it. Notre Dame would have to kick, and Southern Cal punt-returning ace Orv Mohler would put the Trojans in a commanding field position with a strong runback.

With the clock, the crowd and the odds against them, the Trojans struggled back to respectability—and finally, to victory.

Early in the fourth period, Mohler alternated with Gus Shaver as ball carrier and helped drive Southern Cal within sight of the Notre Dame goal line. Shaver carried the ball in from the one-yard line for Southern Cal's first touchdown. Johnny Baker missed the extra point try and Notre Dame's lead was cut to 14-6.

Later in the period, a pass interference call gave Southern Cal the ball on the Notre Dame twenty-four. Shaver and Mohler sliced through to the nine on alternate carries and then Mohler lateraled to his brutish teammate. Shaver soared around left end for another Southern Cal touchdown. This time Baker was true on his kick and the Trojans trailed the Irish by a tenuous 14-13 score with eight minutes to go.

Southern Cal was alive and doing well, as reporter

Braven Dyer pointed out: "The fury of Troy's attack in the second half astounded everybody. Mohler's choice of plays was almost perfect, and the way the 162-pound Orv rammed into the Irish line inspired his mates immensely."

With four minutes remaining, Southern Cal took possession on its twenty-seven-yard line and the first capacity crowd at Notre Dame Stadium—50,731—started to buzz. Shaver faded almost to his goal line and threw a long pass to Ray Sparling, who made a diving catch on Notre Dame's forty-yard line. Later tackle Bob Hall took Shaver's perfect pass over his shoulder for a first down on the eighteen. The Trojans had used up two minutes of precious time on this drive. An offside penalty moved the ball to the thirteen and Sparling drove around end to get the ball into an ideal field-goal position.

At this juncture, Jones sent Homer Griffith charging into the game with the logical instructions. "Field goal, field goal," he said, pushing Griffith onto the field. But Mohler waved back the sideline courier with a dramatic flourish of his hand, as if to say: "I don't need any help. I know what to do." Jones was momentarily taken aback by Mohler's action. "Cold sweat broke out on his brow and an assistant groaned in anguish," said one writer.

Jones need not have worried, however, for Mohler had no other intention but try for the field goal. He took the snap from center and put the ball down on the twenty-three-yard line for Baker and Southern Cal's field goal kicker, who had nearly quit the team earlier after an argument with Jones, kicked the winning points through the uprights and into the bleachers. There was one minute left in the game, but it really was over at that point.

"Great! Boy, great!" Jones yelled, happily embracing Mohler as he came off the field.

In a more tranquil moment, Jones would ask Mohler why he waved Griffith back to the sidelines in that moment of truth at the end. The confident quarterback insisted he needed no help, pointing out: "Baker and I have been practicing that play all year. I knew if it failed I'd be the goat and we'd be licked, but old 'Bake' doesn't miss on those short ones. I knew he wouldn't fail me. Wasn't it a beaut?"

The sound of the final gun sent the Southern Cal players shooting off into the locker room to celebrate. It became a chamber of madmen, the players hugging and dancing, and some even crying. Bruising Ernie Pinckert led the team into the dingy room, his eyes glistening. Gordon Clark followed, the game ball tucked under his soiled, red jersey.

"I knew they couldn't stop us," Pinckert shouted and slapped stocky Tom Mallory on the shoulders. "I've waited two years for this day—but, boy, what revenge!"

A group of alumni had crashed the gate and discovered Baker in the shower. They pulled him out grinning and dripping and snake-danced around the Trojan hero.

Jones lost his usually steely composure, as Southern Cal captain Stan Williams recalls: "My big kick came in the dressing room when I found someone hugging and kissing me, and I kissing back, too," Williams says. "I came to for a moment and saw it was the 'Head Man' himself. I was so excited—and he was, too, that he didn't know it."

Later Jones, his hat mussed and his coat hanging from his shoulder, went around the locker room and shook the hand of each of his players.

"Honestly, I'm too flabbergasted to say a thing," he told reporters. "But I'll tell you that it was the greatest team in the world. I knew I had a ballclub, but the thing that pleases me was that we gave 'em fourteen points and then came back and licked 'em."

The normally grim Jones became giddy during the train ride back to Los Angeles, indulging in playful pranks such as stuffing snow down the neck of the Southern Cal athletic director.

But whatever exuberance prevailed on the long ride home was miniscule compared to the racket at the end of the trail. A crowd of 300,000 cheering citizens welcomed the players when they stepped off the train.

"I never saw anything like it in my life," remembers Ernie Smith, who shared in the victory over Notre Dame and then the victory march afterward.

The Southern Cal players all wore bowler hats, courtesy of a Chicago haberdashery as a tribute to their dramatic victory.

"We were all done up in these fancy hats, and they had these cars waiting for us," Smith recalls. "They put two players in each car, and we started to ride down Fifth Street to Main and then on up to City Hall. It was a real thrill—it was unbelievable. For a football team to get this kind of reception, I mean it *really* was something."

Another participant in the extravagant homecoming celebration recalls people "four and five deep along the curbs throwing all kinds of waste paper."

"I think Ted Husing's national radio broadcast of the game had a lot to do with that welcome," remembers Al Wesson, Southern Cal's sports publicist of the day. "He built up the last quarter to such a dramatic extent that Los Angeles people were running out into the streets during the game and screaming. It was the wildest sports demonstration that the city of Los Angeles ever had. Everyone got a helluva cheer—even me."

The game had been recorded by a movie camera and, as if to certify one of Southern Cal's greatest triumphs, it was soon shown as a full-length feature in Los Angeles theaters. Sportswriter Braven Dyer did the soundtrack narration at the Metro-Goldwyn-Mayer studios between supper one night and the next day's breakfast.

"They rushed the film down to Loew's State theater, then the top movie house in downtown Los Angeles," Dyer recalls. "When the bill first went on, the football game was one-half of the double feature. After the first day's business was so good, and everybody admitted it was the football game that had lured them to the theatre, the manager jerked the second feature and ran the gridiron picture over and over. It broke all house records at Loew's State."

For many years thereafter, the 1931 game was classified as "The Game" in Southern Cal folklore and replayed over the seasons as the headiest of Trojan triumphs. Spiritually deflated by the loss, the Fighting Irish nevertheless found some gratification in the pragmatic side, realizing large profits at the gate. In fact, both teams could look forward to such financial windfalls in the future, now that the young rivalry had grown to command national acclaim.

Jones would taste other close triumphs over Notre Dame in the thirties, but none as sweet, and there would be bitter defeats to swallow as well in one of the nation's most hotly contested rivalries. Before the "Head Man" died prematurely in the summer of 1941, he had won six games, lost eight and tied one against Notre Dame, and eight of the decisions were decided by a touchdown or less.

"That was always the big game," remembers Pappas, "and sensational things always happened."

The games during Pappas's time were marked by typical hard play, and at times it seemed to the halfback that the Fighting Irish went to rude extremes. Horror stories of Notre Dame violence persisted: Trojan tongues cut by well-aimed elbows, punches thrown and shirts shredded, to say nothing of hurt feelings.

It worked both ways, of course. Once, after a bitter half when Notre Dame players used illegal tactics, they got it back from Southern Cal with interest. One Notre Dame player who had been taunting the Trojans had tobacco juice spit in his eyes and was forced to leave the game, half-blinded. The players were on their own, of course. Jones never condoned such buffoonery.

"Jones was very ethical and didn't put up with any dirty football," says Pappas. "You couldn't play for him if you played that way."

By the late forties, Frank Leahy was shaking down the thunder at Notre Dame and producing what many believed to be the best college football dynasty in history. Leahy's teams, perhaps the most stunning array of college talent ever gathered in one period, won national championships in 1946, 1947 and 1949 and except for a 14-14 tie with Southern Cal, probably would have worn the crown in 1948 as well. Some called that tie the "biggest upset of the decade," and it might have been. Notre Dame had gone twenty-seven games without defeat and came into Los Angeles with a richly talented team that included four All-Americans—guards Bill Fischer and Marty Wendell, end Leon Hart and fullback Emil "Six-Yard" Sitko. The Trojans had no All-Americans and were virtually the same team that had been humiliated 38-7 the year before by the Fighting Irish.

But the Irish encountered an inspired Southern California team, which had been skillfully trained by coach Jeff Cravath, in a converging-line defense that made it difficult for them to run the ball. The highly touted Notre Dame players miscued, fumbled and stalled and barely held onto a 7-0 lead as the first half ended.

"Here we were Number One in the Associated Press poll for about seven weeks and we were heavy favorites over Southern Cal," recalls quarterback Frank Tripucka. "But we just couldn't hold onto the ball, for some reason. We never fumbled—yet on that day, a nice, clear, warm day in the Los Angeles Coliseum, we'd work the ball out to midfield, and then we'd fumble. This went on the whole first half."

In the closing minute of the first half, Tripucka decided to kill the clock by stalling. He attempted three quarterback sneaks in a row to use up the time remaining before intermission, and on the third try he danced around and let Southern Cal's big ends and tackles get a crack at him. They did—and Tripucka wound up with two fractured vertebrae and some cracked ribs.

"It seemed like the whole stadium hit me," Tripucka remembers today.

In the locker room between halves, Notre Dame quarterback coach Bernie Grimmins said to inexperienced Bob Williams: "Tripucka can't play. You're in." Nervously, the eighteen-year-old Williams took over in the second half, shouldering the responsibility of preserving Notre Dame's mammoth unbeaten streak.

"I couldn't analyze too well," Williams says. "The

linemen helped me out by telling me what the defensive men were doing."

Late in the third quarter, the resolute Trojans snatched one of Williams's passes out of the air and returned the ball to the Notre Dame eighteen. Pounding away at the Irish line, they finally squeezed Bill Martin over from the one-yard line a few minutes after the fourth quarter began. When the placement tied the score a moment later, a torrential, jubilant storm of noise washed down the terraced walls of the vast arena. As soon as the "7" was hung up next to Southern Cal on the scoreboard, the thousands of USC fans implored the Trojans to do it again. Caught up in the frenzy, they did.

A fumble by Williams, one of seven committed by the Fighting Irish that day, gave the Trojans good field position and when their first assault sputtered, they played it smart and kicked out on the Notre Dame five. When Notre Dame was forced to kick back to the USC forty-two, the Trojans swept down the field in a brilliantly sustained march to go in front 14-7, putting the overjoyed crowd into a "Roman Holiday" mood.

At this point, a meaningful scenario took place on the field when Billy Gay, one of the Irish pony backs, approached a referee.

"Mr. Referee," he said, "how much time is there left to play?"

"Two minutes and thirty-five seconds," replied the referee.

"That will be plenty of time, sir, if they will just kick it to me," Gay responded.

The swaggering football player was as good as his word. He took the ball on his one-yard line and followed blockers down the right sideline until he was dragged down on the Southern Cal thirteen by Don Doll.

The Coliseum crowd was up, yelling, whistling and stamping, imploring the Trojans to "Hold that line . . . hold that line!" Williams cracked through the middle to the five. The quarterback then missed two pass attempts, but a pass interference call on one of them put the ball on the two. Then Williams gave the ball to Sitko and the reliable Notre Dame fullback plunged the final six feet while 100,000 people screamed in a deafening emotional counterpoint to the Irish touchdown.

Now Notre Dame's unbeaten string depended on Steve Oracko, the big tackle who did the extra-point kicking for the Fighting Irish. Picking up his helmet, Oracko jumped off the bench and wisecracked to a teammate: "I'll be right back—I'm going out and tie it up."

Williams knelt on the turf, waiting to receive the snap from center while Oracko made his mental and physical preparations.

"What's everybody so quiet about?" Oracko asked, grinning at Williams in the center of a dead-silent stadium.

Oracko then proceeded to kick the tying point through the uprights and keep alive Notre Dame's three-year unbeaten streak.

It was called a moral victory for Southern California's underprivileged team, and the Trojans needed it against Leahy. They could only beat the famous Irish coach once in ten meetings, and at that only by two points. Leahy's players made amends for the 1948 slump by routing the Trojans 32-0 in 1949 and thus certifying their third national championship in four years.

Terry Brennan, Joe Kuharich and Hugh Devore had nearly similar success against the Trojans in the fifties and early sixties, even if they had problems with everyone else. While Notre Dame's record was a modest 51-48 in the decade following Leahy's stormy resignation, the Irish won seven of ten from the Trojans.

The frustration of playing against the Leahy teams and the continued Notre Dame dominance by his successors brought the Trojans to the boiling point and Parseghian ultimately paid for it in 1964. All season long, while the Fighting Irish piled up victory after victory under their new coach, Parseghian replayed the persistent pessimism: "It is impossible to go through a season undefeated. Teams are too evenly matched these days."

After nine games, however, the only thing that stood between Notre Dame and its first perfect season in fifteen years was a so-so Southern California team that had lost three out of nine games. True, the Trojans had something worth fighting for—a possible Rose Bowl bid. But the Irish had something worth more: the national championship. "This is our Rose Bowl," said Parseghian, and few of the 83,840 fans in the Los Angeles Coliseum could have believed that they were about to witness the upset of the year.

John McKay's clinical viewpoint, however, left him no doubts that the Trojans could take this mighty Notre Dame team. The Southern Cal coach joked about the seemingly impossible task of trying to beat the Irish but, in all seriousness, calculated their destruction.

While Southern Cal's emotional players tore photographs of Notre Dame stars off their lockers and danced on them, McKay provided more practical voodoo to counteract the nation's top-ranked team. All week long prior to the game, McKay was outwardly respectful of Notre Dame's elephantine defensive line, insisting, "We can't run inside on Notre Dame." But, in fact, that would be part of his chief offensive strategy.

"We can gouge our men through," McKay confidentially told his players, "and if we can make our inside running go, we can make our passing go."

Just as passionate about defensing Notre Dame's great passing combination of John Huarte-to-Jack Snow, McKay laid out these plans: "We'll use a confusion rush. We'll loop our tackles outside, use crisscross stunts and play a three-deep secondary—very deep."

Bookmakers made Notre Dame an eleven-point favorite and the Fighting Irish looked every bit as good as their advance notices by taking a 17-0 halftime lead. For all of McKay's elaborate defensive preparations, Huarte had a field day before intermission. The Irish quarterback hit on eleven of fifteen passes for 176 yards and one touchdown, and Notre Dame added a field goal by Ken Ivan and a touchdown run by Bill Worski to take a commanding lead into the locker room.

McKay, still confident, tried to buoy his downhearted Trojans: "If we can score the first time we get the ball in the second half, it's a brand-new ball game."

The seventeen-point deficit did not look all that big to McKay and to any other astute observer who perhaps noiced that the Trojans had indeed been able to run inside on Notre Dame, even if they had not scored. Southern Cal's one good chance in the first half was blown by an errant pitchout.

Remarkably calm, McKay told his team: "Our game plan is working. Keep doing your stuff and we'll get some points. If we can get on the scoreboard quick, we can put some pressure on 'em. They've won nine games without any duress. If we can make this thing close, they might not know how to react."

In the second half, USC's runs continued to work efficiently. The power blocks by Southern Cal's brutish tackles opened holes for Mike Garrett and running mate Ron Heller. When Notre Dame swung its defense to stop the inside running game, quarterback Craig Fertig threw to Rod Sherman over the middle. Fertig's deadly passes moved the Trojans within scoring range and Garrett carried the ball over to cut Notre Dame's lead to 17-7.

Huarte rallied Notre Dame on a crackling drive to the Southern Cal nine, but that failed on a fumble. Later, a holding penalty hurt Notre Dame even more. The Fighting Irish had scored a touchdown, but it was canceled by the penalty and thereafter the momentum of the game shifted to Southern Cal's side. Fertig passed with skill, Sherman and Fred Hill made clawing catches and Garrett continually slipped away from Notre Dame's frustrated tacklers. From his own eight-yard line, Fertig marched the Trojans to the Notre Dame twenty-three. Then he rolled out, lofted a pass to Hill in the end zone, and the Irish lead was cut to 17-13.

McKay was extravagantly optimistic at this point. "I knew we had 'em then," he said. "The momentum was all ours. In a situation like that the Number One rating is a fairly suffocating thing."

With less than five minutes left, Parseghian decided to
eat up the clock. But the aroused Trojans stuffed the ball
down Notre Dame's throat, held for downs and forced the
Irish to kick. At the Irish thirty-five-yard line, Southern
Cal went to desperate work with only two minutes and ten
seconds remaining. A run failed and two passes fell incomplete and now it was fourth down and eight with one
minute and forty-three seconds left.

On the sidelines, Sherman told McKay that he wanted to
run an "84-7 delay." The pass play was an old one in the
Southern Cal playbook. The receiver splits wide to the left,
delays for one second after the snap, sprints straight ahead
for five steps, fakes outside, then cuts sharply down and
across the middle of the field. The quarterback drifts
straight back and throws to the spot.

"I watched the way their halfback reacted and I figured
that I could beat him," Sherman explained later.

The play unfolded perfectly by the book. Chased by Irish
blitzers, Fertig found Sherman clear of defender Tony
Carey and drilled a chest-high pass to his receiver for a
touchdown that made it Southern Cal 20, Notre Dame 17.

"It was a big letdown," recalls Jack Snow. "I thought—
what a way to end up! You could see the guys' faces fall
when Sherman went across for the score. The locker room
was very silent, very still, a great deal of emotion. A lot of
guys were crying, they were so upset. Ara didn't say much
except that we had a good year and came a long way, and
it was a shame that it had to end that way."

Scars of that bitter defeat were still visible many years
later in Parseghian. "Be careful talking about it with Ara,"
a friend said a long time afterward. "I don't think he's gotten over it yet."

Parseghian had his revenge soon enough, though. The
following year, Larry Conjar matched the modern Notre
Dame record with four touchdowns to lead the Irish to a
28-7 romp over the Trojans and their All-American runner,
Mike Garrett. In 1966, the Irish returned to Los Angeles
and administered a blistering 51-0 defeat, the worst humiliation in Trojan history, and the Southern Californians

could blame the Battle of '64 for that embarrassing loss.
Mindful of the agonizing defeat in the same Coliseum two
years before, Parseghian would take no prisoners this time.

"Before that 1966 game, Ara came into the locker room
and wasn't like himself," remembers end Jim Seymour.
"Normally he would leave the ballplayers completely
alone, except for maybe talking to the quarterbacks or the
receivers about certain plays to make sure they had them
down cold. But this time he came into the locker room, and
after we knelt down in prayer, he went over to the blackboard and wrote down '1964' and circled it and said, 'Let's
go!' "

The game was ironically similar to the 1964 game in
some respects, even down to deciding the national championship, but Parseghian was not about to blow his chance
this time.

"We're ahead 17-0 with about two minutes to go before
the half," remembers Seymour, "and Ara was going nuts at
this time. All he could see was that we were going in 17-0
at halftime, just like they did in 1964. Well, the Trojans
fumbled the ball, and Ara called time out. He wanted another touchdown to take into the dressing room. He called
over quarterback Coley O'Brien and asked him, 'How far
can you throw the ball?' and Coley said, 'Way on out to the
end zone.' And Ara said, 'All right, put it up.' He told me,
'Run out there and catch it.' And that's exactly what we
did, and we went ahead and kicked off, and they fumbled
again, and Ara said to get another one. And we went in and
got another touchdown and went in leading at halftime
something like 30-0. Ara told us at the half, 'Don't come
down.' We went out for the second half and just kept going
where we left off. And once he saw we had them beat good,
he finally pulled out the first stringers."

It is said that McKay never forgave Parseghian for that
humiliation. "There's been no love lost between Ara and
McKay," Seymour says. So it was no doubt with great satisfaction that McKay was able to spoil Notre Dame's
perfect year in 1970 with a 38-28 victory on the last day of

the regular season. Nor was it any less pleasurable for McKay to round out a perfect season in 1972 with a 45-23 whipping of Notre Dame as flamboyant Anthony Davis scored six touchdowns. Perhaps just as enjoyable for the Southern Cal coach was the 1974 game, when his Trojans came back from a 24-0 halftime deficit to bury the Fighting Irish 55-24 with a barrage of second-half touchdowns led by the irrepressible Davis.

Parseghian has had his opportunities to puncture McKay's balloon as well. In 1968, Notre Dame cost Southern Cal a perfect regular season with a 21-21 tie. In 1969, the Irish again tied the Trojans, this time by 14-14, and ruined another perfect year for Southern California. And in 1973, Notre Dame's 23-14 victory halted Southern Cal's twenty-three-game unbeaten streak.

All in all, it has boiled down to a lot of heartache and long-distance hate.

"I still think the greatest rivalry in the country is Notre Dame and Southern Cal," says Snow. "They're always screwing each other up. Seems when you're going for a national championship, one team or the other will gum up the works."

13
KANSAS—MISSOURI
The Oldest Rivalry West of the Mississippi

When the first Missouri–Kansas football game was played, overcoats were selling in Kansas City for ten dollars, men's suits for eight dollars, ladies shoes were one dollar and the price of a newspaper was two cents. The stock market was down and the corn market was up and there was a threat of war between Chile and the United States. A reward had been offered for members of the Dalton gang and in Leavenworth a man named Jack Draves had made a contract with the United States marshal to hang a convict named Benson for twenty dollars.

This rivalry goes way back.

Missouri–Kansas games started in 1891, making the series the oldest west of the Mississippi and the fifth oldest among all collegiate rivalries. The series got off the ground ahead of the airplane, preceded Marconi's invention of the wireless and spanned every war from the Spanish-American to the one in Vietnam.

But age alone has not established this as one of the nation's vintage rivalries. Along with the sense of history that is brought to every contest, there is an overriding, uncommon passion. As one writer stated: "Missouri–Kansas games have a way of bringing back memories of the border warfare between the states that supposedly ended in 1863." It has brought lofty, distinguished college leaders down to the level of the lowliest freshmen in terms of fanaticism. Before one Missouri–Kansas game in the sixties, the Kansas chancellor was heard to proclaim in the finest language of the streets: "We'll put Missouri's Tigers so far in the tank they'll never come out."

Similar feelings were exhibited in the early stages of this venerable series, when the confrontation of the student bodies on the neutral streets of Kansas City, Missouri, were every bit as competitive as the battles on the field. The series had been established in that legendary Midwestern metropolis on October 31, 1891, and played there with one exception until 1911, when the locale was moved to the campuses.

Flush with $100 profit from a game with Washington University in 1890, Missouri's first season, the Tigers were urged by their newly formed athletic association "not to meet the small schools, but to engage in activity only with schools of Missouri State University caliber." Though still scheduling such substandard opponents as Drury, Washburn and the Kansas City YMCA the following season, Missouri also began its vital relationship with the University of Kansas in a game at Kansas City's Exposition Park. The *Kansas City Star* heralded this initial meeting as the possible start of something big and proclaimed that Kansas "hopes that this game will open a more intimate relationship with their Missouri rivals and will work to this end."

The Jayhawks, however, did everything to discourage the Tigers from coming back, handing them a solid 22-8 beating before about 3,000 spectators. The *Star* reported that "Kansas outplayed the boys from Columbia at every stage. . . . They were better trained, surer kickers, safer catchers and knew what to do with the ball when they got it. Their victory was marked by more team play. . . ." A victory in that game apparently meant something even then, because after it was over, said the *Star,* "A mighty yell went up from the Kansas delegation and they broke on to the field and carried off the victorious team while the Missourians quietly disappeared."

The obvious elements of an intriguing rivalry were recognized early, for the following year the Missouri–Kansas game was shifted to Thanksgiving Day as a season-ending feature. At this game Missouri sported its first mascot, a bulldog named Grover Cleveland, but the Tigers needed more than a good-luck charm that day to combat the magic of the Kansas defense. They were only able to score once in a 12-4 loss and their only consolation was a $1,000 check.

Those beatings from Kansas became a regularity in the early years of the series, when the Jayhawks held a 13-3-2 edge over the Tigers. Kansas was clearly the superior team in this period, guided by such early coaching lights as Hector Cowan, Fielding Yost and Bert Kennedy, and led by outstanding players in the inspirational mold of Howard "Tub" Reed, Carl Pleasant and Swede Carlson. Not as distinguished in football during this era, Missouri was often the butt of jokes from Kansas. The Tigers' inefficiency against the Jayhawks was especially noted by Kansas basketball coach Phog Allen, who cracked: "Why, even the railroad is so embarrassed that it backs into Columbia."

That was all to change, however, when William W. Roper stepped off that same train to Wabash in 1909 to take the job of Missouri football coach. Greeted by 400 students, Roper's first words thoroughly delighted his audience. "I understand you want to beat Kansas," he said. Roper expressly had been recruited for just that purpose. He had played football, baseball and basketball at Princeton and was twenty-nine when he was offered $2,500 to coach the Tigers. An impressive-looking man, Roper was a lawyer, insurance salesman and a politician as well as a football coach, and he used the one-upmanship qualities from each profession to promote a winning attitude at Missouri. He relied heavily on the emotional aspect to win games. As former Princeton coach Charley Caldwell once said: "Roper felt that football was ninety percent fight and all the rest was ten percent. . . . He was wonderful in talking to the team. He was more than just a coach. He was a great man."

Roper installed a system of walking and talking football with his assistants and players on Sunday afternoons. Often, they covered eight to ten miles on these unique jaunts, and they must have learned something because the Tigers were undefeated coming into the traditional Thanksgiving Day game with Kansas in the season's finale. Both teams, in fact, were unbeaten, and Roper was at the top of his game in inspirational salesmanship for this one. One by one the head coach called Missouri's key players into his room the night before the game and said: "The alumni don't think you can beat Kansas, but I don't believe them."

Then he added a punch line that became one of the most famous in college football: "The team that won't be beat, can't be beat."

The desire to beat Kansas became an all-out team effort by the University of Missouri and its friends. "Beat Kansas" buttons were sold to raise funds to take the scrubs, the band and the cheerleaders to Kansas City. The Princeton trainer came out to help Roper, not to mention the Yale coach and former Missouri stars.

Taking Roper's words quite literally, the Tigers would not be beat that afternoon. Despite the outstanding play of Tommy Johnson, Kansas's great quarterback, Missouri managed at 12-6 victory over the Jayhawks with the help of Ted Hackney's kicking. Hackney's role was so significant that one legend persists he kicked one field goal leftfooted and the other rightfooted. However, one newspaperman, reminiscing in later years about Hackney's drop kicks of forty and thirty-five yards, mentioned only his left foot.

At a celebration that Thanksgiving night in a Kansas City hotel, someone jumped up, drink in hand, and offered a toast, proposing Roper for governor. Perhaps he would have thought twice about it had he had a crystal ball instead of a glass in his hand. Roper only stayed at Missouri that one year, turning his back on the Tigers for a bigger money offer back East from his beloved Princeton. But Roper had given Missouri something to remember in his brief stint there—the only undefeated record in the school's history and a philosophy that was hard to beat.

Missouri did better against Kansas after that, eventually assuming the lead in the series with the help of Don Faurot's long-lived administration and, in modern times, coach Dan Devine. Gwinn Henry also played an important role in helping swing the series Missouri's way, although part of it was inadvertent. Henry was the head coach in both camps. At Missouri from 1923 through 1931, he had a creditable 4-4-1 record against the Tigers' staunchest rivals. But while at Kansas from 1939 through 1942, he lost to Missouri four straight years.

The year after Roper left, the Tigers would not be beat, but they would be tied. Although by most accounts Missouri was the better team that day, the result of the 1910 game was a 5-5 standoff that provoked this editorial comment from one newspaper: "Everyone knows the Tigers were kept from winning by the robbery of the officials—not once, but many times." The most notable of the calls against Missouri was when umpire C. F. Thompson detected that Tiger center and captain, Frank Thatcher, was holding as Hackney kicked what would have been a thirty-yard field goal for the winning points.

Although fans with a Missouri viewpoint might mourn the outcome of that 1910 game, the meeting with Kansas will be far more remembered overall for its historical place in the series. It was the last game played off the campuses of the two universities until a travel restriction in World War II. Before 1911, every Kansas–Missouri game was played in Kansas City, except for one year when the locale was moved to St. Joseph, Missouri.

The 1911 game was played at Rollins Field in Columbia, Missouri, where concrete stands had been newly built and Chester L. Brewer, the Tigers' temperate coach and athletic director, had designated a "Coming Home" day for Missouri alumni. Thus it became the first "Homecoming Game" at Missouri and certainly one of the first in college football history. The Columbia Missourian ran lists daily of former students and friends planning to return. To accommodate the large army of visitors, Columbia threw open its doors, serving buffet luncheons in churches, clubs, fraternity and sorority houses and the homes of private families. The homecomers who filled Rollins Field (a record crowd of 9,000) enjoyed everything that weekend but the outcome of the game, which finished in an unsatisfying 3-3 tie. Missouri, featuring the Anderson twins, Edgar and Elmer, was denied one score by Pete Heil's spectacular first-half tackle. The Kansas safety prevented a breakaway touchdown by Missouri's Gene Hall and this was repaid in kind by Missouri when little Billy Blees made a similar game-saving tackle in the final seconds.

The increasing size of the crowds inspired Missouri University to eventually enlarge Rollins Field, and the 1919 game with Kansas featured an overflow seating capacity of 15,000. The night before the game, Missouri freshmen burned their "beanies" on the baseball ground just south of the football field and the next day, the Missouri football team defeated Kansas 16-7 to continue a marked trend in the series. The victory was Missouri's fifth against three losses along with two ties in the Kansas games dating back to 1909. The Tigers would add a sixth victory to that record by 1920 and by 1922 would win one of the most memorable games in the series.

The Missouri victory in 1922 came, uniquely enough, after Coach Tom Kelly's forced resignation in midseason. Kelly, whose Missouri team had staged a sit-down strike against him at one stage of the season for his rough tactics, had been fired after admitting to cursing and kicking a particular player.

It had been customary for former Missouri men to rally around the flag prior to the Kansas game, but nothing compared with the outpouring that preceded this contest. Even Bill Roper came back from Princeton at the invitation of Missouri friends. The pregame pep rally was unusually vocal as eight thousand people crowded into the south bleachers and the gridiron of Rollins Field. Old

Tigers such as Burton Thompson, the Missouri fullback from the 1890 team, and Oak Hunter, star of the class of 1900, echoed the winning phrase of the great Roper. The rally closed with freshmen charging to the west end of the football field to light a tall bonfire.

The next day, Missouri burned Kansas 9-7 with one of the most famous kicks in its football history, a forty-nine-yard field goal by Al Lincoln. Late in the game, with Missouri losing 7-6, the Tigers faced fourth down in a punting situation when captain Herb Bunker suggested in the huddle, "Let Link try a field goal." Under the circumstances, it was not considered the best of plays to call. The day was wet and the ball extremely heavy, yet Lincoln kicked a school-record field goal to pull the game out for Missouri, and Bunker remembers he hit the ball with such authority that "It would have been good another ten yards if the goal posts had been back on the endline where they are now."

Three years later, another late field goal played a crucial role in the series, but this time the beneficiary of the kick was Kansas. Playing the season finale on a Saturday instead of the traditional Thanksgiving Day, the Tigers and Jayhawks were tied 7-7 when Stoney Wall came off the bench and kicked a field goal for Kansas on the last play of the game. The Kansas defense was cited for notable heroism in this classic game, twice holding the Tigers within their ten-yard line in the third period. After that 10-7 triumph, the victory-hungry Kansas partisans at Lawrence charged onto the field and carried off Wall, the ball and the goal posts. This expression of joy was understandable. In the middle of one of Kansas's football depressions, this inspired Jayhawk team had not only saved the season with a victory over Missouri but spoiled an undefeated year for the hated Tigers as well.

In 1927, Kansas was playing the role of spoiler again, although the Jayhawks could not deny the Tigers a Missouri Valley Conference title that year. In another of the dramatic turnarounds that has been the hallmark of this series, Kansas upset Missouri 14-7 in the final four minutes on a thirty-seven-yard touchdown pass from Arthur Lawrence to Henry Shenk in a game that had the sideline critics howling for the head of Tiger coach Gwinn Henry. Kansas had upset the equilibrium of Missouri with a shift and some tricky faking. And because Henry had used his lighter "Pony Express" backfield rather than his heavier set of backs, called the "Steamrollers," he was the object of displeasure in the Missouri camp that day. Yet, he did win some of his critics over the next week when Missouri, unaccountably playing Oklahoma in the season's finale instead of the traditional Kansas game, beat the Sooners to win the league championship.

That Missouri Valley title, by the way, would be the last one for a long time at Columbia. The Tigers' low point included a stretch of six straight games, from 1930 through 1935, when they could not score a point against Kansas, now a stronger team under the likes of Bill Hargiss and Ad Lindsey. The games were all lost by Missouri except for a scoreless tie in 1935, a symbolic score in that Don Faurot came to Columbia that year and eventually pulled the Tigers even with the Jayhawks in the series. In his nineteen seasons at Missouri, Faurot's teams compiled an overpowering 13-4-2 record against Kansas, one of the big reasons he stayed on the job so long. Of course another one was his expert use of the split-T formation, which Faurot brought to light with his 1941 team. That year, he used it to demolish Kansas 45-6 and his team attended several Bowl games because of its astonishing power.

Before Faurot surfaced at Missouri, Kansas had clearly had its way with the Tigers, starting with a 32-0 rout in 1930 that became a *cause célèbre* between the teams. Later that season, Professor W. A. Tarr, the faculty representative at Missouri, had charged Kansas with illegal recruiting. Tarr essentially pointed to the suspected amateur status of Jim Bausch, the Olympic decathlon star and Jayhawks' irrepressible fullback who had led them to the Big Six title that year. Not long after Tarr's charges were mounted, the Big Six faculty representatives shocked the midlands with an announcement after a meeting at Columbia:

"In view of the practices at the University of Kansas in violating the rules of this conference relating to recruiting and subsidizing athletes, the other five members of this conference decline to schedule any athletic games, not now under contract, against Kansas."

Kansas immediately blasted Missouri, prompting highly regarded sports editors Sec Taylor of the neutral *Des Moines Register* and Fred Ware of the *Omaha World-Herald* to defend Missouri's vigilance. Reinstating Kansas after second thoughts, the Big Six representatives announced a stricter policy of recruiting regulations. But although Kansas was welcomed back into the fold, it is safe to say the Jayhawks did not forget that humiliation caused by a Missouri professor. The subsequent shutout string over the Tigers no doubt gave them great pleasure.

While Kansas was relishing its domination over Missouri during the early thirties, the Tigers were experiencing the bleakest period in their history. Gwinn Henry, who had given them a long period of success and stability, had suddenly fallen on hard times during this period and was forced to resign in the spring of 1932. The athletic committee approved the appointment of Lynn "Pappy" Waldorf as head coach and his brother, John, as his assistant. But the curators overruled the athletic committee and opted for a "name" coach—Notre Dame football star Frank Carideo.

Carideo, the ink barely dry on his press clippings, came to Missouri at the age of twenty-three with all the positive fervor of youth. Yet it was this same traditional youthful idealism and immaturity that eventually undermined his goals. As a player under football genius Knute Rockne, Carideo worked out of an intricate offense that took only the most talented players in the country and the most precise rhythms to execute. He hoped to install this Notre Dame system at Missouri but had neither the manpower nor the patience. His first season was a 1-7-1 disaster. In 1933, the Tigers had a 1-8 record, including an embarrassing 26-6 loss to Kirksville Teachers coached by Faurot, his eventual successor. In 1934, Carideo was winless in nine games while Waldorf was winning the Big Six championship at Kansas State and en route to greater successes.

It did not take Faurot long to improve on Carideo's record. In fact, the first three games of the 1935 season were Missouri victories and that auspicious start gave the Tigers more triumphs than they had had in the entire three-year period under Carideo. Faurot, who had played for Missouri in the twenties, couldn't hide the joy of being reunited with his alma mater. "They paid Henry $8,500, Carideo $6,500 and me, $4,500," he said recently. "Heck, I'd have come for nothing." Faurot remained as head coach until 1956, with three years out for military service, and achieved economic stability and a national reputation for having established Missouri's football program. Faurot's success was immediate against most opponents— against Kansas, it was downright astonishing. The one-time Missouri football hero did not lose to the Jayhawks in his first eight years at Columbia, beating them six times in that span before entering the military service in 1943.

Much of Faurot's success at the start was due to Paul Christman, a big, breezy, crew-cut blond campus hero who quarterbacked Missouri from 1938 through 1940. Christman carried many nicknames, including "Pitchin' Paul" for his passing expertise, the "Merry Magician" for his uncanny knack of leadership in tight situations and "Dooz" for his erratic behavior on the field. " 'Dooz' was short for 'Doozy,' " explains teammate Bud Orf. "He'd come into a huddle, see that the team was tense, and he'd loosen 'em up with something crazy . . . like, 'Hey, Bud, your zipper is open.' " Faurot gave Christman considerable leeway on the field, appointing him his unofficial "coach." The Tigers profited from this direction and Christman expressed his flexibility with many school passing records that are still standing today.

Kansas is certain to remember the 1938 game, when Christman's multifaceted talents led Missouri to a 13-7 victory. Playing the dual role of safety, the Missouri quarter-back returned a punt seventy-six yards for a touchdown after a gorgeous fake handoff to a teammate left the field virtually clear. After using his brains and his legs to tie Kansas, Christman used his arm to beat the Jayhawks with a stunning passing display in the fourth quarter. He capped the winning touchdown drive with a thirty-yard scoring pass to Jim Starmer. A writer marveled in the *Kansas City Star* that Christman had "shadow-boxed his way back to give his receivers time to get downfield." Christman finished his career in style with a personal hand in three touchdowns, 50 yards on the ground and 167 in the air, as Missouri walloped Kansas 45-20 in 1940. Wrote C. E. McBride in the *Star:* "When Coach Faurot called Christman to the Missouri bench shortly before the end of the game, the crowd stood and voiced such an ovation as no other Tiger in Missouri's gridiron history ever heard. . . ."

Caught in the universal sliding scale that affects every football team, Kansas meanwhile was on the down cycle at the end of Ad Lindsey's administration and through the futile years of former Missouri demigods Gwinn Henry and Henry Shenk. The Jayhawks had losing seasons for ten years, from 1936 through 1945, until George Sauer's strong postwar teams. By 1947, Sauer had not only produced his second straight victory over Missouri and a second straight Big Six cochampionship, but he also led Kansas to the Orange Bowl with an undefeated, high-powered team that had scored as many as eighty-six points in one game.

Much of the power source for these unusual Kansas teams came from halfback Ray Evans, a rare All-American in both basketball and football, and end Otto Schnellbacher. The privileged Jayhawks also boasted the likes of quarterback Lynne McNutt, fullback Forrest Griffith, end Dave Schmidt, guard Don Fambrough (a future Kansas coach) and tackle Don Ettinger. Faurot is likely to remember Evans more than any of them, though, for his spectacular broken-field run in the fabled 1946 Kansas–Missouri game. A Big Six cochampionship with Oklahoma was in the balance when Missouri met Kansas that day. The Tigers fumbled seven times but the thing that really killed them was the big play that Evans made seconds before the half ended. Evans faded back to pass and, rushed, he eluded tackler after tackler. As the gun went off, the brilliant Kansas halfback threaded his way sixty-five yards for a touchdown. The play stood out all the more after Kansas had recorded a tense 20-19 decision. "Several Missouri players had more than one chance to make the tackle," recalls Bill Callahan, the Missouri sports information director who acknowledges that contest, as many other respectful observers do, as "the Ray Evans game." "That was one fantastic broken-field run."

Not as spectacular as Evans's memorable run but just as effective were the extra points kicked for the Jayhawks by Fambrough, who in the seventies as Kansas coach would continue to show a knack for knocking off the Tigers. That 1946 Kansas victory, incidentally, was a landmark contest in more than one way. It was the Jayhawks' first seven-victory season since Missouri spoiled their bid for an unbeaten year in 1909 (when they had an 8-1 season). It also was Kansas' first victory at Columbia since 1934 and the first occasion that Faurot had ever lost to the Jayhawks, as player or coach.

Evans also was a last-minute man for Kansas in the 1947 game. The Jayhawks' answer to Missouri's Paul Christman, flamboyant star of an earlier era, Evans drove Kansas to a winning touchdown in the final minute. "Cool, collected and as good as cash in the bank," according to *St. Louis Post-Dispatch* sports editor Bob Broeg, Evans called the perfect plays needed to move the length of the field. Before he had sent Griffith over from the one with sixty-three seconds left on the clock, the ubiquitous Griffith had made a game-saving tackle for the Jayhawks on their four-yard line, just when it seemed that Nick Carras would score for Missouri. "For late excitement colored Red and Blue, that would match anything KU has known since Stoney Wall's final-play field goal cost MU an unbeaten season in

1925," Broeg wrote in *Ol' Mizzou,* his fine book on Missouri football.

Faurot would not lose many more to Kansas after that, in fact only two games (1951 and 1955) in the ensuing nine years. Two of his most enjoyable—and surprising—victories came in 1950 and 1956.

In 1950, heavily favored Kansas came to Columbia to play a senior-studded but disappointing Missouri team. But apparently the Jayhawks did not pack suitable cold-weather gear for the trip and at kickoff time, the temperature had dropped to seventeen degrees. "Don Faurot had gotten long underwear for our players," remembers Callahan, "but apparently Kansas wasn't prepared for any cold weather like that. It was so bitterly cold . . . that we even issued emergency wool socks to anyone in our unheated press box who wanted them—and we had plenty of takers."

Chuck Hoag, one of the frostbitten Jayhawk backs, fumbled on the game's first play, but Missouri recovered and that set the tempo of the game. Frozen-fingered Kansas lost a total of eight fumbles that day—and the Tigers pulled off a 20-6 upset.

The 1956 game provided a storybook ending for Faurot's storybook career as Missouri coach. The contest seemed destined to end in a 13-13 tie with less than two minutes left and Kansas in possession of the ball deep in its own territory. Kansas Coach Chuck Mather misjudged the precise placement of the ball, however, and called for a daring, deep reverse from the Jayhawk four-yard line. (He later explained he thought the ball was on the nine.) Wally Strauch, the Kansas quarterback, slipped the ball to Bobby Robinson but Missouri defensive tackle Chuck Mehrer read the misdirection, barreled across the goal line and dumped Robinson in the end zone for a two-point safety and a 15-13 Missouri victory. That night at a cocktail party, one of many in Columbia where exuberant Missouri fans were toasting the victory, an alumnus made this long-remembered observation to Faurot:

"Well, Don, you lose some—you win some—and every once in a while, one washes up on the beach."

Similar hairbreadth decisions were not uncommon after Faurot's departure. In 1961 Ron Taylor came off the bench and led Missouri to a 10-7 decision. In 1963 (in the midst of a six-game winless Kansas string against Missouri), the Tigers got a superb effort from Gary Lane and beat the Jayhawks 9-7 on a field goal by Bill Leistritz. In 1966, Missouri won 7-0 on a long pass play from Gary Kombrink to Earl Denny. "As much as the play itself," says Callahan, "I remember a Missouri cheerleader running along the sideline—almost keeping up with Denny." In 1968, both schools had excellent teams and played a classic game in Columbia, with Kansas great Bobby Douglass leading Pepper Rodgers's Jayhawks to a tingling 21-19 victory and an Orange Bowl berth.

One of the most notable of the games in this series, at least from the Kansas standpoint, occurred in 1960 when the Jayhawks spoiled Missouri's only chance for a national championship. Ranked Number One in both the Associated Press and United Press International polls, Missouri had only to beat Kansas to finish the season undefeated and keep an Orange Bowl date with Navy. The fever of a possible national title seized the town of Columbia, where even business offices, houses and the radio station answered the phone with: "We're Number One."

If they were, the Kansas football team was not very far behind. The Jayhawks had a tremendously talented team, including three future professional stars—John Hadl, Curtis McClinton and the controversial Bert Coan. They also had a professional-like defense and this proved to be the undoing of Missouri. Kansas stacked a nine-man line against Dan Devine's famous power-sweep play and limited the Tigers to just sixty-one yards on the ground, about 220 under their lofty average. "He was just daring us to pass," Callahan remembers. "We didn't—and we lost." Devine later second-guessed himself on other counts, suggesting that he permitted too many distractions before the

Kansas game and worked a weary squad too hard, depriving the Tigers of a freshness needed to beat a team of such stature.

Ironically, Kansas had to forfeit that 23-7 victory, along with the Big Eight championship. The Jayhawks had defied the league by using Coan in their backfield when the brilliant runner was not eligible.

Devine got even for that bitter defeat many times in the subsequent decade, but never as conclusively as in 1969, when his Tigers buried Rodgers's Jayhawks under an avalanche of touchdowns, 69-21. Rodgers thought that day that Devine had poured it on because of an Orange Bowl bid in the offing, but one could not help suspect that the Missouri coach was thinking back to a dreary November afternoon in 1960 when Kansas cost him a national championship.

Rodgers was quoted later as saying that when he tried to give Devine "the peace sign," the Missouri coach only returned "half of it" from the opposite sidelines.

14
HARVARD-YALE
The Game

Once in the cathedral hush before a Yale–Harvard game, Eli coach Tad Jones is alleged to have told his players: "You are about to play football for Yale. Never again in your lives will you do anything so important."

A couple of world wars have since passed, and America has had several flings at depression and inflation, but the feeling about The Game persists still in those two Ivy League bastions of tradition.

The Yale–Harvard rivalry still is called The Game in deference to its elite stature in the proud Ivies. It remains one of the strongest tribal rites in American football, despite its usual lack of importance in the national standings.

The annual renewal of the Yale–Harvard game inspires an atavistic seasonal excitement each fall, sparking a heavy migration to either New Haven, Connecticut, or Cambridge, Massachusetts. The pull of history, the appeal of school spirit, the social ritual and the clan feelings all are part of the tradition of The Game.

Harvard and Yale were once the Greece and Rome of college football and have been playing one another since 1875. Their contests once decided national championships, produced a new philosophy (the flying wedge), built impressive monuments (the Yale Bowl) and dominated foreign powers (in 1919 Harvard won the Rose Bowl).

The Game brought out uncommon ferocity in everyone concerned. According to legend, a turn-of-the-century Harvard coach inspired his players without uttering a phrase. While they watched in mounting frustration, he slowly and silently choked a bulldog to death and tossed

217

the carcass at their feet. Perhaps the most rabid Harvard fan was John Reed, Class of '10, who wrote a vitriolic song proposing to "twist the bulldog's tail" and "call up the hearse for dear old Yale."

While much of the game's national significance has since evaporated, along with such examples of warlike ferocity, the Harvard–Yale rivalry remains a focal point each year, both as a contest and a social event.

There are rousing reunions, widespread and fervent partying and peripheral sporting contests to go along with the main event.

As game time nears, the pace quickens.

"Before kickoff," writes Roger Angell, "the fields and streets that encircle Yale Bowl will look like a state fair in full swing. Station-Wagon tailgates become picnic tables. Hampers, charcoal grills, folding chairs, steamer rugs, and Thermoses are unpacked. The cocktails begin to flow— Martinis, mostly. Friends are recognized, greetings fly from group to group. Vendors do a brisk business in pennants and programs, and crimson and blue feathers. There is a thump and tootle from somewhere in the distance, where one of the bands is warming up and a picnicker, keeping warm, finds himself stamping his feet in time to, 'Good night, Poor Harvard,' or 'Harvardiana.' "

The cheers battle each other across the field and the long howls begin: "Goooo Har-varrdd, beat Yay-ell!" Then the two bands form together on the field, a huge "Y" locked inside a huge "H," and play the National Anthem.

In addition to his ticket, his program and his flask, every graduate in the stands brings with him his own personal scrapbook of memories. Many can still recall the days, before World War I, when the Harvard–Yale game was of national importance. Often then, their squads would contain an abundance of All-American players. Usually both teams were undefeated and the winner would be certified as the best in the country.

Harvard and Yale had been playing somewhat different

versions of football when they first met at New Haven's Hamilton Park in 1875. The "concessionary rules" agreed upon before the contest somewhat favored Harvard's rugby style of play over Yale's soccerlike game. Indicating the tenor of football in that era, the rules that day specified that "the player carrying the ball may be tackled or shouldered, but not hacked, throttled or pummeled."

The Harvard men wore knee britches, crimson shirts and stockings; the Yales, yellow caps, blue shirts and dark trousers. There were fifteen men on a side and Harvard won by four goals and four touchdowns to nothing.

In 1876, Walter Camp made his debut for Yale and forever changed the face of football, not to mention tormenting Harvard as both a player and coach. As the story goes, the Harvard captain approached the Yale captain before the 1876 game, pointed to a small Yale back and snarled, "You don't mean to let that child play, do you?"

"Look to your business," was the reply from the Yale man. "He may be small, but he is all spirit and a whipcord."

Camp was to become the greatest figure in the sport during his time and for some time afterward. He played halfback for five years, captained the Yale team for two seasons, and coached from 1888 to 1892. Camp helped invent and standardize the basic rules of the game, and took personal charge of the All-American teams in his lifetime. It is hard to speak of Camp's value to Yale football and the college sport in general without indulging in superlatives. But one of Yale's football captains of the early 1900s summed up Camp's overpowering influence in this way:

"When we want to know how the Yale team is doing at any time, we don't go to the newspapers to find out. It makes very little difference to us what the players are doing; we want to know what the coaches are doing evenings. If they are going up to Walter's every night, then we know the team is going to be a good one."

Harvard felt Camp's influence instantaneously. The

brilliance of Yale's little "whipcord" outshone the Crimson's gaudy colors and started a string of eleven Eli victories that finally ended in 1890. After that, Camp's hand was also felt as Yale ran off another string of five and bolted to an early 16-2 lead in the series.

As far as Harvard was concerned, he was the first of a long list of brilliant Yale stars who was to plague the Crimson for the first thirty-six years of the series. During this period Yale won all but five games, led by men like "Pa" Corbin, "Pudge" Heffelfinger, Amos Alonzo Stagg, "Bum" McClung (later treasurer of the United States), Frank Hinkey (four years All-American and called the greatest football player who ever lived), Tom Shevlin and Ted Coy. While Harvard was not able to win many games from Yale during the early years, its players were able to win All-American recognition. The Crimson had its own early luminaries—Marshall Newell, Bernie Trafford, Ben Dibblee, Percy Haughton and Charles Daley.

Harvard was not that bad during this time; it was just that Yale was a little bit better. Ten times between 1876 and 1906 Yale spoiled an otherwise perfect season for Harvard. Yale's power during this period was awesome. After a 12-6 defeat by Harvard in 1890, Yale ran through thirty-five games without giving a single point to opponents and scored 1,265 points in the process.

One of the big reasons for this Yale domination of Harvard and just about every one else was Heffelfinger, not only Yale's best lineman but an athlete some considered the finest guard who ever played the game. Placed on every all-time, All-American team, Heffelfinger was the tower of strength in the middle of Yale's immovable line.

"He stood in an almost erect stance that allowed him to slip blockers and plunge into the enemy backfield," an observer says. "Although his playing weight of 190 to 200 pounds made him a large man for his day, he was always the fastest lineman on the field, which meant that he led most offensive plays and even carried the ball on occasion."

Long after he graduated, Heffelfinger proved that his legendary tales were not exaggerated. For more than forty years, he would come back to New Haven intermittently and scrimmage with the Yale varsity, dumping brash young giants on their backs. When he was sixty-three years old, he played in an exhibition football game, displaying the same exuberance, if not the power, of his younger, gaudier days.

Heffelfinger was one of many titans who came back year after year to teach successors the violent traditions of early football. In 1892, Harvard introduced the controversial flying wedge, but it didn't help the Crimson beat Yale. The following season, Camp adapted the deadly formation to his team and a player named Butterworth used it to carry the ball over the goal for a 6-0 Yale victory. Characteristically, the genius of Camp so disguised the formation that Harvard itself was not able to recognize it during the game.

The monstrous power of the flying wedge typified the ruthlessness of the college game of that era, and the Harvard–Yale battles were stereotypes of this kind of action. The 1894 game was marked by so many bloody sluggings and broken bones that even the fans became indignant. The public uproar caused such a commotion that the colleges were forced to call off the series until 1897. That game resulted in a mighty scoreless tie, highlighted by Percy Haughton's remarkable eighty-six-yard punt through the rain. The standoff with Yale so disappointed Harvard's players, hitherto unbeaten and untied, that they refused to vote themselves varsity letters that year. They felt a lot better about things after a conclusive 17-0 victory the following season.

Football grew wildly after the turn of the century, though still marked by roughness and damaged by public outcry. By 1906 President Theodore Roosevelt threatened to abolish the sport by congressional decree unless new rules were instituted to make football safer and saner. Ironically, the changes that were made might have been different had it not been for Harvard's handsome new stadium, which had been dedicated in 1903. One of the proposed new rules suggested that fields be made a full forty feet wider, leaning toward a lateral, more rugbylike game. Harvard protested, however, pointing out that its stadium was not wide enough to permit this innovation. The rulesmakers capitulated and instead legalized the forward pass, which was to become the basis for modern football.

The game's savagery was considerably lessened after the change of rules, but it was not an overnight occurrence. In the 1909 Harvard–Yale game, blood still flowed, and an excited spectator later said: "At one point of play the two lines were right opposite me. . . . It was the most magnificent sight I ever saw! Every lineman's face was dripping with blood!"

That 1909 game, incidentally, is still considered by old grads to be one of the best ever played between the teams. Ted Coy's unscored-on Yale team defeated Hamilton Fish's Harvard eleven 8-0 in a battle of unbeaten national powers. It was not only one of the best games between Harvard and Yale but also proved to be a turning point in the series, for it marked the end of Yale's dominance. With that victory, Yale had won twenty-two games, lost but five and tied three with Harvard. But in succeeding years, the series would be more evenly matched. In fact, Harvard would hold a slight edge in the seasons that followed.

The change in Harvard's fortunes was brought about mostly by one man, Percy D. Haughton, the former Crimson star, called by some the "first modern football coach." Harvard, which had failed to score on Yale for six straight years after 1901, installed Haughton as its coach in 1908. In Haughton's first year, Harvard achieved an undefeated season culminated by Vic Kennard's left-footed drop kick that beat Yale, 4-0. And after the 1909 defeat

and two scoreless ties, Haughton's Harvards rolled past
Yale for four straight seasons with power and precision
hitherto unseen in American football. In that four-year
stretch, Harvard amazingly outscored mighty Yale 112-5.

Two precedents were set in the 1914 game. Harvard's
36-0 score marked its most lopsided margin in the series
until that point, and the opening of the Yale Bowl attracted
the largest crowd. Although the name itself might have
been considered somewhat undignified by a few, the Bowl
compared favorably in capacity and grace to a Roman am-
phitheater.

Not lost in the immensity of the gargantuan Bowl were
the accomplishments of Haughton. The final score, said
the one writer, "represents the culmination of Mr.
Haughton's efforts in building up a football organization
at Harvard on sound principles and thorough groundwork.
The result of this game is ample testimony for the efficiency
that comes from one-man control of a college's football
policy—particularly if that man happens to be a Mr.
Haughton."

Haughton was one of the leading innovators of his day
and his major contributions to college football included
such unique ideas as the unbalanced backfield, spinner
plays, shifting defenses, five-man defensive lines, defensive
signals and the mousetrap. The "Haughton System" was
built on timing, speed and the perfect execution of relatively few plays. But Haughton's success was built on his total
control over the Harvard players. They always called him
"Mr. Haughton" and practice sessions under this iron-
fisted ruler made game day pleasant by contrast.

"Haughton had a name for each week of practice," said
one observer. "After 'Speed Week' and the hellish 'Fight
Week,' he would relax his players for Yale with the final
'Joy Week.' "

Haughton was fanatically painstaking on the field. Believing that women had better eyes than men, he installed
ladies on the sidelines as Harvard ran plays to see if they
could spot the ball. There is the story that he also tried to

do the same thing with dogs as spotters but it has never been confirmed.

An army of All-Americans marched out of Harvard during Haughton's illustrious time there, including such immortals as Sam Felton, Stan Pennock, Tack Hardwick, Charley Brickley, Packy Mahan and Eddie Casey. They helped Haughton produce one of the best percentage records in college football history (71-7-5) and changed the face of coaching in his era. Yale, for one, stopped encouraging Old Blues to come up and "help the boys" but instead turned over the coaching reins to full-time professionals. Haughton's successor, Bob Fisher, used his system to defeat Yale four straight times and produce an undefeated team in 1919 that went on to win the Rose Bowl game.

Heavy betting, ticket-scalping, Saturday alcoholism and similar foolish excesses marked the Harvard–Yale series in the coon-coat decade of the twenties. Every game in the Yale Bowl was a sellout of 74,000 and it was during this time that Tad Jones could inspire his Elis with stirring speeches and pure college corn.

The fiery confrontations on the field were no more explosive than those among the fanatical flock. After Jones' 1923 team beat Harvard 13-0 to finish the season undefeated, some 800 riotous Elis poured out of the Yale Club in New York City, formed a procession behind a band and marched over to the Harvard Club to rub it in. That game, incidentally, was among the wildest and wettest in the series. The teams, lashed by an unrelenting rain, fumbled a total of twenty-five times and there were fifty-four punts in the game. The difference was Yale's appropriately named Ducky Pond, who scooped up a Harvard fumble and squirmed sixty-eight yards for a touchdown through the Crimson's reservoirlike stadium. A blocked kick and fumble set up Memphis Bill Mallory's two second-half field goals for Yale's other points.

The golden twenties featured not only a rivalry between these two great teams, but also a personal rivalry between two great backs—Yale's little Albie Booth and Harvard's

Barry Wood. Wood, considered one of the best athletes in Harvard's history, had the better of these duels, passing and running the Crimson to three victories over the Bulldogs from 1928 to 1930. Booth, however, had the last laugh when he drop-kicked a field goal that won the 1931 game for Yale, 3-0.

The early thirties marked a turning point for Ivy League football. As viewed from the East, the excesses of the new football factories in the South and Midwest—athletic scholarships, coaches hung in effigy and the Bowl-game fever—seemed of dubious value. Horrified by these seemingly overblown proportions, Ivy League directors stemmed the tide in their area by de-emphasizing college football. The hours of varsity practice were cut down, intramural sports programs were built up, and rules were toughened to guarantee the amateur status of their football players.

This wholesale de-emphasis in Ivy League football did not mean a de-emphasis in the intensity of the Harvard–Yale rivalry. The Game continued without any drop in ferocity or excitement. Harvard later revenged its bitter 1931 disappointment by whipping an unbeaten Yale team 13-6 at Harvard Stadium in 1937. Clint Frank put on one of the greatest shows in a losing cause by making tackles all over the field. But the Crimson, beautifully coached by Dick Harlow, rose above his superb performance at the end.

The Game, with its last vestiges of national significance squirting away, was stopped cold by World War II. When it resumed in the postwar years, Yale assumed command of the series. This was largely due to the fact that the Elis had not abandoned varsity football during the war, while Harvard had to start again from scratch. Actually both squads were lacking compared with the kind of talent found at other schools in the country. In the fifties, when the emphasis on Ivy League football was played down completely, a spirit of rampant amateurism became evident.

In the 1952 game, Yale used a 135-pound student manager by the name of Chuck Yeager to catch the final touchdown pass in a 41-14 romp over Harvard. The hopped-up Yalies carried the new hero off the field in triumph, pummeling and pounding him as though he had scored the deciding point. In 1957, Harvard coach John Yovicsin found his team so riddled by injuries that he had to play a junior varsity quarterback through most of the Yale game. The resulting carnage was so complete that midway through Yale's 54-0 rout, the Harvard Club of Boston sent Yale coach John Olivar a one-word telegram: "PLEASE."

The talent was more equally distributed among the two teams in the sixties, when Yale and Harvard reached a new peak in competitiveness. In one eight-year period, from 1962 through 1969, each school won four games and the biggest margin of victory by either was no more than seventeen points, the precise total by which Harvard outscored Yale in this stretch, 117-100. Two of the most exciting games in the series were played during this time, including one that is considered one of college football's all-time classics, the 29-29 tie in 1968.

Characteristic of this frenzied era, Yale won an electric 24-20 decision in 1967 in the closing minutes on a long, last-chance pass by Brian Dowling, the Elis' newest hero. Dowling did not cut a classic football player's figure. His smooth muscles and relaxed carriage suggested a country-club athlete and his dark eyes and slightly curly hair reminded one of a choirboy. His remark about the winning touchdown pass against Harvard in 1967 showed a dry sense of humor: "The law of averages was with me because I'd thrown so many bad ones earlier."

Dowling was a junior quarterback in 1967 who could run just fast enough to get away from people and throw just well enough to complete the big passes. As one writer observed, his passes "were unpretty but effective." Dowling had resurrected a fresh football spirit at Yale that year. Although he missed the first three games of the season with injury, he eventually led the Bulldogs to the Ivy League championship and was the primary reason that the venerable Yale Bowl creaked with 68,000 fans for the Harvard game.

The enthusiasm in the stands matched the emotional level on the field as Yale and Harvard swarmed after one another in the mud and cold air of New Haven. Dowling was characteristically imperfect, but somehow got the job done. In his first five tries, he had two passes intercepted and no completions. Yet, he eventually led Yale to a 17-0 lead through a maze of mistakes.

Yale managed its first touchdown drive after Dowling finally hit on a pass to end Bruce Weinstein in the middle of a mudhole. Encouraged, Yale continued to slosh down the field and scored an inartistic six points as halfback Jim Fisher fumbled over the goal line and the ball plopped into the hands of Bulldog end Del Marting. In the second quarter, Dowling appeared trapped as he faded back to pass from his own forty-seven, but scrambled through a mosaic of blue and red uniforms and threw a pass to halfback Calvin Hill, who took the ball fifty-three yards for another Yale touchdown. "We do that a lot," Hill later explained. "It's kind of a play. Dowling gets in trouble and I wave my hand and he throws it to me."

A field goal soon provided Yale with a 17-0 lead and all indications pointed to a rout, but the complexion of the game inexplicably turned in the next twenty minutes or so. Led by the running of Ric Zimmerman, Vic Gatton and Ray Hornblower, Harvard scored on three long touchdown drives to move ahead 20-17. Near the end, Yale's position looked quite hopeless, the ball sitting on its own twenty-three yard line with the clock ticking away. But a minute or so was enough for the confident Dowling. "I knew we would score," he said later, even though at that point Dowling had thrown more completions to Harvard than he had to Yale. He had been intercepted four times.

Dowling trotted on the field, appearing almost indifferent, and directed the Bulldogs to the thirty-four-yard line for a first down in two deft plays. Then in the huddle, he called the next play: "Sprint right on two." Marting, his head lowered and limbs rotating, motored down the field as directed by his quarterback and Dowling unloaded a desperation fifty-yard pass that settled in his receiver's eager hands. Marting finished the sixty-six-yard dash for the goal line to provide Yale with a 24-20 victory.

Dowling was also the center of attention for most of the 1968 game, but his gallantry was eventually lost in the story of that spectacular Harvard comeback, which ranks with the most dramatic in college football history.

As the 1968 Harvard–Yale game approached, it was ballyhooed as perhaps the best match in the long history of the series. It had good reason to be typecast that way. Both teams went into the game with 8-0 records. Yale, with sixteen straight victories, sported the nation's longest winning streak. Harvard's defense, called the "Boston Stranglers," was leading the nation in fewest points allowed—sixty-one. The Bulldogs, meanwhile, ranked third in total offense.

The pregame rhetoric from both camps was, predictably enough, heated.

"The biggest reason Harvard is Number One in defense," snarled Yale tackle Tom Bass, "is because they haven't played us yet."

John Emery, the tough, 200-pound Harvard linebacker with a Fu Manchu moustache, countered: "We hope to hit them hard real early, just so they will know."

Led by the ubiquitous Emery, the Crimson defense had allowed the opposition only four touchdowns in a five-game span. "The experts said this was going to be our first losing season," crowed Harvard coach Yovicsin, "but there is something about putting a challenge to Harvard."

In contrast to Harvard's seemingly bleak prospects for the season, Yale's chances had been rated every bit as good as its ultimate record. Most of the Bulldogs' big offensive stars were back from the 1967 Ivy League champions, including Dowling and Hill, two of the best pro prospects in the conference. Dowling, immortalized in a comic strip in the New York *Daily News,* had broken more records than fictitious Yaleman Frank Merriwell. He had completed fifty-seven percent of his passes for 1,438 yards and seventeen touchdowns. He also scrambled for an additional 258 yards. Hill handled much of Yale's running attack, rushing for 588 yards in only 115 carries. In addition, he caught twenty passes for a phenomenal 504 yards and led the Ivy League in scoring.

Scalpers seized the opportunity to make big money on The Game, charging alumni $50 to $175 for a pair of tickets to sit in tired, old Harvard Stadium. One of the 40,280 fans, it was said, paid $1,000 for a block of eight seats. Cambridge was hit by a blizzard of electronic- and print-media stories. Closed-circuit television was hooked up to New Haven, New York, Boston, Washington and Philadelphia. And some 250 journalists, long-accustomed to deriding Ivy League football, poured into town.

What everyone expected at the beginning was a Yale rout as Dowling and Hill helped roll up a 22-0 score and the heralded, classic battle was turning into a laugher at Harvard's stadium. Finally, desperately, Yovicsin turned to Frank Champi, his second-string quarterback. "O.K.," the Harvard coach said, "you try it for a while." Most everyone in the stadium was surprised to see the inexperienced quarterback in a game of such importance, and that included the Harvard football team itself.

"We knew Frank had the arm," said guard Tom Jones, "but we felt he was a little inexperienced for the job. He was a junior and he was sort of nervous all year."

"Frankly, we were surprised to see him," admitted Harvard captain Vic Gatto. "He hadn't played a whole lot that year, and confidence is something you get by playing, not sitting on the bench. But we needed to be shaken up, and he did it."

The first shake Champi gave Harvard was a flip of his wrist, and it resulted in a pretty, fifteen-yard touchdown pass to Bruce Freeman with thirty-nine seconds left in the first half. The Crimson was betrayed by a poor snap from center on the attempted conversion and went into the locker room at halftime trailing 22-6. Despite a sixteen-point deficit, it was a confident locker room.

"At halftime I knew we could win," said Yovicsin. "I told our boys that all we had to do was shut out Yale while getting two touchdowns and a field goal."

The Harvard players felt they could win, too, but not out of any loyalty to the school or to the coach, who was not the most popular man on the team in that particular time zone.

"We weren't playing for him [Yovicsin] and we weren't playing for the school, we were playing for ourselves," said one of the Crimson's twenty-two seniors. "Before this season the majority of the seniors on this team almost walked out. We'd been the forgotten guys on this club. Ever since our freshman year we'd been ignored. We changed our minds about walking out after Vic Gatto was elected captain. We held a meeting in January and decided to rally around Vic, to play for ourselves. We wanted to show the school, the coaches and the experts that we were a lot better than any of them gave us credit for. And we have."

When the second half opened, George Lalich, Harvard's regular quarterback, returned to action for three inoffensive plays and Yovicsin once again resurrected Champi after Yale fumbled the ball back to the Crimson. Harvard took over in first-rate field position on the Yale twenty-five and three plays later, Champi directed a touchdown drive that ended with fullback Gus Crim drilling into the end zone.

The conversion cut Yale's once-significant lead to 22-13 and the crowd began to stir.

Yale fumbled two more times in the third quarter and while Harvard could not convert those mistakes into points, the Crimson was now sure that the Bulldogs were not invincible. Harvard, in fact, had achieved a victory of sorts at this point, stopping Yale's scoring streak, which had reached twenty-two quarters before the Crimson shut down the Bulldogs in the third period. The teams went into the fourth quarter with Yale holding a 22-13 lead, but Harvard holding a noticeable psychological edge.

Perhaps stung by the end of the scoring streak, Dowling started a new one for Yale. It took just eight plays for the Bulldogs to cross the goal line, the inimitable Dowling hauling the ball over on a five-yard rollout. Now Yale coach Carmen Cozza glanced at the scoreboard: Yale 28, Harvard 13. Cozza shrugged and waved in Bob Bayless to kick the extra point, which he did. Earlier Cozza had ordered a two-point conversion after Yale's third touchdown, which Dowling had picked up on a pass to Marting.

"After the third touchdown," said Cozza, "I figured two points would put it out of reach. After the fourth one, I figured what difference does it make? There was no way they could come back. No way they could win."

Cozza's logic appeared mistake-proof. In order to lose the lead, Yale would have to relinquish two touchdowns and a pair of two-point conversions in the space of ten minutes and forty-four seconds. Ten minutes later, the odds had escalated considerably in Yale's favor. The score was still 29-13 in favor of the Elis, only now there was less than a minute remaining in the game and Harvard's chances of erasing that deficit were slight.

Slight for everyone, that is, but Frank Champi.

With Yale rooters waving handkerchiefs and screaming across the field, "You're Number Two," Champi set out to disprove Cozza's theory of conversions. Normally the space-time continuum would not allow for a tied game in those circumstances, but an unlikely chain of events followed. They were triggered by the Yale fans themselves.

"When they started waving those white hankies and yelling," said Gatto, "it got to us."

Champi, a balding, twenty-year-old history major who could throw a football eighty-five yards with his right arm and fifty yards with his left, rallied his troops. Harvard drove downfield with the help of a Yale holding penalty and with forty-two seconds left, Champi threw a fifteen-yard touchdown pass to Freeman. Another Yale penalty gave Harvard two cracks at a two-point conversion and Crim got it the second time for the Crimson on a run.

Yale's lead was now down to 29-21, but only a fanatic would still have given Harvard a chance. The Crimson's only opportunity for a storybook ending would be for Yale to fumble the kickoff, and for Harvard to go in for a lightning touchdown and then pull off another two-point conversion.

"Utterly impossible," said one observer.

But utterly the case.

Harvard booted an onside kick and this was fumbled by a big, lumbering Yale lineman and recovered by the Crimson's Billy Kelly on the Bulldog forty-nine. With Champi running for fourteen yards and getting fifteen more on a face-mask penalty, Harvard eventually advanced to Yale's eight-yard line. Now there were three seconds left. Champi scrambled back and after outrunning a horde of blue shirts, hurled a touchdown pass to Gatto as time ran out.

"What should we do?" screamed an exuberant Harvard fan. "Go for the two points and a tie or settle for one point and a loss?"

"Are you crazy?" shot back another sitting in the Harvard sector.

"Yes! Yes! Yes!"

Champi had the proper Harvard prospective, even though he was drained at this point.

"By this time," said the Harvard quarterback, "I was so tired, I wasn't even nervous."

And so, tiredly, Champi passed to Pete Varney for two points and a stupefying 29-29 tie. But it was a loss as far as Yale was concerned, and this was pointed out in a headline and explained in faultless logic in an editorial the next day in Harvard's campus newspaper, the *Crimson*. The headline read, "Harvard Beats Yale 29-29" and the editorial said:

> Rarely has justice dispensed itself with such timing. Who will remember the team that lumbered ahead to a lopsided lead in the first half? No one. Who can forget the team that

cut the lead to shreds in the last forty-two seconds of the game?

For its efforts, Harvard can lay claim to more than a draw. All save the most fearless of the gambling partisans won their bets and all save the most underhanded of the nation's newspapers (one thinks of the *Yale Daily News*) will surely see fit to play Cambridge well over New Haven in the headlines.

A draw in name only, then. By every other reckoning, a magnificent victory.

Dowling subconsciously sees it that way, too, sometimes. In retrospective conversation about The Game of 1968, he refers to the tie as "the first time I lost at Yale." There is still a trace of bitterness and frustration over that game, and some critics feel he should harbor a feeling of guilt as well. It was Dowling's choice of profligate play-calling in the fourth quarter, rather than a more prudent style of eating up the clock, that probably cost Yale the game. But there were certainly other crucial factors involved, and Dowling is quick to point them out.

"I don't want to take anything from Champi," he says today, "but he fumbled once [Champi says it was a lateral] and his tackle ran twenty-three yards; and that face-mask penalty wasn't any of his doing, either. He didn't pull it out; his team did."

The interference call on Harvard's first two-point conversion continues to irk Dowling, but possibly even more annoying is the mystery of the stopped clock in that last, seemingly eternal minute. Specifically, Dowling recalls Harvard's onside kick near the end, which consumed no time at all on the clock.

"It should have taken at least three seconds to stop and start the clock on the kick," Dowling insists.

Of course those three seconds loom large considering that Champi got his last hike at the three-second mark.

"It just seems that too many calls went their way in the closing minutes," says Dowling, shaking his head. "Not just one call, all of them."

The officials would win no popularity contests in the Yale camp, who looked upon their efforts as strictly partisan. Cozza recites a game-ending story in this regard:

> The referee ran into the Yale locker room looking very scared. "What's the matter, ref?" asked the Yale trainer.
> "Those Yale fans are going to kill me," he replied.
> "Don't you believe in reincarnation?"
> "What's that?" asked the referee.
> "Oh, I can see you returning to earth as a blade of grass. Some cow will come along and munch on you. Then he'll deposit you out his other end. And if I run into you, I'll say, 'Gee, ref, you haven't changed a bit.' "

Cozza's resentment about the officiating still surfaces. "You know how you feel when you're robbed?" he demands. "We *were* robbed. They were looking for bad things to call against us. Harvard had momentum, but they had help. I don't question the integrity of the officials, but they sure as hell got caught up in the emotion of the game. They lost their poise. One of them was president of the Boston Gridiron Club. He was bound to know those Harvard kids."

The matter, however, was entirely out of the officials' hands, if you listen to Champi. He still believes that something unearthly was involved in the affair, and he traces the result to heavenly design. On November 23, 1968, his sun and moon and planets were in the right place and the right time, he insists.

"Astrologically, it was a big day," says Champi.

Embellishing his metaphysical thoughts on that bizarre 1968 game, Champi reflects: "I believe in karma, reincarnation and God. God is divine consciousness and we are sparks of that consciousness. Okay, I see the game in mystical terms. A mystic creates an event by thought. There was a lot of thinking in those stands. It wasn't just the team. Thousands of people wanted us to win."

And what of the intentions of the Yale fans?

"Their energy gave out," Champi explains. "They were

thinking ahead to the victory parties. Therefore, the Harvard fans helped create the tie."

Despite his fierce single-mindedness in the area of officiating, Coach Cozza from time to time gives the supernatural aspect of The Game some serious thought.

"Somebody up there wanted it to happen," he says remorsefully.

15
STANFORD—CALIFORNIA
The Big Game

If we beat Cal every day and twice on Sundays, it wouldn't be enough.

—*Stanford's Don Liebendorfer*

In California, it's known as "Harvard-Yale West," in deference to its widely recognized stature as a somewhat intellectual rivalry. But in all seriousness, the Stanford–California series is that and more, a mélange of many of the good things that college football has to offer.

In truth, both schools are way up there by most academic yardsticks and have produced their share of Noble Prize winners and professional giants. Perhaps the aura of this stunning intellectuality has pervaded the football field itself, bringing an air of tidy civilization to the so-called "Big Game." It is a superb rivalry, to be sure, but one that has for the most part disdained bitterness and violence. As Pappy Waldorf tells it, "I've never seen a questionable play in the series in my years of coaching at California. The series has always been very intense, but always cleanly played, and there's a warm feeling in it. Many times I've seen players walk off the field together after a game. It is a beautiful rivalry."

As a social event, there is probably none bigger in the Bay Area during the last week of the football season. "It's a high point of the student season," says Waldorf. "More classes have a reunion at the time of the Big Game than at graduation time. It means more than just a football game."

Dave Maggard, California's athletic director, describes it as "a happening. It's a game between two great institutions with the same educational philosophy. We're close geographically as well and traditionally, the game brings together a lot of people who work together in the San Francisco Bay area. It's almost a social event as much as a football game."

Enhancing the sportsmanlike atmosphere engendered by these two neighborly California universities has been the quality of play in the game itself. Few rivalries can claim as many pulsating finishes or unbearably close encounters as this one has had in more than eight decades of football. Of the eighty games played through 1977, thirty-seven were decided by a touchdown or less and there were ten ties in this remarkably even series. Stanford held a 37-32 edge in victories and in points led, 1,053 to 1,051.

The Big Game invariably means a big crowd, whether it is played in Berkeley or Palo Alto. Almost without exception, through fat years or lean, capacity crowds have been at every one of these games dating back to 1892 when underdog Stanford pulled off a 14-10 upset in the series opener. Waldorf, a student of football history as well as one of the sport's greatest teachers, points out that the Stanford–Cal series was a crowd magnet from the opening kickoff.

"They hadn't anticipated the crowd they got at that first game," he says, "and they soon ran out of tickets. Admission stubs had to be put in boxes, barrels and tubs, there were so many of them."

Herbert Hoover, later to become President of the United States, was the manager of the Stanford football team that day, and he managed to do everything right but bring a football. Thus the first game of the series was held up and the crowd fidgeted while the proprietor of a local sporting goods store rode back to town to get a ball. Despite forgetting the ball, Hoover did an excellent job of running the gate, and the game netted a nice profit for both schools.

"It wasn't even a complete football that they used," chuckles Waldorf. "It was only the bladder. And California always claimed that was the reason they lost that first game. Of course, Stanford had to use it, too."

They had a better football the second time they met, in December of the same season. "Stanford got football authority Walter Camp to coach and California brought in Thomas McClung, who was later to become U.S. Secretary of the Treasury," says Waldorf. "Camp and McClung not only served as coaches but uniquely enough as officials, splitting the time between halves. Appropriately, the game ended in a 10-10 tie."

The permanence of the rivalry undoubtedly was established in 1898, when the teams produced the biggest gate in West Coast history at the time, taking in the then staggering sum of $16,800.

Since then, the schools have produced many more box-office bonanzas and plenty of golden memories. Although most of the Stanford–Cal battles could be considered football classics in their own right, some tower above the others.

The 1924 game was a battle of unbeatens, California trying to complete its fifth straight undefeated season and Rose Bowl-bound Stanford its first since resuming American football in 1919. Ernie Nevers, Stanford's superlative back, was out of the lineup with a broken ankle suffered the week before in a game against Montana, but the Indians still had two other honored players in Ted Shipkey and Jim Lawson. California was captained by All-American center Edwin "Babe" Horrell. According to one newspaper report, Cal's ailing halfback Tut Imlay was warned he might die if he played. But he replied stoicly, "Fine place to die." With Cal ahead 20-6 and less than six minutes remaining, Stanford rallied to tie the Bears 20-20 on two touchdown passes by Ed Walker. Murray Cuddeback, who caught a desperation eight-yard TD pass from Walker with only seconds left, drop-kicked the conversion for the tying point just before the final gun sounded.

"They say that the 1924 game was the greatest of them all in the Stanford–Cal series," says Don Liebendorfer, the venerable sports information director who set a record for longevity at his job. "I don't know about that, but I do know it was a heck of a ballgame in those last few minutes. After Cal took that 20-6 lead, they took their big horses out of the game, and we were able to come back and tie it. They thought it was all sewed up. It was my understanding that Walter Camp . . . was on the bench congratulating the California coach, Andy Smith, because he thought they were going to win the game easily. What a surprise he got."

Cal was headed for the Rose Bowl in 1928 and there was hope in the Bears' camp that they could end Stanford's three-game winning streak in the series. Steve Bancroft scored on an interception and Russ Avery on a pass from Benny Lom to give Cal a 13-0 halftime lead. But Stanford came back to tie it on a long fourth-quarter pass. Frank Fritz saved the Bears from defeat by blocking the conversion attempt.

The 1947 game was a rude initiation into the Stanford–Cal series for Waldorf. "We had a good team in 1947," he remembers. "We were forty-point favorites or something like 10-1. Actually, there's no such thing. In other words, nobody gave Stanford a chance . . . but they almost beat us."

California had imported Waldorf in 1947 to introduce his blood-and-iron methods of the Big Nine and his Golden Bears piled up frightful scores all season while winning eight of nine games. Meanwhile, Stanford had lost all eight of its games under one-time Notre Dame star Marchie Schwartz. The Bears were ravenous for the Stanford corpse. Newspapers quoted them: "We won't be satisfied with less than sixty points."

But the atmosphere at Stanford belied a loser's image. At practice that week, the sidelines overflowed with students and alumni who shouted exhortations to their football heroes. Piling of wood for the pregame bonfire was usually left to freshmen, but this time most of the student body scoured the hills for brush and "the fire broke ancient records for height and heat," according to one writer.

Before game time, the team stayed in the locker room so long that observers feared something was wrong. When the

Stanford players finally emerged with suffused and contorted faces, privileged old-timers who were with them reported brokenly that Schwartz had delivered the most moving speech in football history.

Predictably, California took the Stanford line apart at the outset, marching to an immediate touchdown. But Stanford rallied and came into the locker room losing by a respectable 14-6 score at the half. Schwartz sketched several plays during the intermission. "You've got what it takes," he concluded quietly. "Go out there and win."

Remarkably, Stanford almost did. Led by Bob Anderson and Wayne Erickson, the outweighed Indians dominated the second half, and four minutes from the end, incredibly held an 18-14 lead. One of the biggest upsets in the fifty-year history of the Big Game was at hand and the electrified crowd of 85,000 in Stanford's stadium knew it.

At that point, Paul Keckley pleaded with Waldorf to send him in. He went in with the ball on the California twenty-one. Dick Erickson lateraled to Jackie Jensen, who stopped and found Keckley all alone on the thirty-five. His pass was low and wobbly but Keckley plucked it off the grass-tops and went the remaining sixty-five yards for the winning touchdown in Cal's breathtaking 21-18 victory. "It was no more than an intramural pass," remembers Liebendorfer. "Everyone in our lineup had a shot at Keckley but they all missed. That might have been the most interesting Big Game of them all."

As the deflated Stanford players left the field, Waldorf told Schwartz, "Your players had the finest spirit I ever saw anywhere." Schwartz thanked him wanly, then turned away and saw the parents of the Stanford back who had failed to stop Cal's winning touchdown pass. He spent the next five minutes telling them that their son had done the right thing on defense. Next, he hurried underneath the stadium to spend some time with a young sophomore lineman who also felt guilty about a terrible blunder he had made. "I don't want any of those people to feel ashamed the rest of their lives," Schwartz later said.

The three-point loss was the epitome of the moral victory. When Schwartz emerged from the stadium, a crowd was waiting to give him a hysterical demonstration. When he appeared the following Monday for the weekly luncheon with the Bay Area's sophisticated football writers, they stood up and cheered a losing coach for the only time in their history. And from all over the world, Schwartz received congratulatory messages, including the following from Dr. Ray Lyman Wilbur, former Stanford president and United States Cabinet member:

> I have had to wait forty-seven years to see a Stanford team really *win* the Big Game. . . . I consider this past season the most successful Stanford ever had. To lose consistently and yet keep fighting is a real achievement, and one that is too seldom recognized.

Stanford continued to lose similar tough ones to Waldorf in the late forties and fifties. The large, jovial man who brought a football renaissance to Berkeley had a field day with Stanford, holding a 7-1-2 edge over the Indians in his ten years at California. Along with the 1947 game, two more of his brightest victories came in 1948 and 1956. Cal, going to the Rose Bowl in 1948, held a 7-6 lead late in the fourth quarter. The Golden Bears were faced with a fourth-and-thirty-one situation deep in their territory when punter Jackie Jensen spied an opening and went thirty-two yards to maintain possession and insure the victory for California. In 1956, John Brodie's pass-minded Indians met Waldorf's last California team quarterbacked by Joe Kapp, but it didn't turn out to be a passer's game. Lou Valli rushed for a Big Game record of 209 yards as Waldorf went out a winner, 20-18.

Several days before that game, incidentally, Waldorf gathered his players around him and informed them that he was retiring at the end of the season. "I didn't want them to feel that my job depended on the game," says Waldorf, who had been experiencing some subpar seasons in the middle fifties. "I didn't want to put any pressure on them." Some suggested that this served as an emotional springboard for the California team that day.

One of the ties Stanford managed against Waldorf came in 1950. The Stanford–Cal contest that year is best remembered for a razzle-dazzle attempt by Stanford in the waning minutes. Bill McColl took a lateral from Gary Kerkorian and threw a sixty-yard pass downfield. The pass was a whisker too long, just missing the outstretched hands of Bob Bryan inside the California ten, and the hard-fought contest ended in a 7-7 tie.

Since then, the brilliance of the series has virtually blinded the eye of the beholder. Most of the games have been so exciting that no one can agree on any specific Big Game as the best of the lot. For instance, in a California football program, the 1959 contest heads a list of the Ten Biggest Games, "unequaled for thrills and excitement." Yet Stanford officials call the 1974 game perhaps "the most exciting ever."

It's an academic tossup, for surely no one would dispute either choice.

In 1959, Stanford quarterback Dick Norman passed for 401 yards (completing thirty-four of thirty-nine attempts) but his team lost to California 20-17. Stanford was driving for the winning touchdown when time ran out with the Indians on the California five-yard line. In 1974, Stanford won 22-20 on Mike Langford's fifty-yard field goal with two seconds left. Stanford was losing 10-3 early in the game but eventually came back to take a 19-10 lead on Guy Benjamin's sixty-yard touchdown pass with 7:36 to play in the game. The Bears then rallied behind All-American quarterback Steve Bartkowski, who set up a field goal with 4:40 to go and then passed for the apparent winning touchdown with twenty-six seconds remaining. The extra point gave California a 20-19 lead at this juncture. But then Stanford's Benjamin did the seemingly impossible, hitting tight ends Ted Pappas and Brad Williams for eighteen and twenty-five-yard gains, setting up Langford's improbable field-goal try. With most of the crowd of 71,866 at California's stadium screaming for him to miss, Langford kicked the ball through the uprights and won everlasting fame in Stanford football lore. "One day nobody knows you and the next day everybody in the Bay Area knows your name," said Langford, struck dumb by his instant fame. "It just isn't right." Langford was flattered a few weeks after that game when he was asked to serve as a model for a department store in the Stanford Shopping Center. Model he did—in a Santa Claus suit.

Since close ones are a trademark of this remarkable series, other theatrical productions punctuate the length and breadth of its gold-plated history. Prod any one of a dozen Stanford–Cal watchers and each might have his own personal Big Game story to tell. And usually, each one is better than the last.

In 1958, for instance, Cal had to win to get a Rose Bowl bid. Joe Kapp and Jack Hart powered the Bears to sixteen points, then they held on for a 16-15 victory as Stanford missed a two-point conversion attempt at the end. In 1969, a Howie Williams touchdown in the final period gave Stanford a breathtaking 29-28 victory in a game marked by Dave Penhall's school record 321 passing yards for California. Indian-killer Penhall directed Cal to a tense 22-14 victory over Rose Bowl-bound Stanford in 1970 as the ferocious Bear defense corraled the brilliant Jim Plunkett. The 1972 game produced a 24-21 victory for California as Vince Ferragamo threw the winning touchdown pass to Steve Sweeney with three seconds left. A crowd on the field after that dramatic play prevented the needless conversion attempt. The 1976 game was not only one of the finest played in the series, but also one of the most emotional. Stanford coach Jack Christiansen, fired the day before the game, was carried onto the field by his players. Stanford was losing 24-19 when, with 2:20 left, the newly annointed "Cardinals" recovered a fumble at the California two-yard line. Two plays later, Ron Inge scored the winning touchdown with 1:31 remaining. Quarterback Mike Cordova, whose presence in the starting lineup triggered heavy criticism of Christiansen for three years, then bulled into the end zone for a two-point conversion that gave Stanford a 27-24 victory.

The consistent excellence of Stanford–California games through the seasons has been an obvious byproduct of first-rate participants. One of the earliest of these was Pop Warner, a colossus of Western football, who brought imagination and invention to his coaching work at Stanford in the twenties. He devised the wingback formations, is credited with creating the reverse and was one of the pioneers of the forward pass. Grantland Rice has stated that it would be hard to say whether Warner or Knute Rockne had a more profound influence on college football. Warner came to Stanford in 1924 through a unique deal that demonstrated his remarkable character. When approached for the Stanford job, Warner accepted with the stipulation that he would first honor the last two years of his contract with Pittsburgh. He sent two assistants to Palo Alto to install the "Warner System" during the 1923 and 1924 seasons. Later, he came out and made it work, producing strong teams with the likes of fullback Ernie Nevers, even now regarded as the Stanford player without equal. After Warner left in the early thirties to start still another career at Temple at the age of sixty-one, the "Vow Boys" came into prominence under Tiny Thornhill at Stanford. This group of athletes, including Bobby Grayson, Monk Moscrip and Bob Reynolds, had vowed as freshmen never to lose to Southern California, a constant nemesis during Warner's tenure. In three seasons, 1933-35, the "Vow Boys" fulfilled their resolution against the Trojans and, in fact, lost to few other teams during their glamorous period.

After the "Vow Boys" came the "Wow Boys" under Clark Shaughnessy, who introduced the T-formation to Stanford as well as an explosive left-handed quarterback in Frankie Albert during the forties. Shaughnessy perfected the T with such players as fullback Norm Standlee, halfback Hugh Gallarneau, tackle Bruno Banducci and Vic

Lindskog, who would be remembered as one of Stanford's finest centers. John Ralston later produced prominent teams at Stanford in the seventies with the flowering of two fine quarterbacks, Jim Plunkett and Don Bunce.

California's glory reaches back to the days of Andy Smith, whose fabulous "Wonder Teams" never knew defeat from 1920 through 1924. During this period, the Golden Bears won forty-four games and were tied four times. Historians say the 1920 team, which beat Stanford 38-0, was the best of the five. It included ends Brick Muller and Brodie Stephens, tackles Stan Barnes and Dan McMillan, guards Cort Majors and Lee Cranner, center Fat Clark, quarterback Charlie Erb, halfbacks Crip Toomey and Pesky Sproutt, and fullbacks Duke Morrison and Archie Nesbit. The quality of the "Wonder Teams" was suggested when Smith was asked to choose an All-Pacific Coast team in 1920. He ignored the rest of the schools and selected his entire varsity, which had averaged sixty points a game that year.

After the Smith era, California gained a reputation as a graveyard for coaches until Waldorf arrived in the forties. He brought instant prosperity with him, developing such gifted players as Jackie Jensen, Les Richter, Johnny Olszewski and Pete Schabarum. Jensen, a superb running back who later became a successful major league baseball player, is regarded by many as without peer in the history of California football. Waldorf's teams went to Rose Bowls three straight years—1949, 1950 and 1951. California again enjoyed the scent of roses in the late fifties after Warner's retirement and later fielded representative teams with the help of his strong foundation.

The tempo of the Stanford–Cal series has added even more luster to the illustrious histories of these two fine institutions. As with most rivalries, there is a coveted symbol attached—in this case, the Stanford Axe.

The axe was first displayed by Stanford at an 1899 baseball game and subsequently stolen many times by both schools. The first theft occurred at that game after Stanford yell leader, Billy Erb, had used the axe to behead a dummy California bear and chop up the opponents' blue and gold ribbons. When the baseball game was over, the guardians of the axe were jumped by a Cal group (including former U. S. Senator Carl Hayden of Arizona), which spirited away the coveted athletic symbol.

"To help sneak it across the Bay on a ferryboat, the Cal group sawed off the handle," points out Gary Cavalli, the Stanford sports information director.

Stanford got even in 1930 when the so-called "Immortal 21" pulled off a daring daylight robbery. Posing as newspaper photographers, they arranged to take a picture of the axe as it was returned to the American Trust Company in Berkeley after a pep rally. In front of the bank, they exploded smoke bombs and tear gas as the cameras clicked, and succeeded in wrestling the axe away from its custodian in the ensuing melee.

Three years later, the administrations of both schools agreed to make the axe a trophy for the winner of the annual Big Game. That judgment put a new price on the axe and, if anything, encouraged more thievery than ever before. The most recent of these heists—and one of the most ingenious—occurred in 1973, pulled off by Stanford's "Infamous Three," representing the Theta Delta Chi fraternity.

One of the group, impersonating California coach Mike White, called the Cal student union manager and arranged to have the axe brought to the weekly football writers meeting for some publicity pictures. Two members of the Stanford group posed as Cal football players and led four representatives of the Cal Rally Committee to the meeting at a restaurant in Palo Alto. After arriving there, one of the rally committee went inside to fetch White. Meanwhile, one of the two "football players" suggested he be allowed to carry the axe inside. Permission granted, he immediately took off with the trophy, as the rally committee gave chase. A flying tackle pinned him to the hood of a car, with the axe bouncing off the vehicle's roof. Suddenly, reinforcements from Theta Delta Chi appeared, and they promptly whisked the axe back to Stanford.

The proximity of the schools, of course, lends itself to such frantic activity, and anything else the students might conjure up. A few years ago, the *Stanford Daily* printed a bogus edition of the California student newspaper and flooded it with denigrating remarks about the Bear football team. "It wasn't for a while that people realized it was a hoax," says Maggard. "There's a lot of one-upmanship involved."

Their geographical makeup as well usually assures a homogeneous crowd at all games. And the schools make sure to keep it that way, alotting almost as many tickets to the visitor as the home team. "We design it so the crowd is a 50-50 split," explains Maggard. "The home team might have a few more, but we try to accommodate both schools equally. That's the reason there's really no home field advantage for either team."

Home fields wouldn't mean much in this rivalry, anyway. It has been an unpredictable kind of affair through the years because of the uncommon emotion involved. The 1977 game as much as any of them underscores the unique psychological power of the Stanford–Cal series. "They beat us 21-3 even though we were big favorites," says the California athletic director. "We were supposed to have one of the hottest offenses in the country and they supposedly had one of the most porous defenses. Yet they held us without a touchdown. You try to explain that on paper, and you can't do it."

Big Game fever always seems to raise the temperatures a notch or two for these schools.

"My job didn't depend on the Stanford game, as the cliché goes, but you just wanted to win because it *was* Stanford," says Waldorf. "It was the last game of the season and that always carried over until the next year. I don't know how you define 'high' for a game, but we always appreciated the tradition of the rivalry and wanted to put forth our very best effort in the Stanford game. It always brought out the best in both teams. I didn't have to tell my players anything except, 'This is Stanford.'"

16
GRAMBLING—SOUTHERN
Black Magic

Beating Grambling is all anybody thinks about around here.
—Emory Hines, athletic director of Southern University

Southern University was created by an act of the Louisiana legislature in 1880 and, since 1914, has been as solidly rooted in Baton Rouge as the live oaks that shade its handsome, yawning campus by the Mississippi River. It is known among academicians as the Harvard of the black Southern colleges, the "peoples' University" among its huge student population and "Jaguarland" in athletic circles.

Grambling is roughly 200 miles north of Southern and several years behind in tradition. Founded in 1901 in a bucolic wilderness, Grambling was long off the beaten path in the academic structure. A rural industrial school and quasi-public institution for many years, Grambling waited until the forties before attaining the status of a four-year college.

Thus the football game between the two Louisiana schools often takes on the appearance of a class war between the supposedly more sophisticated, better-educated Baton Rouge blacks of Southern against the simple country blacks from Grambling's rural area. Being a native of Baton Rouge, coach Eddie Robinson of Grambling is aware of the distinctions made between the schools and this only sharpens his desire to beat Southern. He has done this more often than not in a skyrocketing career at Grambling that spans more than three decades. And, ironically, he has done it with the help of Southern University people and athletes from the Baton Rouge area.

"Our own president, Robert Jones, came from Southern," Robinson reminds you, "and when I first came to Grambling, just about everyone working at the school at that time was from Southern University."

Robinson has been somewhat of a miracle worker at Grambling. When he first arrived in 1941, a psychology of failure hung over the campus and he, himself, was beset with indecision and doubt. He likes to recall, "We didn't have much to look ahead to, but even less to look back on."

Southern, for one, "used to treat Grambling like a little brother," Robinson recalls. "They were not interested in playing us in a regular game but would scrimmage us. They would stop over and play us a practice game a few days before going on to play Wiley or Prairie View [two of the recognized black powers in the South]. Finally, we got Southern to play us in a regular season game, but it was unheard of for us to beat them. They were the most powerful team in the Southwestern Athletic Conference."

Arnett William "Ace" Mumford was the reason that the Jaguars were at the top of their game during this period and for many years thereafter. Mumford was one of the early coaching giants in black football history, producing eleven SWAC champions and four black college football titles in his twenty-five-year career at Southern. His record of 169-57-14 for a .733 winning percentage represents the second highest number of games won in Louisiana football history, trailing only Robinson in that category.

"When they came to play you," Robinson recalls, "you were supposed to be whipped."

The early whippings by Southern began in 1933 when the Jaguars, with tradition and much finer personnel on their side, defeated the Tigers 20-0 in the first game of the series. Southern had been playing since 1915, eleven years before Dr. Jones came over to start a team at Grambling, and ranked among the early leaders of black football. Along with Southern, the foundation for black football was laid by other great teams at Tuskegee Institute (Alabama), Bluefield (West Virginia), Wiley (Texas), Kentucky State, Langsford (Oklahoma), Morgan State (Maryland) and Florida A&M.

Brice Taylor was the Southern coach who acceded to pleas by Grambling for a football game in 1933, an act of nobility considering that nothing could be gained in playing a school of lesser stature. "Taylor said he would play us just the same," Dr. Jones remembers. "It was mighty nice of him. We only had a few men and we did the best we could."

It wasn't until three years later that the teams met again and things hadn't changed much. By this time, Mumford was the Southern coach and began building the foundation for even stronger Jaguar teams. The 1936 result was a predictable 34-0 victory for Southern over Grambling and in 1939, the Jaguars made it three straight shutouts over their "little brothers" by a 39-0 score. Incidentally, Emory Hines, the current athletic director at Southern, was coaching Grambling that year, a fairly common geographical irony that has made the rivalry of these two schools what it is.

Before later changing allegiance, Hines made somewhat of a mark for longevity at Grambling with a five-year stint from 1935 to 1940. Before him, three coaches had come and gone, each after a year following the original seven-year term of Dr. Jones. Hines, a player at Texas College, had been an offensive line coach at Southern under Mumford before taking the Grambling job.

If intermittent in the early years, the Grambling–Southern series was intense on a small scale. The crowds were modest, reflecting the economic growth of black people in America in the thirties. "Many of them [the fans] held menial jobs," points out Collie Nicholson, Grambling's long-time sports information director, "but the pride factor was there. The two schools represented the ultimate for blacks getting education in our state."

The economic explosion following World War II had a spectacular impact on America's growth and this was felt as sharply as anywhere in the black community. The GI Bill provided young blacks with new opportunities for education and, as a sideline bonus, lifted black football to new heights of respectability. Among the returning wartime veterans who went back to school to study and play football was Paul "Tank" Younger. He helped Robinson complete a metamorphosis at Grambling in the mid-forties.

Younger was a spectacular wheelhorse fullback for four seasons at Grambling, scoring sixty touchdowns and earning many honors on his way to a fruitful and revolutionary professional career in the National Football League. Younger became the first athlete from a predominantly black school to sign with an NFL team. After Younger made a substantial impact, pro teams began looking harder at black schools for players. This area was an especially invaluable talent pool for the young American Football League. It changed interest and created a new respect and esteen that black schools had never enjoyed before. By this time, many of the black coaches who had been legends in the early days had either retired or peaked and Robinson was on his way to becoming the apostle of black college football.

"As meticulous as a lawyer preparing a brief," according to Nicholson, Robinson adheres to the theory of attacking in strength. "Old-fashion [sic] head knocking will always be a part of football," Robinson says. The Grambling coach, a firm believer in a strong running game, has had an appetite through the years for big, powerful backs and massive linemen. Robinson has repeated often enough: "I like my players agile, hostile, mobile and elephantine."

It was a great day for Robinson and Grambling when he first beat Southern in 1947. That, of course, had more than local implications, suggesting that Grambling could finally play on a par with any of the nation's best black teams. "It was a very happy day for us," says Dr. Jones. "I felt we had reached the zenith of sportsdom."

Remembers Nicholson: "As far as games go, that 1947 game was the Big Game for Eddie Robinson. I think he feels that was his biggest win in the series. They came into Grambling highly touted, the SWAC champ, and we beat them 21-6 with two long touchdown runs. It was something they thought could never be done."

In his first try against Southern in 1946, the year the series was resumed after a wartime hiatus, Robinson had lost a 38-8 decision. Therefore, his first victory against the Jaguars in 1947 was also the first victory for Grambling in the series and the Southern people were as upset as the oddsmakers. The Jaguars had an honored team that year, led by running star Odie Posey, and were on their way to their second straight SWAC championship. During this euphoric era at Southern, the Jaguars eventually would win three more league championships in a row as well as three straight national titles from 1948 through 1950. Such All-American running backs as Posey, Pelican Hill, Bill Phillips and Buster Welcome made the Jaguars go during this period.

All-conquering Southern would avenge its lone 1947 loss to Grambling with a victory in 1948, and that game proved costly to the Tigers in more than one way. A fight broke out on the field during Southern's 18-0 victory and athletic relations between the schools broke off until 1959. During this period, Grambling tried to enter the SWAC but was shut out, presumably with Southern's blessing. Robinson took his team into the Midwest Conference, producing an undefeated, untied team in 1955 and several other representative powers.

By 1959, the wounds with Southern had healed and the door to the SWAC finally opened for Grambling. The Tigers stepped through those exalted portals to find a ferocious Jaguar team waiting inside. Southern beat

Grambling the first three years of the renewal of their series, although Robinson could console himself with a cochampionship with Southern and Prairie View during the 1960 season.

It wasn't until 1962 that Robinson was able to beat a Southern team and not until 1965, when Robinson's own son, Eddie, Jr., quarterbacked Grambling, that he was able to win a clean SWAC championship. By this time, Robinson's hard recruiting work had begun to bear fruit. Some of the nation's best black players were staying in the South and Robinson was getting most of them in the late sixties. Included among the future pro material was defensive end Billy Newsome, quarterback James Harris, running back Essex Johnson, wide receivers Frank Lewis, Bob Atkins and Charlie Joiner and linebacker Garland Boyette.

These were only a handful of dozens of players that Robinson would groom for a professional career. This proliferation of pro talent from Grambling was brought to America's attention in the early sixties by a television film called, *A Hundred Yards to Glory*. It gave Grambling a national identity that would soon mark the tiny northern Louisiana school as the "Black Notre Dame" of college football. The Tigers enhanced this image by taking their game to the people, playing in metropolitan areas across the country where large black populations were sure to exist. Their appearance in urban centers magnetized large crowds. "They went to Miami while all the other teams in the SWAC were still playing in their backyards," says Buddy Davis, sports editor of the *Ruston* (La.) *Daily Leader*. "There is a joke that if football is ever played on the moon, Grambling will be one of the two teams in the game." That type of thinking has taken Grambling to games in the Houston Astrodome, Los Angeles Coliseum, Cleveland's Municipal Stadium, Soldier Field and Comisky Park in Chicago and Yankee Stadium in New York, as well as the Rose, Sugar, Cotton and Orange Bowl stadiums. Full houses at these parks have not been uncommon.

Southern, though reluctant, was eventually swept up in Grambling's far-sighted passion to move ahead. Ulysses "Dean" Jones, Southern's associate athletic director and a one-time All-American player under the legendary Mumford in 1940, points out that Grambling's motives have been thoroughly altruistic in the Robinson regime. "Grambling tried to take all the schools in the SWAC along with them when they made that film, *A Hundred Yards to Glory*," says Jones. "At that time, though, there was a reluctance on the part of black schools to do it. Grambling begged us to go in on it with them. They brought in specialists and talked to our presidents. But we all refused, afraid, I guess, that we were being used or fearful of criticism from our Board of Supervisors."

It was this Grambling drive that eventually got the game with Southern moved into the gargantuan Superdome in New Orleans and put the rivalry on a different plane than any other of its kind in America. Since its relocation to New Orleans, the Grambling–Southern game has drawn consistently mammoth crowds and worn the appellation of the "Black Super Bowl." Robinson exercised some pressure to pull off this coup, which in his words was an act of financial necessity.

"We weren't making any money playing Southern on our campus because we didn't have enough seats," Robinson says. "People would come and break down the fences because they didn't have seats available for them. I told Dr. Jones that it would be better to play our home game with Southern at Shreveport. We would get larger crowds there and make more money. Dr. Jones agreed with me, but Southern did not—at least, not right away. I told them they couldn't tell us where to play our home games and that I was going to schedule it in Shreveport in 1973 and that they could come if they wanted to."

The Jaguars came, all right, and so did more than 40,000 customers. All of a sudden, both schools knew they had something big here. The Grambling–Southern rivalry was on the verge of blossoming into the number one attraction in black college football. "Starting in Shreveport," notes Robinson, "it took on a different look altogether."

The next year the game went to New Orleans, where it was staged in Tulane's Sugar Bowl Stadium before 80,000. By this time, Grambling had taken over the momentum in the series and won its fifth straight game from Southern, by a 21-0 score. By 1975, Grambling was still winning and the crowds were still coming—only this time it was to the newly built Superdome. A crowd of 76,000 filled the place the first year to watch Grambling's 33-17 victory and have matched that figure in every subsequent season since, despite the boring consistency of a Grambling winning streak that grew to eight games with the Tigers' 55-20 rout in 1977 behind Doug Williams.

Since taking up residence in New Orleans, the Grambling–Southern rivalry has become more than a football game. Actually, it is a sociocultural phenomenon, "the biggest black happening in the United States, if not the world," according to Robinson, who enjoys it even more now that he has turned the tables on his archrivals.

There's a bit of pride, status-seeking and social one-upmanship involved, as some attendants have explained. "It's more than a Mardi Gras to blacks," says one. "Blacks go to the Super Bowl, but it's not theirs. Carnival is great, but it's for everybody. This is ours." A middle-class matron, one of many who has embraced the annual game as the highlight of her social year, put her finger on the answer to the popularity of this colorful pageant when she said, "It is the first time blacks could ever really get together and unite over something that's fun, instead of trying to solve social or political problems."

A "happening," as Robinson says, is about the only way to describe the Grambling–Southern rivalry these days. "It's the Super Bowl with a soul shake, an Ali fight with marching bands," is the way one writer describes it. Hotels and the best nightspots are jammed for the weekend. Reservations for rooms are sometimes made as far in advance as the previous year. There is a "Battle of the Bands" between both schools who boast some of the finest musicians in the country. They parade down Canal Street the evening before the game, then compete the next day with as much fervor as the football teams. There are not only halftime shows, but shows before and after the game. "People just don't leave after the game," says Robinson. "There's still that postgame show to watch. And it's really something."

First-class football is the centerpiece for all this dazzling, peripheral energy. It must be remembered that Grambling and Southern have produced as many players for the National Football League as any of the black colleges in the country, and more than most schools of any kind. Southern has been known for its predominance of fine, wide receivers (Issac Hagins, Harold Carmichael, Frank Pitts and Allen Dunbar), its defensive backs (Raymond Jones, Willie McKelton, Leverne Dickerson, Ken Ellis and Mel Blount) and defensive tackles (Jim Osborne, Alden Roche and James Battle). Grambling has had more than its share of good quarterbacks (James Harris, Frank Holmes and Doug Williams), wide receivers (Charlie Joiner, Frank Lewis and Cliff McNeil) and defensive linemen (Buck Buchanan, Ernie Ladd, John Mendenhall, Al Dotson and Richard Harris).

These players, and many more of their ilk, have provided plenty of artistic games through the modern era of the rivalry. In 1969 Southern won 21-17 but not without a fierce argument from Grambling regarding a controversial play just before the half. Grambling fullback William O'Neil got into the end zone on a one-yard drive, but fumbled the ball as he went over. Robinson argued that his player had "broken the plane" going over the top and therefore should have been awarded the touchdown. He was not and it eventually cost the Tigers the game. Davis remembers: "Most writers in the press box thought he scored." That was to be the last time Southern would beat Grambling through 1977. The next season, the Tigers won 37-24 behind the running of Virgil Robinson to start the series' longest winning streak.

That 1969 game, by the way, served as one more reason for Grambling to move the Southern game to more spacious surroundings.

"We had 27,000 people squeezed into a facility built for 18,000," recalls Nicholson. "We were determined never to play a Southern game again in our stadium if we could help it. The towns of Grambling and Ruston ran out of gasoline. People had to stay the weekend. There was no food . . . no room for anybody. People were sleeping in their cars."

There are plenty of facilities, of course, now that the Grambling–Southern game is showcased in New Orleans. And every corner of the Crescent City is needed to fill the demands of the populace.

"From the time they shoot the gun at the end of the game until the next year, they're talking about The Game," says Robinson. "Grambling alumni in Detroit, California or any place bring in planes and make plans to meet each other in New Orleans the following year. The Southern people do, too. I'm just so happy we have this rivalry. It's the greatest thing that ever happened for black football."

Jones is happy, too, except Southern's associate athletic director would like to see the scoreboard come up with different numbers in future years.

"We had better days in the thirties and forties and Grambling started wondering if they would ever beat us," he says. "Now we're wondering the same thing."

17
OKLAHOMA—TEXAS
The Battle of Big D

Bud Wilkinson never underestimated the importance of a Texas–Oklahoma game. "To put the Oklahoma coaching job in its proper perspective as a coach," he once said, "you have to beat Texas to have a good year. If you're good enough to beat Texas, you can win the national championship. It's just that simple, because Texas is that good. You base what you're going on what it takes to beat Texas."

The statement by the one-time Oklahoma football coach was made many years ago, but the words are never truer today. The Sooners still have to beat Texas if they are going to go anywhere in the national polls. Actually, the same holds true for the Longhorns.

Southwesterners call the annual Texas–Oklahoma game the "Battle of Big D" or the "Battle of the Red River," but mostly it is just a Battle of Huge Hearts. Or as long-time Texas coach Darrell Royal emphatically puts it: "It is no place for the timid."

The night before the game is played in the Cotton Bowl, the town of Dallas becomes a kind of "Dodge City." Pedestrians who brave the wild downtown area must be ready to dodge both cars on the street or missiles thrown from hotel windows. The army of visitors are there not only for the game, but for the Texas State Fair that engulfs the football action and donates a handsome trophy, the Cowboy Hat, to the winner. In recent years, that hat has been worn mostly by Oklahoma, but there was a time that the Sooners went hatless for a long, cold period. That was from 1958 through 1970, when Royal had brilliant success against the Sooners, losing only once in thirteen games.

Before that, Wilkinson had gone through a wildly successful period. In one stretch, from 1948 through 1957, Wilkinson's supreme Oklahoma teams won nine of ten games from the Longhorns, including a string of six straight at the end.

The towering figures of Wilkinson and Royal stand the tallest in this series and their rivalry was made all the more unique by their interlacing lives. Royal was an All-American quarterback under Wilkinson in 1949 and even after beating him six straight times as Texas coach from 1958 through 1963, continued to call him "Coach."

"Royal was a fine passer, runner and kicker, and he was possibly even stronger on defense," remembers one writer from Royal's Oklahoma playing days. "First of all, however, he was a student of the game. He was usually the last to leave the locker room after practice. He would sit there mulling over the day's practice, analyzing the reason for everything."

Royal served as an assistant coach at North Carolina State, Tulsa and Mississippi State, and as head coach of Edmonton in the Canadian Professional League, Mississippi State and Washington before accepting the position at Texas. In obtaining Royal after the 1956 season, Texas applied a modification of the philosophy: "If you can't beat 'em, join 'em." Royal was not only Wilkinson-taught and an Oklahoma graduate but a native Sooner. He was born in Hollis, in the southwestern corner of Oklahoma, tucked in between the legendary Red River on the south and the Texas Panhandle on the west.

When Royal came to Texas, he was well aware of Oklahoma's recent domination in the series. While Wilkinson continued to knock over the Longhorns, he was helping to knock Texas coaches out of their jobs. Among the casualties were Blair Cherry and Ed Price, Royal's predecessors.

Ironically, Royal would ultimately turn the Oklahoma philosophy against its own progenitor. From Wilkinson, Royal got his respect for the virtues of sound defense, supported by a strong kicking game. The Sooner philosophy dictated that the pass was subordinate to the running game, that "exciting" football would not be played at the expense of sound football. In Wilkinson's words:

"Superior execution of the basic fundamentals will usually insure victory. The main emphasis of the coaching staff should be on the proper development of blocking, tackling and running."

After Wilkinson spelled them out, Royal carried them out to the letter with vibrant Texas teams that soon became the cream of college football. The emphasis of movement, blocking, tackling, running, supported by a strong kicking game—in short, the field-position game—was never put to more classic use than in the 1962 contest with Oklahoma. Ernie Koy of Texas and Joe Don Looney of Oklahoma engaged in a kicking duel before the Longhorns emerged 9-6 winners with the help of two costly Sooner fumbles near their goal line.

Along with Wilkinson's philosophy, Royal brought some of his own to Texas. When he first moved into his office on the campus in Austin, Royal claimed a discarded, dusty picture of a scrawny longhorn and put it on his wall. "I'm fond of that painting," he said. "I don't want any fenced-in, fat Longhorns around here. Just look at him. He doesn't know where his next meal is coming from. He's hungry, and he's not afraid to kick up a little dust. That's the way I want my football teams."

He added a Knute Rockne-type touch to his team chats and a funny new language of phrases patently described as "Royalisms." At halftime of the 1968 Oklahoma game, the Longhorns were in a depressed mood in the locker room because of their 7-0 deficit. "There's a heckuva fight going on out there in the Cotton Bowl," Royal told his team. "Why don't you get in on it?" Texas won the game 9-7.

Even while on the short end of the series during Royal's

brilliant administration (12-7 in favor of Texas), Oklahoma could still laugh at Royal's witticisms. Included among his best "Royalisms":

"He's so rich he could burn a wet elephant."

"We live one day at a time and scratch where it itches."

"We're not exactly a rolling ball of butcher knives."

And, on rating a close game as even, "It's a hoss and a hoss."

Wilkinson was never as successful against Royal-coached teams at Texas as he would have liked. He was beaten by his protégé six times in seven meetings, including a stinging 28-7 defeat in his farewell year in 1963.

The Cotton Bowl was packed so solid that day that one desperate housewife offered all her Green Stamps to get in, "anything for just two tickets." Oklahoma was favored, but Texas emerged as the nation's Number One team 4 ½ hours later in the battle of unbeatens. The Longhorns beat the Sooners with the simplest offense that Royal could dream up: the hoary split-T option that had been Oklahoma's bread and butter for more than a decade under Wilkinson.

That was the sixth straight victory for Royal over his former teacher, a string that started in 1958 with a 15-14 Texas triumph fashioned with a miracle finish usually associated with Oklahoma in those years. Texas quarterback Bobby Lackey passed sixteen yards to end Bob Bryant for a touchdown, and then Lackey kicked the winning point with just three minutes and ten seconds remaining in the game. By then the stature of the series had grown substantially, enhanced by the added feature of the personal rivalry between teacher and student. For the thirteenth straight year the Cotton Bowl was sold out for the game and each school took home $130,000, a figure usually associated with postseason Bowls.

Royal had learned his lessons well from Wilkinson, who despite his basic defensive approach to football, would occasionally reach out for a "barnyard" type of play to distract opponents and score touchdowns. That was how

Oklahoma got its only score against Texas in 1962. With less than two minutes to play in the first half, Ron Fletcher, a 159-pound, third-string quarterback, lined up as a halfback, took pitchouts and completed two long passes. The second went for a score, to halfback Lance Rentzel, who deployed as a flanked end. The pass receiver twice got behind the containing portion of the Texas defense, something rarely accomplished.

Wilkinson was a strong organizational man whose teams were always well prepared, poised and confident of victory. He was influenced strongly by Robert Neyland, the famous defensive master of Tennessee, and two of the General's Lieutenants, Bobby Dodd of Georgia Tech and Ray Graves of Florida. Wilkinson's organizational powers received the supreme compliment once when Graves, then a Georgia Tech assistant to Dodd, made an inspection tour of spring practices at other schools and rated Oklahoma by far the best.

Wilkinson was a study in polite, dignified conservatism and his introverted personality was a marked contrast to the man he replaced at Oklahoma in 1947, Jim Tatum. Wade Walker, the Sooner captain in 1947, recalls the most apparent differences: "Tatum was a lot more outgoing. He would bring himself down to the players' level a lot easier than Coach Wilkinson would. Coach Wilkinson was a person that you didn't feel like you could sit down and talk to."

As a dashing, thirty-year-old head coach, perhaps Wilkinson had some identity problems. As youthful-looking as his players, Wilkinson was sometimes mistaken for one. Walker recalls the first time they met, Wilkinson was an assistant coach and the player asked him, "Bud, what position do you play?"

When Wilkinson first took over the Oklahoma job, the Sooners had little glamour attached to their name. They had appeared in the wire service polls just once in the eleven years of rankings. However, when he resigned seventeen years later, Oklahoma had won just about every college

football honor that existed and was firmly established as
one of the nation's superpowers. The high point of the
Wilkinson dynasty came during the fifties, when he was
consistently beating Texas and everyone else. During this
reign of terror, Oklahoma won three mythical national
championships and posted a gorgeous record of ninety-
three victories, ten losses and two ties. Included in that
brilliant streak was the NCAA record for consecutive victories with forty-seven. Wilkinson and Royal have been the
dominating influences in the Texas–Oklahoma series for
obvious reasons, and both in their time studiously sought
to keep the rivalry at white heat competitively, without any
slides into barbarism. A brief free-for-all just before the
final whistle of the 1962 game was one of the few times in
the series that combatants failed to heed instructions and
stop fighting. Considering the Wild West atmosphere that
surrounds the field, the lack of brawls and bad blood in
this series has been quite remarkable.

Wildness was an element of the 1952 game, won 49-20 by
the Sooners, but none of it came from the field.
Oklahoma's backfield of quarterback Eddie Crowder, halfbacks Billy Vessels and Buddy Leake and fullback Buck
McPhail, one of the most effective put together anywhere,
broke the game open early with four touchdowns in the
first quarter. After each score, Oklahoma's "Roughnecks,"
a special group of rooters clad in red-flannel shirts and
white trousers, fired blanks from double-barreled shotguns
behind the Texas bench. Harley Sewell, the Longhorns'
All-American guard who had recently returned from service in the Korean War, happened to be taking a breather
on the bench when the Roughnecks saluted one of the
Sooner scores with their ear-splitting gun shots. Texas
coach Price called, "Harley, are you rested? Want to go
back in?"

"Yeah, Coach," said Sewell with a pained grimace, "but
this is worse than Korea."

The battle fury of the Texas–Oklahoma games inspired
the weekly "Ug" Award during Wilkinson's reign. It went

to the Oklahoma player who put on the best display of rock 'em, sock 'em defensive play during the contest. "Ug," a fictional all-star guard, was an Indian who performed at Carlisle and later transferred to a many-storied institution in Oklahoma, "Geronimo's Finishing School." After the 24-0 loss to Texas in 1960, Wilkinson was hard-put to point out a defensive hero for Oklahoma. "Ug got ugged," was all he could say, dismissing the award for that particular week.

The Texas–Oklahoma battles transcend the field and the respective coaches wage a different kind of war in the arena of recruiting. Because the states are so close, it is only natural that they sometimes prowl each other's territory in their blue-blood–thirsty hunt for top players. It was especially true in Wilkinson's case during his decade of ascendancy, when he got many of his winning players from Texas. Some Texas backers went so far as to claim that Wilkinson kept a squadron of planes, at a hidden airfield somewhere north of the Red River, on constant alert, to take off and corral any top high-school prospect in west Texas or the Texas Panhandle. It seemed a slight exaggeration, however, when these self-styled spotters insisted that the reputed red-colored planes were equipped with machine guns, à la the German flying ace, Baron von Richthofen.

Whether or not Wilkinson used a football airborne command to shanghai talented Texans is open to debate, but truly, many of them have decorated the Sooner honor rolls. Among the Texas greats were center Jerry Tubbs and tackle Ed Gray, the cocaptains of the 1956 team (perhaps Wilkinson's greatest), which drubbed the Longhorns 45-0; tackle Jim Weatherall, selected on All-American teams in both 1950 and 1951; guard J. D. Roberts, a 1953 All-American choice; and center Bob Harrison, another of Wilkinson's stars in a bright football galaxy.

Although the help of such Texans cannot be dismissed, the best Sooner elevens always contained a sizeable portion of Oklahoma high-school boys. A key factor in the brief Sooner football downcurve, which hit bottom in 1960, was

the temporary fall in athletic quality at Oklahoma high
schools. The plunge at Muskogee's Central High was especially painful, for Central had contributed more than its
share of Oklahoma All-Americans down through the
years. The direct result of this was seen most dramatically
in Oklahoma's series with Texas in the late fifties and early
sixties, when Royal started his domination of Sooner
teams.

Oklahomans always had a hard time accepting Royal's
success over Sooner teams, especially since he was
Oklahoma-bred. But they have great fun with their rivals,
underscoring the fact that before Texas could beat Oklahoma, it had to requisition an Oklahoman to coach.

Of course, that's not entirely true. Long before
Wilkinson and Royal came on the scene, Texas had dominated the series, and actually it didn't matter who was
coaching. From 1900 through 1946, the Longhorns held a
dramatic 28-11-2 edge in the series with a combination of
twenty-one coaches, many of whom didn't last more than
a season or two. Among the ones who did, Dana X. Bible,
Clyde Littlefield and Jack Chevigny had notable success
against Oklahoma. Bible beat the Sooners seven straight
times (1940-1946), Littlefield did it four in a row
(1929-1932) and Chevigny was undefeated in three tries
with Oklahoma (1934-1936).

Oklahoma fans have a ready-made excuse for the Longhorns' early domination—the home-field advantage.
Sooners have been known to prod Longhorns with the reminder that in all the time of this gargantuan series, the
game has been played in Oklahoma only six times. The last
was at Norman in 1922, when Texas won 32-7.

The Norman game before that, in 1908, was memorable
for several reasons. The Sooners that day set the record
high score and margin of victory for the series with a 50-0
victory. The game was played on Friday the thirteenth, the
coldest day that Norman had experienced in ten years. Despite the exquisitely cold weather, some 300 Sooner
rooters, led by Professor D. W. Ohern, head of the geology

department, did a snake dance in celebration of a 17-0 half-time lead and climaxed it by throwing their hats over a goal post at old Boyd Field.

Incidentally, that was only Oklahoma's second victory in the series. The Sooners had won the first in 1905 after six Texas victories and a tie.

The gadfly for the trailblazing Sooners was Bennie Owen, a keen strategist and tactician and the only one who had any real success against Texas in the pre-Wilkinson era. After breaking that seven-game Longhorn unbeaten streak with a 2-0 victory in 1905, Owen proceeded to win five of the next eight games against Texas and his overall 8-8 record in the series was a landmark achievement for the times.

Owen built his 1908 offense on a tackle-around play, because he was blessed with two exceptionally talented offensive tackles in Ralph Campbell and Willard Douglas. Between them, they gained 401 yards that season. The most exciting play of the 1908 Texas–Oklahoma game, however, was a ninety-yard runback on a punt by Oklahoma's Charley Wantland. (This stood as a school record until Royal ran a punt back ninety-five yards against Kansas State in 1948.) Wantland's father, an old cowman, was watching his first football game that day and was nearly shocked out of his seat by the Texas–Oklahoma mayhem. Not long before, a humane society had succeeded in gaining legislation to prevent roping of steers at rodeos, and Wantland, Sr., commented: "This is the roughest thing I ever saw. They ought to make them cut this out instead of steer roping."

No doubt Wantland would have been even more upset had he witnessed the earlier Texas–Oklahoma games, prior to the widespread change of rules in 1906 that kicked much of the brutality out of college football. The Longhorns had been at this bloody business a few years earlier than the Sooners (1893 to 1895) and apparently had a little bit more on the ball when they met for the first time in 1900. Actually, 1900 was virtually Oklahoma's first full season, since the Sooners had played no more than three games in any previous year.

Texas won the first game at Austin, 28-2, and established an early superiority. Uniquely, the teams played two games each in 1901 and 1903, when finally Oklahoma could claim any kind of parity with a 6-6 tie.

Once Owen came on the scene, however, things were a little different. Among his most significant accomplishments was a three-year win streak over Texas that included a 6-3 decision in 1911. The victory completed an undefeated season for the Sooners and handed the Longhorns only their second loss of the year. In that one, Oklahoma captain Fred Capshaw scored a touchdown to bring the Sooners from behind in the first half.

Like the powerful 1911 team, the 1915 Sooners were all-conquering. They not only beat opponents that year, they rubbed their noses in the dirt with such astonishing margins of victory as 102-0 over Alva Normal, 67-0 over Kingfisher College and 55-0 over Weatherford Normal. Prior to their game with Texas, the Sooners had embarrassed four opponents by a collective score of 248-0.

This crippling offensive machine paid a visit to Dallas on the fifth weekend of the season with every hope of dismembering the Longhorns, a new colleague in the Southwest Conference. The game, enhanced by the Texas State Fair, attracted 11,000 fans, reportedly the largest crowd to see a football game in the state to that time.

The favored Sooners won, but not with the explosiveness expected of them. They had to come from behind in the last quarter on the wings of Forest Park Geyer's passing. Geyer, nicknamed "Spot" because of his throwing accuracy, passed to Montford "Hap" Johnson for a touchdown, tying the score at 13-13. In those days the extra point was tried from the spot on the goal line at which the touchdown was scored and Geyer kicked the conversion from an extreme right angle for a 14-13 Oklahoma triumph. When they returned to Norman by train Sunday afternoon, the Sooners were met at the railroad station by a crowd estimated at 4,000, a staggering figure for the day.

The series was interrupted for the first time in 1918, although neither school would have wished it that way. When a Spanish influenza epidemic reached Oklahoma, it forced cancellation of games with Texas, Missouri and Alva Normal. But in the remaining schedule, the Sooners won two Southwest Conference games and tied Texas for the championship. Thus the epidemic had forced cancellation of what might have been the championship tie-breaker between Texas and Oklahoma.

The complications of new directions for Oklahoma presaged any real structure in its series with Texas for the next ten years. During this time, the Sooners first joined the Missouri Valley Conference and then the Big Six, forerunner of the present Big Eight, and a total of three games were played between the Sooners and the Longhorns from 1919 through 1928. However, a five-year drought at the end of that period was the last time this fabled rivalry was interrupted.

Since then, the series has been college football's version of the Hatfields and McCoys—a feud in the very real sense. Significantly, both teams have often been undefeated, usually ranked high in the national polls and always ready to tear each other's throats out in the circus atmosphere of the Texas State Fair, the permanent home of the series since 1929.

The feuds attached to the games have sometimes been as interesting as the games themselves. The 1947 contest, won 34-14 by Texas, featured the so-called "Sisco incident." With the score tied 7-7, Texas had moved fifty-seven yards to the Oklahoma three-yard line with only seconds remaining in the first half. Longhorn runner Randall Clay was stopped for no gain on the next play, and the field clock showed no time remaining. However, Jack Sisco, one of the game officials, declared that Texas had called timeout with three seconds remaining and gave the Longhorns another play.

On the second-chance play, Texas halfback Jim Canady was stopped at the line of scrimmage and fumbled the ball. But Longhorn quarterback Bobby Layne was able to recover the fumble and throw a touchdown pass to Clay for a 14-7 Texas lead at halftime. Wilkinson protested the play, claiming that Layne's knees touched the ground when he recovered the fumble and that the play should have ended there.

The disputed play appeared to turn the tempo of the game in favor of the Longhorns. In the third quarter, when an Oklahoma gain was nullified by a holding penalty, Sooner fans threw bottles and seat cushions on the field. After the game, the officials had to be escorted to safety by the police. The following Monday, Sisco was burned in effigy on the Oklahoma campus, and no one would have blamed Wilkinson had he lit the torch himself. The Oklahoma coach said that the coaches and officials had agreed before the game that the field clock would indicate the official time. On that basis, he believed that Sisco had no right to give Texas the extra play.

"If I had been a more experienced coach, I would have taken our team off the field and let Sisco decide what he was going to do," said Wilkinson, who of course was only in his first year at Oklahoma that season.

Of course the proximity of the states didn't make the relationship between the schools any easier, nor did Wilkinson's continual recruiting raids into Texas territory. After Wilkinson's time, the feuds were just as intense and sometimes far more complicated.

The game of 1975 featured the "Great Lie-Detecting And Guitar-Picking Debate," as one sportswriter put it. Royal implied that Oklahoma had used illegal or at least unethical tactics in luring promising Texas high-school players north of the Red River, the demarcation line between Oklahoma and Texas. Royal and others in the Southwest Conference helped push through an NCAA rule limiting the number of visits to a prospect's home. Of course, Oklahoma and its Big Eight friends opposed this legislation. Then, in the spring of 1975, Oklahoma coach

Barry Switzer had his entire staff take lie-detector tests, which he said proved "no sinning." Royal's staff followed suit.

This did not allay the bitter feelings between the schools or the coaches, however. Losing four straight games to Oklahoma and losing lots of prospects were upsetting enough to Royal, but he really hit the roof when he heard subsequent deprecating remarks by Switzer. Speaking to an Oklahoma alumni group, the Sooner coach sharply criticized the visitation rule and spoke of coaches who "would rather sit home and listen to guitar pickers," an obvious dig at the country-music–loving Royal.

There was even more bitterness between Royal and Switzer before the 1976 game, when there were charges and countercharges about spies and recruiting. At one point, the enflamed Royal reportedly offered to give $10,000 each to Switzer and Larry Lacewell, Switzer's number-one assistant, if they would pass a lie-detector test proving that they did not use a spy on Royal's secret practices before the game. Royal and Switzer flanked President Gerald Ford as the three walked on the field for the ceremonial coin toss before the 1976 game, but their feelings were dramatically evident when the coaches refused to shake hands with each other.

The 1975 game, incidentally, was typically hot-blooded to the end and provided the usual sellout crowd at the Cotton Bowl with a dramatic last-quarter rally so familiar to fans of this series. Oklahoma twice took ten-point leads, but Texas fought back to tie the score at 17-17 in the final period. Aided by a face-mask penalty that seemed to take the heart out of the Longhorns, the Sooners moved down the field on runs by Horace Ivory, Joe Washington and quarterback Steve Davis. From the Texas thirty-three, Ivory shot through left tackle, cut to his left and fled down the sideline for a touchdown with just 5½ minutes left. That gave Oklahoma the game, 24-17.

In terms of history, it was proper that the game should have a Hollywood ending. The keen competitiveness of the

Oklahoma–Texas series has sponsored many other outstanding finishes.

In 1950, Billy Vessels scored a touchdown with only three minutes, forty-six seconds remaining to tie the game for Oklahoma at 13-13. Then Jim Weatherall kicked the extra point for a 14-13 Sooner victory. "The goal posts looked like they were nearly together," remembers Weatherall in savoring the moment.

Led by quarterback Jimmy Harris, Oklahoma came from behind to defeat Texas 14-7 in 1954. The 1958 game was marked by a miracle finish, with Bob Lackey leading the Sooners to a 15-14 victory in the last four minutes. Texas, smarting from an 18-9 Oklahoma upset in 1966, defeated the Sooners 9-7 in 1967 on quarterback Bill Bradley's touchdown run in the last quarter. And in one of the rivalry's greatest games, Texas stopped Oklahoma 26-20 in 1968 as fullback Steve Worster, running from the newly devised wishbone-T, scored a touchdown on a two-yard run with only thirty-nine seconds left.

The Texas–Oklahoma series, still a bone-rattler, promises more artistic football to come, with the contest's most distinguishing factor being the close state rivalry.

"I just hate Okies, to put it bluntly," Texas tackle Brad Shearer had said at the time of the 1975 game. "They hate me just as bad and that's what makes it a great game."

Johnny Treadwell, the Longhorns' All-American linebacker of the early sixties, puts it more diplomatically but just as dramatically: "The Oklahoma–Texas game is an experience. It's nothing like anything you've been in before."

18

ALABAMA—TENNESSEE

A Matter of Respect

Of all the heroic names attached to the Alabama–Tennessee series, one is etched a bit deeper than the rest in the rich fabric: Gene McEver. In 1928, McEver was a stocky, vibrant fullback called "The Wild Bull" who was to become a symbol of power football at Tennessee and the conduit through which electricity would run in this high-voltage rivalry.

Until that 1928 game, the Alabama–Tennessee series was a desultory one, creating almost as much apathy as inspiration. But McEver pushed the button that set it all in motion. His historic contribution was a ninety-eight-yard kickoff return for a touchdown that will be remembered as long as football is played at the two institutions. McEver's run not only helped Tennessee beat a heavily favored Alabama team that day, but soon became known as the prototype of such feats.

While films of that run have long since been faded by time, McEver's memory has not. Clear images of one of Tennessee's most historic games continually run through his mind.

"Somehow," McEver says, "the Major [Coach Robert Neyland] had us convinced that we were going to win. I don't know to this day how he did it. Alabama was already a big name in college football. They were undefeated, as we were, but they had beaten Ole Miss 27-0 and we had beaten them just 13-12. I don't think that anyone, except Neyland and the team, believed that we could do it."

When McEver and the sophomore-studded Volunteers took the field at Tuscaloosa, they were twenty-five-point underdogs to Wallace Wade's team. Wade had given the Crimson Tide new national status with Rose Bowl teams in the twenties while Tennessee was still considered a growing Southern power under Neyland, who had been assigned to the Knoxville school by the War Department as an instructor in military science and tactics in 1925. Neyland, ever the psychologist, approached Wade before the game and suggested that, to keep the Crimson Tide from "routing" his Vols, the third and fourth quarters be shortened. Wade responded that he did not expect his team to win as easily as Neyland thought, but agreed to play the abbreviated second half if Alabama's lead justified it.

Of course, Wade never had that luxury. McEver cut back to his own two-yard line to haul in the opening kickoff—and was on his way.

"Two of them converging on me," he says. "I kind of 'split' them. One of them bumped from one side, and then the next one from the other. But then I was clear and there wasn't any doubt about it after that."

There was some doubt as to the outcome of the game, though. In less than two minutes, Alabama had retaliated with a quick touchdown drive that cut Tennessee's lead to 7-6. "A lot of people don't remember that Alabama came back to score a touchdown three plays after we had scored," points out McEver. "They just took the kickoff and marched right through us, and I remember thinking, 'Uh-Oh, this is going to be one of those games where we lead for one minute and that's all.' "

The Volunteers improved their lead to 9-6 when Hobo Thayer fell on a fumble outside the end zone for a safety. Bobby Dodd later hurled a short touchdown pass to McEver, but the Crimson Tide came back with another touchdown to trim Tennessee's lead at the half to 15-13. Needless to say, the teams went on to play two full fifteen-minute quarters in the second half, but 15-13 was the way it ended. Never again would the Volunteers catch a team looking the other way after that game. In one brilliant October afternoon, they had moved into Dixie's football penthouse alongside the redoubtable Crimson Tide. "I suppose," notes McEver, "you could say that is when it all started for us. After that we went on to some great years."

Not only did McEver become a household word with his dramatic runback, but Neyland was soon recognized for his football genius. A lieutenant fresh from West Point in 1925, Neyland had Tennessee's football flying higher than it ever had before. He launched his storied career by winning sixty-six of his first sixty-eight games. Five of his first seven teams were undefeated and he was soon acclaimed as the greatest of defensive coaches, particularly after his 1939 team did not yield a point in the regular season. Overall, he had an imposing record of 173-31-12, although his coaching career was interrupted three times by military service before he retired in 1952. A brigadier general in World War II, Neyland was similarly militaristic in his approach to football. "You had to walk the straight line with him," recalls George Cafego, an All-American tailback for Tennessee in the thirties. "There was no horseplay when he was around. He certainly had the complete respect of his players."

Strong figures such as Neyland have given the Alabama –Tennessee rivalry a deeper dimension through the years and marked it as much as anything as a series manipulated by dominating personalities. Neyland, the most imposing figure in Tennessee football history, was always center stage with Alabama's Wade or Frank Thomas, both coaching giants in their own right. Historians generally agree that Wade's 1927 Rose Bowl team played the most important game in Alabama's proud football history when the Crimson Tide scored three touchdowns in six minutes to beat the University of Washington 20-19. Johnny Mack Brown, who was to become a cowboy movie star, Pooley Hubert and Grant Gillis were among the Alabama heroes who gave the South the national exposure it had long hungered for. When Wade moved to Duke in 1931, after compiling an eight-year record of 61-13-3 at Tuscaloosa, he recommended Thomas as his successor. A former Notre

Dame quarterback who had played for Knute Rockne and roomed with the legendary George Gipp, Thomas gave Alabama alumni little reason to bemoan the loss of Wade. Thomas responded nobly to the challenge of replacing a big-name coach, and his Alabama teams recorded a glamorous 115-24-7 mark in fifteen seasons before ill health forced his retirement in 1947 at the peak of his career. Thomas's teams played in the Rose, Cotton, Orange and Sugar Bowls and his team that upset Stanford 29-13 in the 1935 Rose Bowl was generally considered to be his most memorable. The Crimson Tide featured the famous battery of tailback Dixie Howell and end Don Hutson, who was later to become an All-Pro at Green Bay. The other end on that squad was Paul "Bear" Bryant, who would subsequently become the most successful coach in Alabama's history.

Bryant picked Alabama up after it had fallen flat on its fortunes in the mid-fifties. Crimson Tide football was approaching its lowest ebb in this period when Bryant began restoring prestige to his alma mater in 1958. He had produced winning teams at Maryland, Kentucky and Texas A&M and was hailed as "the Great Rehabilitator" at Tuscaloosa. He fulfilled that promise with haste, turning out a winning team in his first year and a national champion by 1961. Tackle Billy Neighbors in 1958 was the first of many All-Americans developed by Bryant at Alabama. The honor roll also includes such stars as Joe Namath, Lee Roy Jordan, Pat Trammel, Steve Sloan, Ken "Snake" Stabler, Terry Davis, Dennis Homan, Ray Perkins, Johnny Musso and John Hannah. By the seventies, Bryant had won three more national championships and had become college football's winningest active coach and the third biggest winner in the history of the sport. Ironically, though Bryant produced four Bowl teams in eight seasons at Kentucky, he could never beat Neyland's Tennessee team and, as a matter of fact, had problems with the Volunteers until the seventies. Bryant went through a four-game losing streak with Tennessee teams coached by Doug Dickey and

Bill Battle until 1971, when he started a winning string that extended through the 1977 season and finally gave him the edge over his one-time nemesis.

The early years of chasing Tennessee were among Bryant's most frustrating moments in football. He says it used to get to him and that he often "overcoached" against the Volunteers. One year, looking hard for inspiration, he even decided to have all the Alabama dummies painted Tennessee Orange. All except one, he said. "I overcoached again, and got beat."

That it has taken a coach of Bryant's stature all these years to get a grip on Tennessee tells you something about the competitiveness of this rivalry. But it has an even deeper dimension. The series has developed a special character, because of the special teams involved. Both have produced so much first-class football through the years that there is a mutual respect that disdains the usual bitterness found in other top rivalries. As Tim Siler, sports editor of the *Knoxville News-Sentinel*, explains it: "The two schools have a great relationship. The loser always goes home and shuts up . . . no criticism of the officials, no bitterness. Just, 'We'll get 'em next year.' They admire each other too much to sling mud. That's why this rivalry has been on such a high plane through the years. They are two high-class operations."

This warm relationship was underscored recently when Johnny Majors, the new Tennessee coach, spoke to a meeting of the Tuscaloosa Quarterback Club and later paid a visit to an Alabama practice session. "Of course, it was after Tennessee had played Alabama that year," said Siler, "but that probably wouldn't happen anywhere else in college football—one coach in a Conference visiting another during the season. Majors was asked why he went and he said that he just wanted to see how the Bear ran practice. They were up in the tower together for three hours, talking and having a good time. That's the kind of spirit that's been engendered by this rivalry."

The competitive edge is, of course, one of the sharpest in

America. All of their mutual energies are directed at beating each other. This includes not only football but every other sport. "Some time ago, Tennessee went out after a good track program," recalls Siler. "Bryant didn't like this . . . and he started to raise the other programs at Alabama to a higher level. He didn't want to see Tennessee do better than Alabama at *any* sport. Neither wants to lose to the other at *anything*. An Alabama swimmer said recently: 'We don't care how we beat Tennessee—as long as we beat them.' "

Similar sentiments have been expressed in varying degrees by both sides through the years, especially about the football rivalry.

"When Neyland came to Tennessee," Cafego recalls, "he was told that the team he had to beat was Alabama. If you want to go anywhere, do anything, you had to beat Alabama. That was the rallying cry on campus. . . . That was all anybody talked about all summer."

Says Bryant of the Alabama–Tennessee game: "Neither coaching staff has to work hard at motivation. Actually, the toughest thing is keeping things from reaching a peak too early."

In a recent poll taken of Tennessee fans, former players and coaches, a tremendous majority said they'd rather mash Alabama's nose than any opponent on the Volunteer schedule. Dr. Andy Kozar, who played fullback for Tennessee in the early fifties, was one of those who answered the widely distributed questionnaire. "When I was playing, it was the game we measured it all by," he replied. "If we got past Alabama, we started thinking we might have a pretty good year."

Since starting in 1901 with an appropriate 6-6 tie, it has been a series of streaks. In the early 1900s, Alabama won seven straight games at one point, all by shutouts. A Tennessee "jinx" beguiled Alabama from 1948 through 1960, when the Crimson Tide could only win one of thirteen games. Starting in 1961, however, Alabama won five games and tied one. Later in the sixties, Tennessee defeated Alabama four straight times before Bryant started his recent streak against the Vols.

Given new stature by the 1928 game, the Alabama–Tennessee rivalry produced volcanic meetings in subsequent years, displaying some of the most memorable football the South—or the nation—had ever seen.

Of the 225 games that Neyland coached, he considered the 1932 duel with Alabama, playing under coach Frank Thomas, the most memorable. In a hard rain in Birmingham, Tennessee's Beattie Feathers and Johnny Cain of Alabama staged one of the greatest punting duels in college football history. Each kicked twenty times, Feathers averaging forty-eight yards and Cain forty-five. Tennessee won 7-3 when Feathers scored the game's only touchdown on a play that one newsman described as "one they will tell about when you and I are old, Maggie." Running from the twelve-yard line, Feathers slammed into the end zone through the mud of Legion Field. Up in the press box, Tennessee assistant coach Bill Britton was manning a telephone to the bench and startled everyone by shouting, "That's the one! That's the play!"

Bryant will no doubt remember the 1935 game, and for more reason than a 25-0 Alabama victory. He played with a broken leg, providing college football lore with one of its most colorful stories. Actually, he hadn't planned to play —he was forced into action by circumstance. Bryant had broken a bone in his leg the week before in a game with Mississippi State and was told by a doctor that he could dress for the Tennessee game, if nothing else. In the locker room before the game, assistant coach Hank Crisp—talking with a cigarette dangling casually from his mouth— delivered one of the most inspirational pep talks Bryant could remember. At the end, Crisp pointed to several players and said: "I'll tell you gentlemen one thing. I don't know about the rest of you, I don't know what you're going to do. But I know one damn thing. Old 34 will be after 'em, he'll be after their asses."

Bryant, whose number fluctuated from week to week,

looked down at his uniform shirt and, to his surprise, saw No. 34.

"I had no idea of playing," Bryant relates. "So we go out there and cold chills are running up my back. He done bragged on old 34. Ben McLeod, whose son played for us at Alabama a few years ago, had never started a game in his life, and he was starting in my place. They lined up for the kickoff and Coach Thomas turned to me and said, 'Bryant, can you play?' Well, shoot, what are you going to say? I just ran on out there. McLeod was so mad he could spit."

Bryant would later protest that "it was just one little bone." Red Drew, another assistant coach at Alabama in those days, would answer that with, "How many bones do you need to have a broken leg?"

With both teams at the top of their game in the thirties, the Alabama–Tennessee rivalry heated up considerably in this period. At the end of the decade, Tennessee was a bit hotter, constructing three straight unbeaten regular seasons with defensive giants that stood as tall as any in football. The Volunteers shut out a total of twenty-six opponents during a three-year high, extending from 1938 through 1940; they went to the Orange, Rose and Sugar bowls during this high-powered period. Alabama, a Rose Bowl team in 1937, only found a path of thorns against Tennessee in the subsequent three years.

Football historians generally agree that Johnny Butler's fifty-six-yard touchdown run in the 1939 game, won 21-0 by Tennessee, was one of the most brilliant broken-field maneuvers in the sport's history. He made much of it without benefit of blocking and not a single Alabama player was able to lay a finger on him as he circuitously threaded his way downfield.

"It has always been known as 'The Run,'" says Ben Byrd, sports editor of the *Knoxville Journal*. "You don't have to say anything else around here. Everyone knows what you're talking about. For years, it was used by Hollywood in movies whenever they wanted to show the classic running scene in a football picture."

Alabama–Tennessee games introduced more astonishing individual talents such as Harry Gilmer in the forties. Gilmer, one of the originators of the running-passing play, was equally heroic in Alabama's 12-0 defeat by Tennessee in 1946 and the Crimson Tide's 10-0 victory in 1947. After watching the slender Alabama star complete sixteen passes for 157 yards although spending some of the afternoon on the seat of his pants, courtesy of Tennessee tackle Dick Huffman, Neyland said of Gilmer after the 1946 game: "I doubt that football has or ever will see his equal. Gilmer is all they said he was and more, too. Don't let anyone tell you any different." It was the supreme compliment from a man rarely given to absolutes.

Byrd recalls that Huffman "must have had Gilmer down thirty or forty times in that 1946 game, but the little fellow kept getting up. And when he left, the Tennessee fans applauded him." That contest, by the way, marked the last game between one of the South's most colorful coaching rivalries, Robert Neyland vs. Frank Thomas, which had begun back in 1931. The Tennessee coach compiled six victories and a tie in ten meetings with Thomas. Neyland was just as tough on the other Alabama coaches he faced, forging a 12-5-2 record against his fiercest rival before he retired in the early fifties. Bowden Wyatt, a legendary player at Tennessee who returned to coach in the mid-fifties after producing championship teams at Wyoming and Arkansas, built on Neyland's success with five victories and a tie against Alabama in his first six tries. That made Bryant mad enough to kill himself recruiting players and he came up with an armload of great quarterbacks for the sixties in Joe Namath, Steve Sloan and Ken "Snake" Stabler.

Bryant won more than he lost against Tennessee in this decade, but few of the victories came easy. In 1965, the teams played to a 7-7 tie that will be long remembered for an unlikely Stabler goof as much as anything else. The Alabama quarterback, thinking it was first and goal to go, threw a pass out of bounds inside the Tennessee ten-yard line to stop the clock with six seconds left in the game. Actually, it had been fourth down, and the Crimson Tide lost possession of the ball.

Stabler made up for that mistake, and any others he might have made as a sophomore, the next year when he led Alabama to the national championship. Along the way, the Crimson Tide stepped over Tennessee's body after a death struggle in the rain at Knoxville's Neyland Stadium. The Volunteers, the best team Alabama would see that year, held a 10-0 lead in the first half, but finally succumbed 11-10 as the cool, persistent Stabler led Alabama back with a gallant, second-half rally. A Steve Davis field goal in the fourth quarter provided Alabama with its winning points, but was almost anticlimactic compared to the frantic ending. Key plays by quarterback Dewey Warren and halfback Charlie Fulton led Tennessee inexorably downfield in the closing minutes and with sixteen seconds left, the Volunteers had the ball in excellent field-goal position on the Alabama three-yard line, much to the amazement and joy of their passionate fans. But also to their disbelief, kicker Gary Wright missed this easy shot. A Tennessee professor later calculated that the angle at which the ball was snapped, from the right hashmark, had reduced the width of the kicker's target by about a foot and a half. Wright's attempt missed only by inches. "If Gary had had the opportunity to kick head-on, from the middle of the field, there is no way he would have missed," said one observer. "But the bad angle was just enough to throw him off."

Reverse déjà vu occurred for Bryant in 1968 when a short field-goal try failed for Alabama, costing the Crimson Tide a similar one-point loss. This time, Tennessee held on, 10-9.

The balance of power switched dramatically to Alabama in the seventies, but Tennessee hired Majors in 1977 with the hope that he could be their Bryant. It's felt that the rivalry has affected the past, present and future of the two schools, that Tennessee domination in the fifties helped bring Bryant to Tuscaloosa and that the circumstances were similar in the seventies for Majors, a go-getter who produced a national champion at Pitt in four short years.

The hard emphasis on this game has been a fact of football life among the interstate neighbors. Tennessee's Harvey Robinson, who played against Alabama in the early thirties, polished Neyland's single-wing attack as backfield coach and eventually became head coach of the Volunteers, says that Alabama–Tennessee is "a player's game . . . a game of concentration to avoid mistakes, fierce but clean hitting, tremendous fan enthusiasm." And Bryant gives the ultimate compliment to the rivalry when he says that he always judges a player as to whether "he'll play in a fourth quarter against Tennessee."

19
ARMY—NAVY

The Best of Friends,
The Worst of Enemies

From the beginning, the Army–Navy game has been all-out war. No football rivalry has ever been a more complete natural than this fierce competition, which embraces the competitive urgency of an armed skirmish and the flaming color of a Roman circus.

There may be contests with more intensified local appeal and annual games with higher national stakes, but the Army–Navy series has the broadest base of all and therefore what must be assumed to be the largest following.

A show with a unique flavor and powerful emotional wallop, the Army–Navy game might still be considered college football's top national attraction, as its publicists claim. Certainly no other annual one-day event draws such an influx, nor requires such a multiplicity of advance preparations or governmental concern.

Of the 100,000 or so who see the game annually in Philadelphia's John F. Kennedy Stadium, it's modestly estimated that more than half come to the city from other parts of the country. Railroads have worked out the complex logistics of carrying 25,000 to 30,000 passengers to the stadium from New York and Washington within a two-hour period and Philadelphia hotels brace for a blizzard of visitors.

The stature of the game is mirrored by the variety of emergency directives issued by federal and local agencies. Without special clearance, no aircraft may fly within three miles of the stadium the afternoon of the game. All drawbridges must stay down, so as not to impede the flow of traffic. Certain factories in New Jersey whose smoke sometimes drifts across the Delaware River to the stadium are told to suspend operations. Philadelphia firemen hose down nearby city dumps to suppress any fumes.

Abnormal concern is given to the care of the field, continually polished with green dye, and the concessionaires store everything from 150,000 hot dogs to 10,000 chrysanthemums for the glorified event.

Insignias of high rank are commonplace the day of the game, including the highest of all—the President of the United States. Teddy Roosevelt was the first chief executive to attend in 1901, and it is essential for the country's number-one citizen to display total objectivity. Traditionally, the President splits his allegiance, sitting one half of the game on Navy's side and the other half on Army's.

Starting with the President, some of the country's most eminent citizens have been Army–Navy fans.

The late Douglas MacArthur was a student manager of the 1902 West Point team and his interest never diminished, even in time of war. When the first of Army's great teams of the Second World War–period broke a five-game losing streak against Navy in 1944, MacArthur radioed from his headquarters as supreme commander in the Southwest Pacific: "The Greatest of All Army Teams Stop We have Stopped the War to Celebrate Your Magnificent Success."

President Franklin D. Roosevelt never attended an Army–Navy game, obviously because his physical disability prevented him from observing the custom of changing sides at halftime. But this did not prevent him from betting sizable sums of money on the game with his military aide, Maj. Gen. Edwin "Pa" Watson.

Roosevelt, a dedicated Navy rooter, was able to use his high office one time to bring aid and comfort to his ailing Middies. Several years before Roosevelt's term, Army and Navy stopped playing in a dispute over player eligibility. Annapolis had adopted the prevailing rule that limited a player to three years of college football, while West Point insisted on its right to field any bona fide Cadet, even if he had already played four full years at a civilian college before entering the Military Academy. Such veteran athletes as "Light Horse" Harry Wilson and Red Cagle allowed Army to run off a long string of victories against Navy in this period.

With the Depression setting in during 1930, President Herbert Hoover ordered an Army–Navy game to be played to raise money for charity. In 1931 the same thing happened, so the service academies decided to resume their heated rivalry on their own. The difference in opinion on eligibility remained, though, until 1938 when F.D.R. abruptly invoked his authority as commander-in-chief to settle the issue in Navy's favor. He handed Pa Watson a note for delivery to the Military Academy, which said: "From now on West Point will abide by the three-year rule."

Loyalty runs so deep in this series that partisans will do anything to stay in touch with the game, no matter where they are on the planet. At military outposts around the world, Army and Navy men arrange parties to hear the game broadcast on Saturday, whether it comes on at breakfast time, as in Hawaii; in the evening, as in Europe; or at three o'clock in the morning, as in the Far East. Each year, the two academies fill requests for party kits—pennants, pictures of players, "Beat Army" or "Beat Navy" posters, and flyers with school insignias—from not only all over the continental United States but just about every service installation abroad.

Wherever partisans gather, passions run high. In the Army–Navy Club in Manila during the 1926 game, a typically frenetic scene took place. The game, which was played in Chicago that year, was being broadcast via Navy radio. Game time in Manila was the early hours of the morning and the party had been going for some time before kickoff. While waiting for the contest to begin, some Army officers dressed as white Russian princesses, a mocking of the Navy officers from the Asiatic fleet who had

been known to have dated Russian women. Not to be out-
done, Navy officers wheeled kiddie carts around the
ballroom floor in a game of polo, thus imitating a favorite
Army pastime of the day.

The broadcast of the game was lost when the radio went
dead in the second quarter, and of course Army followers
accused Navy rooters of chicanery. It finally came back on
during the last few plays, including a touchdown by Navy
and Tom Hamilton's tying extra point that made the final
score 21-21. Characteristically, a big fight broke out among
the revelers in the club.

The ingenuity of one Navy officer stationed in Hong
Kong shows to what lengths loyalists will go to keep in
touch with the Army–Navy game. The officer took a radio
to his room with all the intentions of hearing the contest,
but the connection wouldn't fit and he was unable to plug
it in. He ended up getting reports via walkie-talkie to his
ship in the harbor.

No one, however, can match the imagination of the
American POWs in a Hanoi prison during the Vietnam
War. Commander Jack Fellows, a 1956 graduate of the
Naval Academy and a prisoner of war for six years, seven
months, relates that he and his fellow prisoners had "an
Army–Navy weekend every year. We'd tap on the wall that
everyone should come over to a certain room for make-
believe beer and pretzels," he says. "And would we dream
up magnificent menus for the postgame celebrations!"

These special "mind parties," plus pleasant recollections
of past Army–Navy games, kept Fellow's psyche intact
during his long, hard ordeal. He even made "bets" with Air
Force men who were graduates of West Point.

"We'd tap fake scores to each other through the wall,"
he explains. "The one who got the first tap in usually was
the winner."

The Joint Defense Force in Iceland has little else to do
but wait for the annual Army–Navy game and its attending
revelry. A recent request for a variety of material included
the following letter:

Dear Sir,

Once again it is time for the senior half of the Army in Iceland to come to you for help. Some years ago an enterprising Army officer made the Army–Navy game one of the big social events of the year, and it falls upon his successor each year to chair the effort at the Officers' Club. What really happens is that we tune in on Armed Forces Radio and Television Systems, run it through the speakers in the ballroom, get a gaggle of good-looking gals to move a football up and down a pseudo-gridiron on the floor, con some of the other gals to lead cheers, and have a grand old time.

While the Army–Navy game steams up backers everywhere, it is at the schools themselves that temperatures come to full boil.

There are football rallies at both Annapolis and West Point every week of the regular season, but before the Army–Navy game, everything is magnified considerably. Traditionally, the teams have two weeks before their climax game and the intensity in that period is downright mind-boggling.

"One thing about the Army–Navy game you always remember is the two weeks of buildup," says Navy coach George Welsh. "It's endless. It seems as if the game is never going to get here."

Signs shoot up on campus buildings, expressing the "Beat Army" or "Beat Navy" theme, and the big Thursday night rally before the game usually features "name" speakers. One year at West Point, Dwight Eisenhower, still a general then, addressed the Cadets by phone from Washington with the reminder: "The Army and the Navy are the best friends in the world 364½ days a year, but on this one Saturday afternoon, we're the worst of enemies."

At Annapolis, the Midshipmen prepare for the traditional event by applying war paint to Tecumseh, the bust of the old Indian chief that sits inside the so-called "Yard." The bronze replica of a wooden figurehead from the old warship Delaware is a talisman to whom generations of Midshipmen have made obeisance in appealing for favors—a passing mark in exams, a victory over Army. As a regiment of Midshipmen parades by on the eve of the game, each man slings a penny with his left hand at the face of the old warrior as a gesture of good luck. Meanwhile, West Pointers await the outcome of the annual Goats–Engineers game—a contest between teams drawn from the lowest-ranking and highest-ranking students. A victory for the goats is always perversely regarded as a good sign for Army against Navy.

On Friday morning, the teams leave for Philadelphia—"If only to get them away from the bedlam around here!" says one Naval officer. The same day, tractor trailers pull out with displays and stunts rigged up for the game by the Middies and Cadets.

Among the more appealing stunts are those surrounding the Navy goat and the Army mule, perhaps the most famous mascots in college football. One year the goat came on the field in a float designed to represent a perfume bottle and another time he emerged from a Trojan horse. A pair of mules one time rode in together on a trailer truck billed as "Army's Answer to Atomic Warfare." To the delight of the Midshipmen, the truck got stuck in the mud near one of the end zones.

Incidentally, the choice of the mule as the Army mascot reflects the longstanding usefulness of the animal in military operations—hauling guns, supplies and ammunition. The first Army mule, however, pulled an ice wagon and became a mascot when an officer at the Philadephia Quartermaster Depot decided that Army needed something to counteract the Navy goat. Just exactly when the Navy football team enlisted the goat as mascot is an uncertainty. But there is a legend that the Naval Cadets (as they were known then), on their march from the ferry station at Highland Falls up the steep hill to West Point to play the first Army–Navy game in 1890, saw a goat outside the noncom's houses at West Point and promptly shanghaied "Billy" for their mascot.

Kidnapping the Navy goat has always ranked among the Cadets' most prized Army–Navy pranks. There was the successful "goatnapping" of Billy XIV by Cadets in 1953. Professing deep regret, West Point finally sent the animal back to Annapolis with a diplomatic escort commanded by a colonel, who issued this statement upon his arrival: "They say in the Army there are four general classes of officers—aides, aviators, asses or adjutants. I am adjutant at West Point, have been playing aide to a goat all day, and feel like a bit of an ass." Another goatnapping one year spawned this ad by the Cadets in the *New York Times:* "Hey, Navy! Do you know where your 'kid' is today? . . . The Corps does."

The Navy goat, so often the victim, was used as a weapon of ridicule against the Army in 1971. There had been rumors all week prior to the Army–Navy game that President Richard Nixon would attend the contest. Just prior to the game, a limousine pulled into J.F.K. Stadium, bearing the presidential flags with Secret Service agents running alongside it. As the car tooled past the Cadets, they all rose and saluted. It proceeded around the huge arena, triggering a stir among the thousands of spectators, and stopped in front of the brigade of Midshipmen. When the door of the car opened, however, out came the Navy goat, much to the displeasure of the offended Cadets.

One of the most classic pranks relating to the Army–Navy game is the "ghost story" of 1972. An apparition resembling a cavalry soldier from the 1830s was supposed to have appeared several times in one of the West Point barracks. Five Cadets were witness to its shocking appearance.

Turned out, there was an earthly explanation for it. Two days before the game, Midshipman William Gravell came forth to publicly confess that he had pulled off the prank with a flashlight, photographic slide and a fire extinguisher. The thing everyone reported seeing, Gravell explained, was a slide of a Midshipman dressed in bits and pieces of old uniforms. The cold supposedly felt by one Cadet was produced by the fire extinguisher full of carbon dioxide.

Everyone is fair game for pranksters during the buildup to the Army–Navy contest, but no one receives more abuse than the exchange officer who is stationed at the opposite academy. Major Charles Wuerple, a recent Army exchange officer stationed at the Naval Academy, has been locked in his room, had it painted a Navy blue and gold, and found a mule in it that had been fed Ex-Lax. On one occasion, the Midshipmen took his car to the mess hall and filled it with cereal.

The Army exchange officer at Annapolis in 1969 was no less miserable for awhile. One night, Midshipmen surrounded his house and announced that they were going to demolish his car with sledgehammers. As he looked on in horror, the sailor boys hammered away until the vehicle was all but dust. But that mind-bending experience had a happy ending for the Army man. The Brigade had all chipped in one dollar apiece and handed the exchange officer a check for $4,000, sufficient to replace his old car with a better model.

Once the Middies and Cadets take their seats at the game, they supplement their organized cheers and songs with an endless bag of tricks.

One year, the Cadet cheerleaders, called the "Rabble Rousers," distributed air horns and tiny, tin clickers that made sounds resembling crickets.

"Those 8,000 clickers [two per man] made some racket," notes a fan who sat in the West Point section that day. "Then the air horns joined in and there really was some noise."

Another year, at kickoff, the corps of Cadets took off their gray jackets on signal and revealed T-shirts with the No. 12 on the front and the back. It was the start of the "Twelfth Man" tradition at Army.

"The Twelfth Man tradition puts the other team at a disadvantage right away," explains one Cadet, "because the other team has only eleven men on its side. Army has its Twelfth Man—the Corps—always ready."

There is a crossfire of ribbing shooting across the field. One season when Army was being criticized for a light schedule, the Navy came up with this parody of the West Point song, "On, Brave Old Army Team":

"We don't play Notre Dame,
 We don't play Tulane,
 But we play Davidson,
 For that's the fearless Army team."

If Navy wins on Saturday, relays of Midshipmen will keep two bells ringing at Annapolis for twenty-four hours. If Army wins, the players will be met at West Point Sunday afternoon and hauled up the hill to the grounds by hundreds of Cadets in the venerable "victory wagon."

While passions erupt on both sides and serve as a maniacal framework for the game, there is pragmatism afoot as well. The Army–Navy game is a financial must for both schools and often constitutes the difference between profit and loss for a season. It explains why the academies prefer to play at J.F.K. Stadium (formerly Municipal Stadium), which has been the scene of the game since 1936, except for a three-year period during the Second World War. Along with its obvious asset of convenient location, it has the most compelling advantage of size. The gargantuan stadium seats more people—about 100,000—than any other on the Eastern seaboard. And the city of Philadelphia demands only token rental and hands over other extra-profit sources, even those derived from the concessions sales.

Since the Second World War, the game has been the artistic as well as the financial salvation for Navy.

The 1946 Navy team won only a single game while Army, bursting with talents such as Doc Blanchard and Glenn Davis, was headed for its third straight undefeated season. The Cadets were a huge favorite and looked every bit as good as their advance notices by running up a 21-6 halftime lead. But in the second half, the game took a startling turn and the Midshipmen pulled the score up to 21-12 and then 21-18. With Municipal Stadium a madhouse, and frenzied spectators pouring down from the stands, Navy almost pulled it out with a frantic drive that ended on Army's two-yard line. This moral victory for Navy cost Army the national championship, which went that year to Notre Dame.

In 1948, Navy was winless and Army was undefeated, but the Middies proceeded to battle the Cadets to a rousing 21-21 tie. Then in 1950 came one of the biggest upsets in the series. The Cadets had gone through twenty-eight games without a loss by this time and Navy's record for the season showed merely two victories in eight games. Yet Navy pounded out a 14-2 triumph that year over a shocked Army team.

Upsets have usually been a hallmark of this wonderful series, especially during the intelligent administration of Earl Blaik at Army. The late coaching great once gave the matter considerable thought and came up with this analytical conclusion: "In 1946, we started out to annihilate them, then just staved them off. When we took them in 1947, they were expecting to beat us. Before that 1948 tie, practically our entire squad was weakened by nausea from some tainted turkey on Thanksgiving Day. In 1949 we trounced Navy. When Navy beat us in 1950, I guess you could call that an upset. But it was no upset when they won in 1951 and 1952. Our 1953 victory was an upset for Army. So that makes two upsets for us and one for them."

If someone had perhaps approached Eddie Erdelatz for a vote in the matter, he no doubt would have adjusted the upset score to read 2-2. The Navy coach of that era, and just about everyone else in camp, saw the 1946 cliffhanger as Navy's day, even though the final score didn't look that way.

Like Blaik at West Point, Erdelatz took over at Annapolis when football had reached low ebb and built a strong program. Erdelatz modestly declined any personal credit for that upsurge, but rather pointed to the untamed spirit of the players and the entire Naval Academy for this change in fortunes.

Such an intensity of spirit on both sides has created sparks and electricity from the beginning of this brilliant rivalry, when Annapolis challenged West Point to football combat in 1890.

The Army–Navy series opened on the parade grounds at West Point on November 29, 1890, but not before some enterprising work by a Cadet named Dennis Mahan Michie. Following the pioneering example of Rutgers and Princeton, the Naval Academy had played its first outside opponent in football in 1879. But the Military Academy, on the other hand, had been shut out from the sport by a hardnosed, policy-setting academic board, which branded college football as "a frivolous distraction." Michie was the most responsible for breaking through this highly prejudiced barrier. Michie knew and loved football, having played it at Lawrenceville Academy. But more important, his father was a leading member of the academic board and the youngster talked him into getting sanction for the game, in answer to the Navy challenge.

Along with the 270-man corps of Cadets, the audience included, according to the *New York Sun,* a delegation from New York City consisting of "about 150 officers of the Navy, the Army, and the naval reserve, with not a few ladies." Michie—in whose honor the modern West Point stadium is named—had organized a healthy-looking Army squad of fifteen, including said the *Sun,* "a line of giants." They were not strong enough to withstand the Naval attack that day, however, succumbing by a 24-0 score after the Midshipmen launched their powerful V-wedge. Charley Emrich, the Navy captain, became the first high-scoring player of the series with four touchdowns, worth four points apiece at that time.

The central element of interest was established on the spot, even if it did take some time for the trimmings to evolve. At the conclusion of that first game, a contemporary account reports: "The Annapolis men went wild over their victory. When the score reached Annapolis last night the naval Cadets were so delighted with the victory of their team that they fired twenty-four guns and then paraded the streets with horns." Similarly, when the news of Army's 32-16 victory at Annapolis the following year reached West Point, "the pent-up enthusiasm of the corps broke forth. The cadets marched around the post. The superintendent extended his congratulations, the band played, guns were fired (eleven, one for each member of the team), bonfires were lighted with fine effect."

The ferocity of those early games matched the interest. The 1893 contest at Annapolis, witnessed by 10,000 fans, was decided 6-4 in Navy's favor but not before some disturbing violent play. The players' ferociousness seemed to heat up the crowd as well and one row between a brigadier general and an admiral wound up in a challenge to a duel. Whether or not the duel came off is not known, but the incident caused a break in relations for six years. This was the first—and longest—of four interruptions in the series. In 1909 a game was canceled because of a player's death; games were called off in 1917 and 1918 because of the First World War; the final break took place in 1928 and 1929 because of the aforementioned dispute over player eligibility.

After Army and Navy resumed their series in 1899, they made up for lost time with a succession of exciting meetings that produced some of the most appealing football players of the age. Among them were Charley Daly, a dynamic little Army quarterback at the turn of the century who later became a West Point coach, and Navy's Jack Dalton and Babe Brown, who were involved in a string of shutout victories for the Middies in 1910, 1911 and 1912. Dalton, especially, was a romantic figure after he was dubbed "Three-To-Nothing" Jack Dalton for his field-goal kicking expertise. Dalton's field goals in 1910 and 1911 gave the Navy successive 3-0 victories, while Brown kicked two field goals as the Midshipmen made it three in a row over Army with a 6-0 decision in 1912.

Elmer Oliphant was the most visible player in the series for a while thereafter. In the young giant's first appearance against Navy in 1915, he scored all the points in a 14-0 Army victory. The next year, the orders of the day at Annapolis read like this the morning of the game: "6:00 a.m. —Rise; Stop Oliphant!; 7:00 a.m.—Breakfast, Stop Oliphant!" But the Midshipmen just weren't able to follow orders in 1916 and lost 15-7 as Oliphant starred again.

The 1922 game at Franklin Field in Philadelphia was generally accepted as the most exciting of the series until that point. The lead changed hands three times and Army won a 17-14 thriller on a last-minute touchdown pass from George Smythe to Pat Timberlake.

Four years later, the teams played what is considered the number-one classic of their rivalry, a 21-21 tie before 110,000 at Soldier Field in Chicago.

Navy was unbeaten that year and Army had lost only a 7-0 decision to Notre Dame, but there were other intriguing and significant aspects of that meeting. It was the only Army–Navy game played west of the Appalachians and it was watched by the biggest crowd ever to see a college football game. Both teams had new coaches—Biff Jones for Army and Bill Ingram for Navy. There was even a brother vs. brother rivalry, with Navy guard Art Born confronting Army end Chuck Born.

The field had to be cleared of snow shortly before game time and although the ball soon became waterlogged, there was a remarkable exhibition of passing and the now forgotten art of drop kicking.

Using an old Knute Rockne tactic, Jones started seven of his second-stringers in the role of "Shock Troops," but this looked like an error in judgment when Navy broke away to a 14-0 lead on touchdown runs by Howard Caldwell and J. B. Schuber.

"At this pulsating juncture you would have rated the Army's chances as being worth something less than a plugged Mexican nickle," observed one writer.

Army looked as good as gold, however, when "Lighthorse" Harry Wilson and Chris Cagle led a cavalry charge for the Cadets that tied the game 14-14 at the half and final-

ly sent them into the lead, 21-14, in the third period. The
go-ahead touchdown was scored on a brilliant forty-three-
yard dash by Cagle, one of the storied names in Army football history.

Back came Navy. From their own forty-four-yard line,
the gallant Middies ran, passed and plunged through an
Army team that yielded space grudgingly, and finally
scored on a superb, eight-yard run by Alan Shapley around
the Cadets' left flank.

All of the remaining drama belonged to Tom Hamilton,
who drop-kicked the tying extra point in a "field almost as
silent as a tomb," according to one observer.

More than half a century after that glorious Navy comeback, the game is still fresh in Hamilton's mind. Among
the slices of memorable conversation he heard that day was
a piece of advice from Coach Ingram and an inspirational
order from Navy captain Frank Wickhorst. Remembers
Hamilton:

"Ingram told us, 'In going out for your warmups, I want
you to stop at the end of the runway and look as long as
you want at the largest crowd ever to witness a football
game, 110,000 people, and then to forget the crowd."

In the game's most crucial moment, just before Navy's
tying touchdown drive in the fourth quarter, Hamilton recalls that Wickhorst took a time out, got the team together,
pointed at the goal line sixty-five yards away and said: "We
are going across that goal line without losing the ball. Let's
go!"

The tie spoiled an otherwise perfect season for Navy, but
the Middies could console themselves with the national
championship that year. Ironically, the tie game was as
close as Navy came to beating Army in the period from
1922 until 1934—the longest either team has gone without
a victory in the series. During that period of Army dominance, the Cadets won eight times and there were two ties.
Navy finally broke through with a 3-0 victory in 1934 on a
field goal by Slade Cutter and a fine all-around
performance by Fred "Buzz" Borries, the quarterback and

safetyman. "Borries made about ten last-man tackles in that game," recalled E. E. "Rip" Miller, who was an assistant coach in 1934.

Eventually the balance of power shifted and Navy went on a streak of its own with the help of coach Emery "Swede" Larson, who never lost to Army either as a player or a coach. The Middies won five straight games from the Cadets from 1939 through 1943, with three of those victories coming at the beginning under Larson's administration. In 1939, the positive-thinking coach had a big sign put up over the main entrance to Bancroft Hall at Annapolis: "It Can, It Shall Be Done. Beat Army."

In 1944, the Blanchard–Davis era began at Army and triggered three defeatless years and a span of domination over Navy. During this period, Navy produced some of its best squads in history, with the help of transfers due to the war. But if the Midshipmen were good in 1944 and 1945, Army was even better with such players as Felix Anthony "Doc" Blanchard and Glenn Woodward "Junior" Davis in the backfield, called by Cadet coach Earl Blaik "the best one-two punch that college football ever saw." The combined wallop of fullback Blanchard ("Mr. Inside") and halfback Davis ("Mr. Outside") meant trouble for Navy and every other football team on Army's schedule.

"Blanchard was the best-built athlete I ever saw," Blaik once said of the six-foot, 208-pounder. "There was not an ounce of fat on him, with slim waist and Atlas-like shoulders and legs. For a big man, he was the quickest starter I ever saw. He could catch passes, punt and kick off exceptionally well. Twice in Navy games, I saw him run through a head-on tackle without breaking stride and race on to a touchdown. He had great, instinctive football sense, supreme confidence and pride."

Blaik was equally profuse in his praise of Davis: "Glenn Davis was emphatically the fastest halfback I ever saw. He was not so much a dodger and side-stepper as a blazing runner, who had a fourth and even a fifth gear in reserve, could change directions at top speed and fly away from tacklers as if jet-propelled. He could also throw and catch passes and was a superior blocker and tackler."

Combined with Tucker and halfback Rip Rowan, this celebrated quartet was given the sobriquet of Army's "Million Dollar Backfield" and generally recognized as the best in West Point's history. It was Navy's misfortune to be in the way of this unique Army machine, but nevertheless the Midshipmen gave the Cadets all they could handle in 1944 and 1946, two of the best games in the series.

In 1944, the two giants of college football went through a ferocious defensive first period, during which each made only one first down and advanced no further than six yards inside the other's territory. But Army won the quarter if only because the Cadets put out of action one of their principal 1943 tormentors, hard-running Navy left halfback Bob Jenkins. Jenkins, who started the game on an uncertain knee, was racked up by the Cadets and was unable to return to action until the fourth quarter, when he was of little use.

In the second period, Navy suffered its second crucial casualty when tackle Don Whitmire was sent limping off the field after a series of brutal blocks by Army end Hank Foldberg and tackle Tex Coulter. The Cadets added insult to injury with a twenty-three-yard touchdown dash by reserve Dale Hall to take a 7-0 lead at the half.

When guard Joe Stanowicz blocked a kick for a safety and a 9-0 margin in the third quarter, it appeared that Army would be on its way to an easy victory. But Hal Hamberg, a diminutive halfback who ran and passed with equal dexterity, sparked Navy on a seventy-two-yard drive that resulted in a one-yard touchdown plunge by Clyde Scott, cutting the Cadet edge to a tenuous 9-7.

The score remained that way until the fourth quarter, when the indefatigable Blanchard ceaselessly hammered away at Navy's middle until he scored standing up from the ten. Davis later got around Navy's right end and ran fifty-two yards for a touchdown on a special play cooked up for him called "The California Special." Blanchard flanked to the right, Max Minor went in motion to the left and reserve quarterback Tom Lombardo pitched out to Davis, heading to his left. The mercurial halfback just outdistanced Hamberg, who tried to head him off. Dick Walterhouse place-kicked the extra point for a 23-7 Army final and the Corps of Cadets sang on key:

"We are the kings of the gridiron—
And the conquerers of every foe we meet."

Except for a titanic scoreless tie with Notre Dame in 1946, the Cadets also were conquerers of every foe they met. But Navy had the Corps singing a different tune after going down to a bitter 21-18 defeat that ended with the Midshipmen on the threshold of scoring the winning touchdown.

Most observers looked at the game as a monumental mismatch, some listing the point spread in Army's favor at thirty and above. This was the end of the glory road for the brilliant Cadet seniors, who had played twenty-six games without defeat over a three-year period, outscoring opponents over this stretch, 1,158 points to 143, and winning national championships in 1944 and 1945. The Midshipmen had nothing to match this remarkably strong Army team, having lost many of their wartime stars, including the celebrated "Smackover" Scott. After squeezing through a 7-0 victory in one game, Navy lost seven straight times and arrived at the Army contest with one of its sorriest records in recent history.

No one expected what happened next, with the possible exception of Navy coach Tom Hamilton, who had a secret weapon—the power of spirit.

"The support of the Brigade of Midshipmen was unbelievable," Hamilton recalls. "They practically went berserk for two weeks working into a frenzy for the game. Leon Bramlett [the Navy captain] had a secret meeting the night before the game at the Pine Valley Club where the Navy team was secluded."

Whatever inspiration Bramlett gave his teammates was not evident in the first half, as the Cadets built their lead to 21-6 with the help of a fifty-four-yard run by Blanchard and a twenty-seven-yard pass to him from Davis. But the Middies still displayed sublime arrogance in the locker room at intermission, as Hamilton remembers.

"During the halftime, the Navy team reaffirmed its confidence to win the game, and couldn't wait to take the field against this supposedly unbeatable Army team."

With sophomore quarterback Reaves Baysinger mixing his plays beautifully, and "Pistol Pete" Williams and Bill Hawkins doing the running, Navy scored on a seventy-eight-yard drive capped by Hawkins's three-yard buck. Army gambled on a fourth-down play and lost the ball on Navy's thirty-five-yard line, giving the Midshipmen the opportunity to move the ball to the Army five as the third quarter ended. Only moments later, the Middies had their third touchdown of the day, on a pass from Bill Earl to Bramlett.

The Midshipmen missed their third extra point after the touchdown, but it seemed to be academic when they expressed new energy and began sailing downfield toward another apparent touchdown in the later stages of the fourth quarter. They launched their final attack with seven minutes and thirty seconds left, finally arriving at the Army three with the help of a stunning twenty-yard run on fourth down by fullback Lynn Chewning. Now a minute and a half remained and the crowd of 102,000 literally went wild. With many of the guards removed to escort President Harry Truman, a large chunk of the audience burst over the sidelines and end zone. Play was delayed, but the crowd retreated only a few feet.

"The noise was terrific," recalls Hamilton. "It took forever to get the signals heard."

It also took forever, it seemed, for Navy to move the ball. Chewning tried twice to pierce the Army line but was flattened, first by Goble Bryant and Foldberg, and then by Barney Poole. Then Hamilton, in his own words, "made the fateful decision that probably took the game away from the gamest bunch of players. . . ."

What Hamilton did was stop the clock by sending in Hawkins and the result of this gesture cost Navy a five-yard, delay-of-game penalty. Navy got the five yards back when Hawkins back-lateraled to Williams, but the time ran out as the runner attempted to hit the out-of-bounds line on the two and ran into Poole and the crowd.

"This should have stopped the clock as a de facto out-of-bounds," Hamilton says. "In the nine seconds left, I think Baysinger would have hit Hawkins on a check-off pass for the score."

Hamilton made a vain effort at the end to stop the clock by sending in a substitute, but Billy Earl was unable to get the officials' attention. And what might have been the greatest upset of the era fell short.

Eddie Erdelatz had better luck against Army, winning five games and tying one in nine meetings. The one the successful Navy coach might remember most is the 14-2 victory in 1950 that stopped a Cadet winning streak of twenty-eight games. Erdelatz called that one "the greatest team effort I've ever seen" and no doubt it took the Middies just that to beat this great Army squad. The teams came into the game following a pattern developed in those years—Army a winner of eight straight and Navy, winner of only two in eight. Blaik, somewhat inexperienced in analyzing Army defeats (three in his last seven years on the job), detected signs of fine coaching in Navy's behalf.

"We were well scouted offensively," he said after his first loss in twenty-nine games.

But the biggest determining factor to Blaik was the one unregimentable item that had haunted Army before: spirit.

"They outcharged us," Blaik said. "They overwhelmed us."

Some observers might attach some symbolic meaning to that significant 1950 upset, for it established a new era of Navy supremacy that took hold right through the seven-

ties. Included in Navy's upper hand was a five-game winning streak, established from 1959 through 1963, during
Roger Staubach's princely reign at Annapolis.

Even before Staubach came on the scene, the Middies
were manhandling strong Army teams. The most notable
of these Navy victories was a 27-20 decision in 1954, when
Army had rebuilt into one of the country's top teams after
the alleged cribbing scandal at West Point in the early fifties had decimated Blaik's squads. That particular year,
Army was the top offensive club in the country and Navy
first in defense.

"Scalpers were asking between $50 and $125 for a pair of
tickets and getting their price," noted one writer. "The
game truly had captured the nation's spotlight and when it
ended, was worth every bit of the buildup."

George Welsh, who later returned to coach at Annapolis, had a hand in all four Navy touchdowns and won
the game with a scoring pass in the third quarter. In a typically frantic Army–Navy finish, the heralded Middie defenders withstood a Cadet challenge on their eight-yard
line late in the contest and lived up to their colorful
nickname, "A Team Named Desire."

Another big Naval hero during the fifties, when the Midshipmen had a 6-3-1 record against Army, was Joe Bellino.
The sturdy five-foot-eight halfback became the first Navy
man in history to score three touchdowns in a game against
Army as he led the Midshipmen to a 43-12 rout in 1959.
Navy's point total was the highest by either team in the
series, until the Midshipmen swamped the Cadets 51-0 in
1973. Called Navy's greatest prospect in twenty-five years
when he entered the Academy in the fall of 1957, Bellino
was a bruising, cocky runner ("I figure I've got at least one
fifty-yard run in me in every game"). He was content to
settle for a forty-seven-yarder on one of his touchdown
runs in that particular Army game and was even more delighted with a fifteen-yard score on which he used some
field expediency. He crashed through right tackle, found a
gaping hole, swung to the right sideline, and scored. That

wasn't the way the play was planned, however. "I was supposed to cut toward the middle," he said of his first-quarter touchdown burst. "But it's easier to go outside—especially when there's no one there."

Then along came Staubach, the Heisman Trophy–winning quarterback who led some of Navy's strongest teams since the World War II era. Staubach, who as a sophomore directed a 34-14 rout of Army in 1962, emerged as college football's glamour player of 1963. His stature, in fact, loomed so large that Navy coach Wayne Hardin decided that a ban on interviews was necessary to give Navy's leading man some piece of mind and some quiet time in which to pursue his studies.

"More people would like to see Roger Staubach right now than any celebrity," Hardin said at the time, explaining the unusual ban on professional visitors. "If we opened the doors, do you have any idea how many writers and photographers would show up at our practice? A dozen? It would be closer to 5,000."

There were times, it appeared, when not even that many tacklers could chase Staubach down. The lithe, six-foot-two quarterback was the country's foremost practitioner of the art of scrambling, rolling out with deceptive speed and long, powerful strides.

The more Staubach got into trouble, the better he was, it seemed. Always hard to pin down, Staubach passed proficiently with tacklers tearing off his jersey or clawing at his legs.

"He is, in the final sense, that splendid combination of runner-passer who can invest every play with unbearable excitement," one observer decided.

Staubach's style was decidedly perfect for Hardin's football philosophy, which was wide-open and occasionally bordered on the razzle-dazzle. In stark contrast to Hardin was the new Army coach, Paul Dietzel, who attached breezy labels to his various teams such as the "Go Unit," "The Chinese Bandits," and "The Regulars" but actually was content with a more conventional game than Hardin.

The contrast in styles in itself made the 1963 meeting between Army and Navy intriguing, let alone the added ingredients of Navy's best season in many years, and a Bowl bid in the offing. The winner would join top-ranked Texas in the Cotton Bowl on January 1, and if the Cadets needed more incentive, they got it from Hardin's arrogant statement prior to the game.

"We think we are the Number-One team in the nation," Hardin had said. "We want to prove it."

Dietzel mockingly agreed. "Don't panic," he told his Army players with a grin.

Army was lusting for blood as well, since Navy had won four straight games from the Cadets and was installed as an eleven-point favorite to make it five. To rub it in, Navy's gold uniforms had "Go For Five" lettered on the back.

From the opening moments, it appeared that this sixty-fourth annual game might be memorable. Texas coach Darrell Royal, scouting his Cotton Bowl opponent, was impressed with the action while watching from the press box.

"I'll tell you one thing," he said. "Nobody's backing off down there. They're trying to maim each other."

For the first three quarters, the game went according to form. Army quarterback Rollie Stichweh (it rhymes with "which way") sliced over from the ten after driving his team sixty-five yards and the Cadets had a 7-0 lead. But the gifted Staubach responded to the gravity of the situation with the help of fullback Pat Donnelly. Throwing just enough to keep the Army defense honest, Staubach kept mostly on the ground and put together three drives of forty-seven, eighty and ninety-one yards, capping each with a touchdown by Donnelly. Navy had what looked like a safe 21-7 lead with 10:32 remaining.

"I had no idea Staubach was that quick," Royal said. "You've got to be under control when you rush him. He loves to come out of there, doesn't he? Well, one reason he gets away with it is because the linebackers are dropping off to defend against the pass, and when he decides to run he's quick enough to get away from those old clubfooted tackles and guards."

Just when Royal was adjusted to the idea of meeting Navy in the Cotton Bowl, a series of crises confronted the Midshipmen. These were engineered by the ubiquitous Stichweh, who very nearly out-Staubached the Navy. He moved the Cadets smartly to a quick touchdown with the help of halfback Ken Waldrop. When Navy beefed up its flanks, Stichweh sent Waldrop cracking through tackle for big yardage. When the Middies stacked up the middle, Stichweh scampered around end. From the Navy five, the Army quarterback rolled out to his right and leaped into the end zone for the Cadets' second touchdown of the day. Moments later, another Stichweh rollout gave Army a two-point conversion and cut the Navy lead to 21-15.

"They're going to try an onside kick just as soon as the referee gives them the ball," Royal suggested. "What we do in a situation like this is put our backs and ends up on the front line. They're more agile."

Navy made no such move, and the agility belonged to Army on this particular play. The Cadets recovered their own kick at the Navy forty-nine-yard line with a play that they had practiced for two years. As Ray Hawkins, the regular kicker, lined up behind the ball at the forty-yard line, Dick Heydt suddenly swung in at an angle and booted the ball across the field to where Stichweh fell on it. This type of razzle-dazzle was expected from Hardin, but hardly from Dietzel.

Now Army had the ball and the momentum, and six minutes and thirteen seconds left—"plenty of time to score its first victory over Navy since 1958, and its first ever over Navy coach Wayne Hardin," observed one writer.

There was still plenty of time left for the Cadets after they had scratched their way to three first downs and the Navy seven-yard line. That left one minute and thirty-eight seconds for Army to score, but the Cadets would have had even more time had they put more care and planning into their drive and used their precious seconds wisely. Once

when time was called for a first-down measurement on the
Navy twenty-two, Army had not taken advantage of the
interlude to call its next play but huddled only after the
clock had restarted. Possibly more than twenty seconds
could have been saved in that instance. Further, Army never deliberately threw the ball behind a receiver's hand in
order to stop the clock or go into what most teams call a
"two-minute drill," which requires calling a series of plays
in the huddle and running them in sequence to save time.

The Cadets were finally undone not only by their own
lack of diligence but with the help of the fans as well. As
the seconds ticked off, Army rooters screamed, "Touchdown! Touchdown!" and Navy fans cried, "Stop Them!
Stop Them!" and this combined noise with the roar of the
crowd forced twenty more precious seconds to be wasted
because the Army team could not hear Stichweh's signals.
Referee Barney Finn stopped the clock momentarily so
that Stichweh's signals might be heard. This could have
been a break for the Cadets, who had no more timeouts
left. But they unwisely rehuddled, unaware that the clock
had restarted. When play resumed Waldrop barreled to the
two. Now there were sixteen seconds remaining. Quickly,
Army lined up. Once more, the din drowned Stichweh's
signals and there was no margin left for Army.

During the last play, on which Waldrop plowed to the
two, the Navy players were understandably slow in getting
untangled from the pile-up of players.

"I was underneath all of it," said Navy tackle Jim Freeman, "and I had sort of a peephole to look at the clock. I
was in no hurry to get up." Navy guard Alex Krekick, also
in the tangle, noted, "I don't think any Navy player was in
a hurry to get up." Added Navy guard Fred Marlin: "I
think Army caused some of the confusion. They were
scrambling around, trying to get up, and kept knocking
everyone back down."

Staubach also was in that tangled web of tacklers, if only
in spirit. He watched from the sidelines, helpless but happy, as the gun went off and Navy had its 21-15 victory and

Cotton Bowl bid. "I must have said a hundred 'Hail Marys,' " Staubach told a reporter later.

In artistic terms, the end of the game hardly satisfied purists who would demand for the sake of argument that a last play was needed to tie a neat ribbon on the affair. They, of course, either wanted a dramatic Army touch-down or a gallant goal-line stand by Navy. But the exciting finish nevertheless elevated the game to a high position in Army–Navy annals, perhaps matching the unusual drama of the 1946 contest.

By an ironic coincidence, the two finishes were exactly parallel—the losing team running out of time on the threshold of victory. Only in 1963, it was Army who came out on the short end.

20
EPILOGUE
Jugs, Mugs, and Hugs

The Little Brown Jug is among America's most famous college football trophies, but most fans would flunk a quiz to name the origins of the Little Brown Stein. The Little Brown Stein? Why, yes, it is about eighteen inches high and cost about twenty-five dollars to make in 1938. Idaho and Montana annually play for possession of that vessel and spare no passion doing it.

It is just this type of circumstance that separates the boys from the men or, more precisely, the colleges from the pros. Tradition and trophies are words that belong almost exclusively to the vernacular of college football. And because they do, every fan has *somebody* he especially wants to see beaten. The week of their game, Wabash feels about DePauw the way Ohio State feels about Michigan, and so forth.

There are all kinds of rivalries to keep spirits up during the football season. There are interstate rivalries, intrastate rivalries, border rivalries, crosstown rivalries and cross-country rivalries. Their relative worth is academic, of course, because after all, at one time or other they have all burned brightly in the hearts of their followers. If the flame is currently not at a roaring pitch, as it may be in some cases, then at least the tradition and the trophies are still there.

The Minnesota–Michigan game, for the Little Brown Jug, may be put in such a niche. At one time the modest crockery vessel was a trophy for titans and the Little Brown Jug became football's best-known art object. Michigan and Minnesota have played a lot of games and produced an army of good teams through the years. The jug, which is 2½ feet tall, was originally an old gray plaster crock that Michigan coach Fielding Yost carried around so that his players could drink fresh Ann Arbor spring water while drowning the opposition in points. The tradition of Minnesota playing Michigan for the jug began with one of the most exotic upsets in college football history in 1903. That year, Michigan had arrived in Minneapolis with its fabulous "Point a Minute" team and a twenty-nine-game winning streak. But Minnesota clawed its way to a 6-6 tie on old Northrup Field and Yost and his team were in apparently such a hurry to get out of town that they went off and forgot their crock of water. It led to the immediate joke among Minnesota Swedes: "Jost left his yug."

A janitor, Oscar Munson, found the Michigan water jug the following Monday morning while cleaning up and took it to the athletic director. It was labeled "Michigan Jug 'Captured' by Oscar." When Michigan later inquired about the jug, Minnesota promptly replied: "If you want it, come up and win it." They have been fighting for it ever since and if the rivalry improved with age, so did the jug. It is now painted maroon (for Minnesota) and blue (for Michigan) and all the scores of the games are printed on it.

The most famous modern contest for the jug came in 1940, when Michigan was ranked Number One and Minnesota Number Two in the national polls. There was only one thing wrong with what could have been a splendid game. It rained hard that day, turning the Minnesota stadium into the world's largest swimming pool. The bad field conditions hurt Michigan more that day, especially slowing down the usually meteoric Tommy Harmon. He had a forgettable afternoon, slipping and sloshing around and missing an extra point that still makes him irritable when he talks about it. He did pass for a touchdown that gave Michigan a 6-0 lead, but later Bruce Smith slithered eighty yards through the muck and mire for a touchdown and Minnesota became Number One by that very margin of one point, 7-6. Near the end Harmon had a chance to win

the game for Michigan when he drove his team down to
Minnesota's goal line in the fourth quarter. However,
when a wide hole opened up for Harmon, he slipped in the
mud. "I can still see the hole," Harmon says today. "It's
bigger than a room, but I just can't get in there."

The "Victory Bell," *objet d'art* of the series between the
University of Cincinnati and the University of Miami of
Ohio, is another of college football's hallowed trophies.
Originally, the bell hung in the famous twin towers of Harrison Hall, the "Old Main" that in 1824 became Miami
University. Early in Miami's football history, it became
customary to celebrate football victories by ringing the
bell. And the "borrowing" of the bell by some University
of Cincinnati rooters in the 1890s was one of the many
incidents that made sparks in this rivalry, the oldest west
of the Alleghenies and among the Top Ten for longevity in
the country. The series is one of a handful that have currently topped the eighty-game mark.

The Miami–Cincinnati bell was a victory symbol for
many years, changing hands according to the outcome of
the annual Thanksgiving Day game. Then, sometime in the
thirties, the bell disappeared. Circumstances are vague. Miami supporters circulated the theory that "some of the Cin-
cy boys got tired of always passing the prize to Miami and
decided to remedy the situation by hiding it." But the results of that era weren't consistent enough to support the
theory, although Miami does hold the overall edge in the
series thus far. In 1946, the bell just happened to turn up
beneath the visiting team's bench at Cincinnati's Nippert
Stadium. It stayed with the Bearcats that year as Cincinnati
won one of the most exciting and important games of the
series, 13-7, and went on to the Sun Bowl. Brought back to
Oxford, Ohio, after a victory by Miami in 1947, the bell
was inscribed with the scores of the series that year. In
1950, after Miami defeated Cincinnati in a game renowned
as the "Blizzard Bowl" for its icy weather conditions, the
bell was dressed up. It was hung in a new wood framework,
painted with a red "C" on a black background on one side

and a red "M on a white background on the other, with each team's victories indicated on its side of the bell.

Notre Dame and Purdue play for something called "The Shillelagh." It was donated to the series in 1957 by the late Joe McLaughlin, a merchant seaman and an Irish fan who brought the club from Ireland. Although Purdue and Notre Dame are neighbors in the state of Indiana, they didn't start playing football with each other until 1946. They have made up for lost time, however, with some of the most intriguing games of the modern era. One of the best games in this closely fought series came in 1948, when the Fighting Irish edged the Boilermakers 28-27 in what one sportswriter called "one of the finest college games of all time." Steve Oracko missed three out of four extra-point conversion attempts that day and then kicked a long and difficult field goal to give Notre Dame what turned out to be the winning points. Purdue certainly savors its 1965 victory, when the Boilermakers moved the length of the field on Bob Griese's passes to win, 25-21. But the game that Purdue loyalists are apt to remember the most is the 28-14 victory in 1950 that stopped Notre Dame's thirty-nine-game unbeaten streak and signaled the end of an era as well.

Because of their stature in college football, the Fighting Irish find that they have more than one natural enemy. Their rivalries with Southern Cal and Army made headlines for years, but just about everyone else considers Notre Dame the team they would like to beat the most. Along with the aforementioned series, the Notre Dame–Michigan State game has been very intense in the modern era and Notre Dame's rivalry with Navy is certainly one of the most enduring. The highlight of Notre Dame's battles with Michigan State was probably the 1966 game when the Fighting Irish and Spartans fought to a 10-10 tie with a national championship at stake. Notre Dame eventually won the title with the help of a crushing defeat of Southern Cal at the end of the season. Navy has stayed on the Notre Dame schedule through thick and thin, mostly thin, in the longest continuous intersectional rivalry in college football. The two have met annually since the start of the series in 1927. One of their most celebrated, and controversial, games occurred in 1945. With the score tied at 6-6 and the contest in its final seconds, Notre Dame quarterback Frank Dancewicz hit Phil Colella with a pass deep in Navy territory. Tony Minisi, a Navy defensive back, managed to shove Colella out of bounds. But many fans, particularly those of Notre Dame, thought that Colella had crossed the goal line while still inside the sideline chalk mark.

"We thought we had that one," recalls one-time Notre Dame coach Hugh Devore. "But the officials ruled that Colella went out on the one-foot line. We tried two sneaks and still didn't get the touchdown."

Though many still contend that both Colella and Dancewicz (on the second sneak) scored, the game went into the record books as a 6-6 tie.

Winner of the Wabash–DePauw game gets to keep an old locomotive bell called the "Monon Bell," assuming it is not stolen by overzealous students first. The bell was donated in 1932 by the Monon Railroad in Indiana. If the Cincinnati–Miami propagandists claim to have the "oldest rivalry west of the Alleghenies," then the Wabash–DePauw drum-beaters go them one better. They call their series "the oldest *continuous* rivalry west of the Alleghenies." At any rate, it is one of the continually best small college rivalries in the country. Being in the same ballpark competitively over the years, Wabash and DePauw have beaten each other about the same number of times and harassed each other even more. A Wabash professor says that every time the DePauw mascot—a student dressed in a $300 tiger suit—gets near the Wabash stands he loses his tail, or worse.

Any self-respecting, persevering rivalry should have growing pains, of course, and some bitter seeds were planted early in the Wabash–DePauw series. DePauw claimed a forfeit of the 1891 game because Wabash didn't show. Wabash has no record of it but has been unable to get it off the books. When DePauw lost at Wabash one year, its student newspaper reported that "the best team cannot win when playing against thirteen men, two of them officials ... [who] were personal friends of the Wabash coach." Wabash backed out of another game because of an incident the year before when Wabash fielded a black player. When DePauw records showed a victory over Wabash that year, Wabash officials investigated and discovered that the losing team was actually Wabash High School.

There is no specific trophy involved in the Bowling Green–Toledo game, just the bragging rights of northwest Ohio. This notable Midwestern rivalry began with Bowling Green's first game ever, in 1919, when Toledo scored a first-period touchdown and outlasted the Falcons, 6-0. The series continued until 1935, when athletic relations broke off because of "poor sportsmanship" by the respective teams in football and Bowling Green's general inability to keep up with Toledo's rapidly growing football program. By 1948, the football rivalry resumed after a long cooling-off period ironically enough through the efforts of a basketball man, Toledo coach Harold Anderson.

Anderson served as the gadfly to get Toledo and Bowling Green together again on a basketball court during the 1947-48 season, and this eventually led to the resumption of football relations. One of the unique aspects involved in the resumption of the basketball rivalry was the "Peace Pipe" trophy, which was donated by the journalism societies of both schools. The pipe is approximately seven feet long, has a fourteen-inch high bowl and holds several cans of tobacco. The pipe was traded back and forth between the school newspapers on the basis of which basketball team won the first game of the season between the two clubs.

One of the most controversial and well-remembered games in the football series is the 1951 contest. Toledo won a grim battle, 12-6, but the most prominent element of the game was a free-for-all that erupted in the last minutes between players and fans. The factor that triggered the big fight was a heated argument between Toledo coach Don Greenwood and referee Ray Wisecup. Greenwood felt that a Bowling Green player had used an illegal block on his halfback, and he continually criticized Wisecup throughout the contest. Perhaps the game that really set the tempo for the rivalry was played in 1955 when Doyt Perry's Bowling Green team routed Toledo 39-0 and started a spectacular string of twelve victories over the Rockets.

"The Bowling Green–Toledo rivalry has been a great rivalry ever since I first became acquainted with it when I started school at Bowling Green in 1929," says Perry. "As a coach, I considered it the most important game on our schedule. A number of things entered into the picture when we prepared for Toledo. One thing was that the kids were naturally up for the game. Another important thing was the . . . proximity of campuses. We undoubtedly had more kids from Toledo than anywhere else, at least when I was coach. When I first started in 1955, all three halfbacks, both fullbacks, and two or three linemen were from Toledo. Some of those kids played with or against some of the Toledo players while in high school, so there was no real problem in getting the kids up for the game."

Bear Bryant will also tell you the same thing whenever his Alabama team meets intrastate rival Auburn in one of the South's most intriguing series. "I'd rather beat Auburn than Ohio State five times," Bryant says. The coach's wife, Mary Harmon Bryant, is more definitive. "Auburn–Alabama is just *everything*," she elaborates. "We don't have riots, or folks don't burn each other's cars or anything like that. But an awful lot of people get their *feelings* hurt."

The game was first played in 1892. Auburn won 32-22 and a breathless newspaper account reported that the crowd "was too large to be handled by one man." But in 1907, an "incident" occurred that broke off the series for forty-one years. No one seems to remember what precipitated the break in relations—exaggerations range from "just a little old-fashioned hell-raising" to "some killing and maiming"—but the schools did not get together again until 1948. Since then, they have been beating each other's brains out on the field and sniping at each other off it. "An Auburn man to an Alabama man is a guy who has plowman's stoop and drives a pickup truck to the game on Saturday," says one writer. "To Alabama, Auburn is a cow college. Auburn people call Alabama people country-clubbers and silly sophisticates."

During Shug Jordan's successful and elongated tenure at Auburn from the fifties through the seventies, a natural coaching rivalry developed with Bryant. The two maintained a cordial relationship and occasionally even got together for a grin-and-bear-it round of golf, but they battled each other hard for the state's best high school players. It was generally felt that Bryant had the recruiting edge because of the image of the schools. Auburn has been sometimes thought of as basically a technical and agricultural school, although it is much more than that. Alabama's image is more sophisticated, even though it is planted in a typically small Southern town. "When you've got doctors and lawyers recruiting against farmers," says one Auburn man, simplistically, "the doctors and lawyers win every time."

Bitter intrastate rivalries are a hallmark of Southern football. Mississippi State plays Mississippi each year for possession of the "Golden Egg," a lustrous trophy that was invented in the twenties to bring an end to some of the altercations that had been breaking out after each game. The egg, a gold-plated football mounted on a gold-plated stand with the scores of each year's game inscribed on the base, is passed to the winner each year in an elaborate ceremony involving the presidents of each school. Actually, the upper part of the trophy is more egg-shaped than football-shaped, thus the apropos title. Despite its intentions, however, there is still some question whether the egg had in-.deed fostered peace between the two Mississippi universities. Warfare among the student body seems to have picked up rather noticeably in modern times.

"Both student bodies annually get into a great deal of serious mischief on the week before the game," notes Bo Carter, the assistant sports information director at Mississippi State. "Students have water balloon raids and egg 'bombings' of each campus on the Thursday and Friday before the contest, and, invariably, the Golden Egg or Mississippi State's live bulldog mascots disappear during the course of Game Week. Usually, just before kickoff the missing bulldogs or the Egg miraculously reappear with a grand entrance into the stadium with the cheerleaders or some reasonable facsimile."

Both school's cheering sections arrive at least an hour before game time and exchange verbal jabs. The traditional cheer from Ole Miss pours from its side of the field: "Hoddy, Toddy, gosh almighty, who the hell are we? Whim, wham, bim, bam, Ole Miss, by damn!" Mississippi State's student body counters with its own version: "Hoddy, Toddy, gosh almighty, who the hell are they? Whim, wham, bim, bam, who the hell gives a damn!"

The inherent rivalry has a way of making both coaches and players put forth superhuman efforts. Coach Bob Tyler came out of a hospital bed to coach in Mississippi State's 13-7 loss to Ole Miss in 1975. Tyler had been suffering with a kidney stone for the previous two weeks and was hospitalized in a Columbus, Mississippi, facility all week before the contest. "Even though he still retained the stone," remembers Carter, "he remained on the field for the whole game and had to check back into the hospital for further tests the following day." In 1976 Mississippi State linebacker Mike Lawrence played and was the defensive star although doctors had told him shortly before spring practice he would never play football again after two serious knee injuries in the previous two years. Lawrence ended the game with six tackles, four assists and three sacks for minus four yards. Offensively, the greatest accomplishment in the series was by Arnold "Showboat" Boykin of Ole Miss, who set a national Division I record for touchdowns scored in one game. He had seven scoring runs in 1951 when Ole Miss buried Mississippi State 49-7.

Whether the teams are up or down, the stadium figures are always high for this game. Barney Poole, a former All American end at Ole Miss who is now manager of the Rebel's Memorial Stadium, vouched that the ticket demand for the 1976 game was at least 80,000 for the 46,000-seat stadium. "We could have enlarged it and filled it to the brim," noted Poole.

Student unrest similar to the Ole Miss–Mississippi State rivalry was the mother of invention for "The Rag," the prized trophy of the Tulane–Louisiana State game. "The Rag," a flag split diagonally, with half designed in LSU colors and half in Tulane colors, was instituted after a free-for-all erupted after the 1939 game. These Louisiana neighbors have provided some of college football's greatest battles, particularly when Tulane was in its golden years during the thirties and forties.

Although Tennessee has been one of the winningest teams in Southeastern Conference history and Vanderbilt one of the losingest, it has not interfered with the competitiveness of this intense rivalry through the years. Tennessee holds the overall edge, to be sure, but more than occasionally Vanderbilt has risen up and delivered a haymaker to its loftier state rival. The 1975 game, won 17-14 by Vanderbilt, was one of the most emotional in the series for the Commodores. The game was played at Knoxville, a wasteland that had produced no victories in the series for Vanderbilt since 1959. Vanderbilt's Barry Burton had the misfortune to misplay punt snaps in the Tennessee games of 1973 and 1974, costing victories each year for the Commodores. And it was this same Burton who ironically stood in the end zone again in 1975 waiting to kick with the Volunteers bent on pulling out another game. The Neyland Stadium public-address announcer had the partisan Tennessee crowd in an uproar by blaring, "Back in the end zone to punt, And it's—Barry Burton!" This time, however, Burton fielded the snap cleanly and kicked the ball forty-one yards out of the end zone.

Tennessee's Stanley Morgan caught Burton's punt and headed down the sideline only to be knocked out of bounds by Burton at the Vanderbilt thirty-yard line. Burton was the last player who could have tackled him. Otherwise it was a touchdown. The defense held the Volunteers three downs and then was not fooled by a fake field goal attempt on fourth down.

"Another interesting feature of the game," remembers Vanderbilt sports information director Lew Harris, "was that Vanderbilt coach Fred Pancoast read the lyrics to the song, 'Blind Man In The Bleachers,' before the game started. It was a rather heartrending country and western song that was popular at the time and it may have helped to motivate the team. Coach Pancoast is a big country-and-western fan and on this occasion it may have helped to win a game."

Kentucky has been another longtime colleague of Tennessee's. Their rivalry, like the one with Vanderbilt, started around the same time in the early 1890s and produced about as many legendary moments. The Volunteers and Wildcats beat each other's brains out each year for a trophy called the "Beer Barrel," an honored *objet d'art* instituted in 1925 without the blessing of the Women's Christian Temperance Union and the Anti-Saloon League. Kentucky alumni Guy Huguelet and Rollie M. Guthrie hoped to stimulate the Wildcat–Volunteer rivalry to greater heights with the introduction of a game trophy and first hit upon a whiskey barrel as the most symbolic prize. "We wanted to come up with something symbolic of both states, and we immediately thought of moonshine whiskey and started to hunt a whiskey barrel," Guthrie explains. But when the league, the WCTU and other similar organizations got wind of the plan, they protested vigorously and Guthrie and Huguelet had to settle for a beer keg, which they obtained from a Lexington distributor. But even this did not placate the anti-liquor groups, who evidenced horror at the thought of even a beer barrel symbolizing this fine football rivalry. So, the keg was carried onto the field with "Ice Water" painted on it, to the tune of, "How Dry I Am." In future years, the rotating trophy stimulated the

rivalry, as Guthrie and Huguelet had hoped, and sparked
endless confrontations between the student bodies of the
schools, as Guthrie and Huguelet perhaps would never
have imagined. The barrel was always being carted off to
one campus or another in a series of imaginative "kegnap-
pings" through the years and this triggered other acts of
reprisals such as the theft of the Tennessee coon dog
mascot, Smoky, and Kentucky's stuffed Wildcat mascot,
Colonel. At one point Tennessee was beating Kentucky so
methodically that even when the Wildcats did occasionally
sneak in a victory, they had little use for the trophy. When
the keg turned up missing in 1953, one Kentucky man said:
"We hope they bury it. It carries mostly memories of head-
aches for Kentucky. Virtually nothing but Tennessee
wins."

Another traditional Southern rivalry is the Florida–
Georgia series, most widely known as the "world's largest
outdoor cocktail party" before a law recently prohibited
alcoholic beverages in the Gator Bowl. However, the city
of Jacksonville, Florida, is still wild over the game, which
annually draws 70,000 brawling, squalling fans whose passions reach uncommon peaks. The highlight of the Jacksonville social season, the Florida–Georgia confrontation
is as much a happening as it is a football game. Festivities
in Jacksonville's downtown Hemming Park usually get underway a full five days before the game as tumblers, bands
and other entertainers from high schools and junior highs
perform from 11 a.m. daily Monday through Friday. Then
the parties take over and burn straight through Sunday.
Restaurants generally order double the usual weekend pro-
visions and squeeze in a few extra tables, if possible. Hotels
and motels in the Jacksonville area are usually booked full
for months, and in some cases reservations are made a year
in advance. A good many Georgians party for the weekend
at the sea islands off Brunswick, seventy-five miles north of
Jacksonville, then either take a bus or drive to the game.
The Greater Jacksonville Chamber of Commerce estimates
the game has an annual economic impact of $1.6 million.

That doesn't include the $700,000 ticket receipts, split between the two universities. Meanwhile, the game itself more often than not matches the accompanying hoopla. In 1976, the teams played for the Southeastern Conference championship and Georgia wound up a 41-27 winner with an astonishing twenty-eight-point rally in the second half. Historically, the game has been one of dramatic, fourth-quarter rallies. At one point, a statistician revealed that eleven of thirteen games were won in the last period, some of them on a play drawn and sent in on a napkin.

Out in America's midlands, the Oklahoma–Oklahoma State series still stirs up quite a lot of dust, even though the Sooners have dominated that rivalry. There, the tradition of the "Bell Clapper" trophy goes back to 1917. When Oklahoma State defeated Oklahoma for the first time in football that year, students rang the old prairie school house bell throughout the night. In 1930, during an imminent Oklahoma State victory, Sooner fans stole away from the stadium, climbed into the belfry of Oklahoma State's Old Central and stole the bell. It was made an official trophy of the series the following year.

The two major institutions in the state of North Dakota have also developed an august rivalry. North Dakota State and the University of North Dakota are involved in a yearly confrontation for the "Nickel Trophy," an exact replica of the once-minted U.S. coin with the Indian head on it. Two inches thick, twenty-two inches in diameter and seventy-five pounds in weight, the trophy as prize was inaugurated in 1938 and like many others, has been the object of intercampus raids. The series is such that many of those involved are wont to call the contest the "game of the year" no matter what year it is, and one North Dakota State coach said recently, "It's not just a game, but a matter of life or death."

Because of the dominating effect these two teams have had in the North Central Conference and on a national scale in Division II football, they are usually playing in midseason when one or both clubs are ranked in the Top Ten. And how they play!

"The series is bitter," notes George Ellis, the sports information director of North Dakota State. "I remember the 1975 game where on one play five athletes were on the ground and had to be assisted off the field. One was admitted to a hospital where he underwent surgery to save his life after a crushing block ruptured his liver in at least seven different places."

The contest captures the attention and emotion of nearly everyone in the state of North Dakota. "The feeling developed is almost one of civil war with the major state newspapers devoting extensive pre- and postgame coverage," says Ellis. The game is televised throughout the state on a seven-station network and the news media gets as worked up about it as everyone else. In Fargo one year, a television sportscaster served as a psychological prop for the North Dakota State team. With the knowledge of the North Dakota State coach, he picked the Bison to lose to the Sioux in his midweek prediction show in hopes of motivating the team. It was his contribution to the victory and after the game, he came into the winning North Dakota State locker room and was nearly ripped to pieces by angry North Dakota State players for picking against them. Coaches had to interfere to save this well-intending sportscaster.

North Dakota State and North Dakota have been meeting every year since 1894 with a few minor exceptions around the turn of the century, and their series currently is in the eighty-game range, one of the highest in the country. This has been a lot of time to produce a lot of significant football games and two of the most important in the series occurred in 1965 and 1971. In 1965, North Dakota State won its first national title with a 6-3 victory over North Dakota, although some contend the Bison had to use an illegal play to do it. "It was a crackback block by a wide receiver that was planned especially for that situation," points out Ellis. "It helped score the touchdown to win the game, the Conference and the national title. Of course our people will deny now that we ever used it." In 1971, North Dakota State had been unbeaten in thirty-six games, longest streak in the nation at that moment, but was knocked from the top of the national standings by a 23-7 loss to North Dakota.

Arkansas and Texas have been playing each other since 1894, but it took about thirty years before it became pretty much of an annual affair and another thirty or so before it became a red-hot rivalry. This finally came to pass in 1958, Darrell Royal's second year at Texas and Frank Broyles' first at Arkansas. Since then, it has been the kind of game, Royal once said, "where you screw your belly to the ground."

Royal and Broyles were considered the Young Turks of the Southwest Conference in their formative years there. They were devoted friends and incurable golf partners, a relationship that added color and charm to the rivalry of their teams. The most essential part of this rivalry, however, was built on the excellence of their players and the high treasure for which they competed during the torrid sixties, when almost every game involved a Conference championship and national standing. They were usually worthy of their buildup, too.

With the exception of one or two games during this period, all of the matchups between Arkansas and Texas featured rich suspense and flights of dazzle.

In 1959, with Arkansas ahead 12-7 and Texas with its back to the wall, Jack Collins completed a running, off-balance pass for a key first down that started the Longhorns to a dramatic 13-12 victory. In 1960, Mickey Cissell's field goal all but died on the crossbar, but was good by inches to give Arkansas a 24-23 triumph with only fifteen seconds remaining. Losing 3-0 in 1962, Texas drove nearly the length of the field to pull out a 7-3 victory at the end. Texas was on top in 1963, but not by much, with a tense 17-13 victory. In 1964, Royal gambled everything—the Conference title, the Number-One ranking in the country and a fifteen-game winning streak—on a two-point conversion. But it failed, and Arkansas beat Texas 14-13.

The 1965 and 1969 meetings were the ultimate expression of what this fine series has become in modern times. Converting two fumbles into immediate touchdowns, Arkansas swaggered to a 20-0 lead in the 1965 game. But Texas rallied, as Marvin Kristynik directed the Longhorns with inspiration and David Conway kicked three field goals. It was 24-20 Texas when Jon Brittenum began completing passes to the acrobatic Bobby Crockett, six of them, to wing the Razorbacks to a 27-24 victory. At the start of the winning touchdown drive, Jim Lindsey, a poised and unselfish senior halfback, talked earnestly to his teammates and exhorted them to give Brittenum the blocking he would need to throw his passes. "Jim Lindsey is the one who rallied our team," Broyles said later. "Not me. I was a babbling idiot."

In the so-called "Big Shootout" of 1969, the eyes of Texas and just about everyone else in the nation were on the Longhorns and Razorbacks. Texas was the Number-One team in the country and Arkansas not far behind, but it looked like their positions should have been reversed after three quarters. At this point, Arkansas had been pushing Texas around the field all day and held what looked like an insurmountable 14-0 lead. However, that evaporated in the heat of a fourth-quarter Longhorn rally led by James Street, called "Slick" because of his good looks, flashy clothes and, most importantly to Royal, his ball-handling ability. Street ran for one score and a two-point conversion, then directed the winning touchdown drive in the dying minutes for a 15-14 victory that gave Texas the national championship.

The big play in the rally at the end was a forty-four-yard bomb, which Street unleashed to Randy Peschel, the Texas tight end. The play was virtually picked out of a hat by Royal when the Longhorns had a fourth and three on their own forty-three with less than five minutes to play. "In a case like that, you just suck it up and pick a number," Royal said later after receiving a presidential citation for

Number-One ranking from Richard Nixon. "There's no logic to it. Just a hunch."

The recent Texas–Arkansas wars are indicative of the type of rivalries existing in the Southwest Conference over the years. At one point, the Southern Methodist–Texas Christian series was a virtual furnace of passions. Before the Texas–Arkansas game of 1969 came along, few in the SWC believed there was a better contest ever played than the SMU–TCU game of 1935. It featured the Number-One and Number-Two teams in the country, both undefeated, with the winner going to the Rose Bowl and the loser to the Sugar Bowl. Bob Finley, who recently retired as the SMU baseball coach, threw a fifty-yard touchdown pass to Bobby Wilson on fourth and thirteen from punt formation for the Mustangs' game-winning touchdown. SMU finished the regular season with a 12-0 record, Number-One ranking and a berth against Stanford in the Rose Bowl. The series inspired the fans to deep and fervent emotions. During one game in the career of SMU's Don Meredith, a man stood up in the crowd at Fort Worth, Texas, pulled out a gun and said, "Meredith, I'm going to kill you." A policeman standing nearby jumped the gun-waving fanatic and took him to the station.

The feelings are just as volatile in the Arizona–Arizona State series, particularly since Frank Kush took over the head coaching job at Arizona State in 1958. Both institutions surfaced in the 1880s and began playing football around the turn of the century. Arizona dominated the early years, until 1949, and Arizona State has had the upper hand since then. The bitterness of this rivalry became apparent as the result of an academic matter in the late fifties, when Arizona State attempted to reach university status and was rebuffed by regents, legislators and others of the power structure—mostly made up of University of Arizona lawyers. Thus thwarted, the Arizona State crowd got its proposition on the general ballot and touched off what is remembered as one of the bitterest and most expensive campaigns ever staged in Arizona. Among those involved was Kush, an ex-Michigan Stater who recalls putting up pro-Arizona State posters in southern Arizona towns and having them immediately torn down by irate U of A alumni.

In the crucial 1958 election-year game, Arizona State humiliated the University of Arizona 47-0. Notes an embittered University of Arizona man: "State's real argument was that their football team had kicked hell out of us, so they deserved to be a university." This might not have been the strongest of academic reasons, but it may have carried some clout with the electorate, which subsequently voted two to one in favor of making Arizona State a full-fledged university.

Back in the East, where it all began with Princeton and Rutgers, those two New Jersey schools are still at it after more than 100 years. Their first game in 1869, indeed the first officially recognized version of the American game, was nothing to compare with the slick perfection of later years. But it did furnish seeds for lasting contributions. The fans saw "uniforms" for the first time—red turbans worn by the Rutgers players—and they heard the first football yell, some vague sort of chant the cheerleaders remembered from a few years earlier when New York's Seventh Regiment marched through town on its way to fight in the Civil War.

A Revolutionary War cannon was the spark that set off the nation's oldest football rivalry. The two schools had been fighting over this cannon for a long time and finally decided that a football game would be a better way to determine who got it annually. After a few years Princeton got smart and cemented the relic in a bed of concrete, but in later seasons, a Centennial Trophy eventually took its place as the official game trophy. It's a single monolithic slab, ruggedly finished and engraved from artwork representing early football by Frederick Remington, a noted American artist. In the base is soil from the field where the first game was played in New Brunswick, New Jersey.

Until the late thirties, the game belonged to Princeton.

But in 1938 Rutgers showed a new spirit and a fine passing attack to shock the Tigers 20-18 and begin an era of close competition. The fifties had some of the series' best games and the one in 1967 could have been the best one of all. The 1951 meeting featured a high-scoring duel as Princeton outlasted Rutgers 34-28 behind the ubiquitous Dick Kazmaier. In 1953, the Tigers won 9-7 when a substitute fullback named Art Pitts blocked a punt for a safety, and the next year Princeton put on three goal-line stands to preserve a bitter, nerve-racking 10-8 victory. In the 1967 game, Princeton forged an early 14-0 lead, then had to fight for its life at the end to endure by a point, 22-21. Bryant Mitchell led a late Rutgers rally, finally springing loose on a thirty-three-yard touchdown run to give the Scarlet Knights a 21-14 lead with but two minutes left. But then Bob Weber took charge of the Princeton attack and led the Tigers to a score in the space of a minute. Princeton coach Dick Colman sent in Scott MacBean with a special play for the two-point conversion, and the sophomore, making his varsity debut, lobbed a pass to Weber in the left flat for the winning points.

While Princeton's oldest rival is Rutgers, there are others on the Tigers' schedule with more continuity. The most notable of these, of course, is Ivy League colleague Yale. They played for the first time in 1873 and the 1978 game marked the historic 100th meeting of these venerable foes. Rutgers, by sheer strength of its longevity, has established great relations with an armful of Eastern schools—among the most notable, Columbia. If for no other reason, it deserves mention as the nation's second oldest rivalry, started in 1870.

New York City is not currently especially known for college football, but it was back in the twenties and thirties when the annual "Battle of the Bronx" took place between Fordham and New York University. These were especially notable directly after the First World War when the increased size of the crowds made it imperative to move the annual battle to Yankee Stadium and the Polo Grounds.

Gargantuan crowds of 80,000 were not uncommon for this superb rivalry.

Fordham was the early dominator of the series that started in 1899, but NYU stopped playing the part of shrinking violets as soon as Chick Meehan became coach in 1925. Meehan, a star player and successful head coach at Syracuse, was recruited to breathe new life into the NYU football program and his arrival did indeed bring a breath of fresh air. In his seven years on University Heights, Meehan never had a losing season and produced several national powers.

Two years after Meehan came from Syracuse to NYU, Major Frank Cavanaugh came from Boston College to Fordham. And thus came the days of the "Violent Violets" and the original "Seven Blocks of Granite." The Rams and Violets then began to stage the "Battle of the Bronx" before pulsating, sellout crowds. Louis J. Madow, a Fordham Road jeweler, put up the Madow Trophy, which went to the most valuable player in the game, and was the forerunner of the Lambert Trophy, which annually goes to the best team in the East.

Fordham's "Seven Blocks" were as rough-hewn as their famous appellation, helping to wear down some of the best teams in the country. There were interchangeable parts through the thirties, but though the names changed, Fordham's memorable line was always a collection of tough, hard-hitting players. In 1935 and 1936 this uncompromising crew was composed of Leo Paquin and Johnny Druze at the ends, Ed Franco and Al Barbartsky at the tackles, Nate Pierce and Vince Lombardi at the guards and Alex Wojciechowicz at center. These great players made history, but it took an honored foe like NYU to knock them off their pedestal in 1936. The "Seven Blocks" didn't surrender a touchdown to such potent offenses as Southern Methodist, St. Mary's, Purdue and Pitt, and the cry at Fordham that year was "From Rose Hill to the Rose Bowl." But, unhappily, the Rams blew it when they lost their last game to old rival NYU, 7-6. Pitt, instead, went to the Rose Bowl and beat Washington, 21-0.

Before Meehan went to Fordham, he was involved in another of America's special early football rivalries—the Syracuse–Colgate game. Until its end in 1961, the Syracuse –Colgate series was one of the most colorful rivalries in the country. Colgate dominated the early years, and Syracuse was the more powerful of the two in the modern era. The so-called Colgate "hoodoo," when Syracuse was not able to beat the Red Raiders from 1925 to 1937, has gained a place in college football legend. An inability to beat Colgate and sometimes not even cross the Red Raiders' goal line cost some Syracuse coaches sleepless nights, and, eventually, their jobs.

The series was touched by some oddity and tragedy, but never a lack of interest. In 1894, the game was enlivened by a Colgate player who ran the wrong way and inadvertently scored for Syracuse. The 1897 game was punctuated by a tackle made by a spectator, who pulled off the play without so much as the formality of removing his hat. The pandemonium that followed provoked a cessation of athletic relations between the schools and they did not resume playing until 1902. The 1906 game was marked by tragedy when a portion of the bleachers at Star Park in Syracuse collapsed and more than 100 persons were hurt, many of them seriously. Financial disagreements interrupted the series for a while in the early 1900s, and there were no games played in 1918 and 1943 because of the wars. But neither side ever lost its enthusiasm for this remarkable game, as spectators have shown with expressions of extreme passion through the years. Once a fan threw a snowball at the Colgate center and caused him to make a bad pass. Fortunately for the Red Raiders, they recovered the ball. Uniquely, though, the series had relatively few unpleasant incidents despite the blazing heat of the rivalry. "This is remarkable, when one considers the pressure under which they were playing and the wrought-up student bodies of both universities," Dexter Reed, the former publicity director at Colgate, once reflected.

Equally as bitter is Syracuse's rivalry with Penn State nowadays. The series started in 1922 and continued with intensity each year into modern times, never missing a beat until one year during the Second World War. The teams then resumed their competition with a fervor unlike few rivalries in America and this was fanned into flaming battles in the fifties and sixties. The game always produced stark drama and usually produced the Eastern champion. Players on both sides will confess that they never got hit so hard as in Penn State–Syracuse games. The 1965 game, won 28-21 by the Orangemen, was typical of the bitter, bizarre series that sometimes strains logical thinking. Penn State dominated everything but the points, controlling the ball ninety-one plays to thirty-six for Syracuse, and out-gaining the Orangemen 387 yards to 193. But Floyd Little personally made up for those lopsided figures with three touchdown runs for Syracuse. One sportswriter pointed out that it was a "strange sort of contest . . . but exciting all the way."

The series has featured many other such battles royal, not to mention a lot of wild arguments and controversies, both on and off the field. There was the Penn State accusation after the 1958 game that the Eastern College Athletic Conference assigned a "Syracuse referee." Actually, he was a Princeton man. There was the infamous "shoe episode" in the 1960 game when Penn State quarterback Don Hoak threw his shoe out of bounds to stop the clock. Rightfully, he was denied by referee Frank Brennan. There were hard feelings developed between the schools after Penn State refused to let Syracuse use a video tape monitoring machine in the press box for the 1966 game. And then there was the granddaddy of all the Penn State–Syracuse rhubarbs—the one in 1956 when coach Rip Engle made an illegal substitution of quarterback Milt Plum. Syracuse raised a fuss about it and won the argument, resulting in a fifteen-yard penalty for Penn State. But the debate simmered long after the game was over and resulted in a rules change. The following winter, it was made mandatory for all substitutes to sign in so that the officials, and not the team's bench, would keep the record of such maneuvering.

As for the artistry of the games themselves in the sixties, Syracuse's All-American defensive back Tony Kyasky says, "Where Bowl bids were concerned it always came down to Penn State and Syracuse. The Southern Bowls liked to get the best teams in the East, and those two teams usually were the best."

The Harvard–Yale game may be the most honored rivalry in the New England sector, but there is no less zeal when Middlebury meets Norwich on a football field. Closing in on the ninety-game level, this ancient small college series that began in 1893 is the sixth oldest in New England—predated only by Harvard–Yale, Yale–Brown, Harvard–Dartmouth, Williams–Amherst and Bowdoin–Colby. This is one of those rivalries that made popular that time-honored football cliché, "You can throw out the record book when these two teams meet." Actually, you can. It has been impossible to predict the outcome of the Norwich–Middlebury games because of the ferocity of the rivalry. Several times in the sixties, Duke Nelson's Middlebury teams upset favored Norwich squads, and Norwich ended a long losing streak in 1960 by upsetting the undefeated Panthers 26-0. Middlebury's undefeated and untied 1972 team did the unpredictable, shutting out Norwich 49-0 in a game that had been billed an as "even" matchup. The next year, Norwich snapped Middlebury's fourteen-game winning streak by a 19-12 score.

One of the greatest passing duels of the series took place in 1967 between Middlebury's Charlie Brush and Ray Potter of Norwich. Potter set the Norwich mark of passes completed in a game by hitting on 20 and Brush set the Middlebury record for most yards passing in connecting for 358. Middlebury finally won the frantic game, 40-38, on a last-minute touchdown pass by Brush.

The Middlebury–Norwich game is usually played in November in a northern climate which brings snow more often than not to the scene. That, however, is not the only sideline color annually added to these often brilliant games. In the thirties and forties when rail passenger service was the way to travel, Norwich chartered a train and brought its entire Cadet Corps along for the Middlebury game. Their marches from the railroad station through the main streets of Middlebury to the field added to the excitement of the occasion. "After one game at Middlebury the Cadets tore down the goal posts on the field and also on the intramural field as a result of a loss," remembers Max Petersen, editor of the Middlebury news services bureau. "Nelson, who was athletic director as well as coach at Middlebury, said he sent Norwich a bill the next day."

Along with Middlebury, Norwich considers the U. S. Coast Guard Academy another of its vital foes. This contest, played for a prize known simply as "The Mug," is best known as the "Little Army–Navy" series. Usually included in the fun and games of this series are kidnappings of the Coast Guard's cub bear mascot, as well as the Middies and Cadets themselves, "bombings" of campuses with propaganda leaflets and rolls of toilet paper, and the painting of salty slogans on symbols and military equipment.

The "Little Three" rivalry is a triangular love-hate affair that has been rocking along nicely between Wesleyan, Williams and Amherst since the early 1880s. It proves that you can have more than two to make a good rivalry. Williams has been the dominant school of late in this well-known small college series, having won the mythical title five straight years from 1971 through 1975. There have been so many upsets in the games between these teams that bigtime gamblers are said to keep strictly away from "Little Three" contests. "Even when one team seems to be greatly superior, there have been so many reverses that what little money is bet on the games is placed purely from sentimental reasons," a football historian once pointed out.

Of course every other football fan from Austin to Boston has a favorite rivalry that stirs similar feelings in his breast. Trophies, jugs, mugs and hugs—all of these make up the game's tradition and it doesn't really matter who's playing, whether it's Army vs. Navy for the Commander-in-Chief's Trophy or Minnesota–Duluth against Wisconsin–Superior for "Gertie The Goose." No one has been able to figure out exactly when the sport of football started, except that it goes back 2,000 years and perhaps the Egyptians may have once played for the Old Wooden Sphinx. But what is really on display is the essence of the sport. As one writer said, "No wonder the millions who thrive on college football like to think that it wasn't Columbus who discovered America—Princeton and Rutgers did."